D0765697

ESPIONAGE IN THE DIVIDED
STUART DYNASTY
1685–1715

Dedication

To DM

ESPIONAGE IN THE DIVIDED
STUART DYNASTY
1685–1715

JULIAN WHITEHEAD

PEN & SWORD
HISTORY

AN IMPRINT OF PEN & SWORD BOOKS LTD.
YORKSHIRE – PHILADELPHIA

First published in Great Britain in 2020 by
PEN AND SWORD HISTORY
An imprint of
Pen & Sword Books Ltd
Yorkshire - Philadelphia

ISBN: 978 1 52674 852 2

Typeset in Times New Roman 11.5/14 by
Aura Technology and Software Services, India.
Printed and bound in the UK by TJ International Ltd.

Pen & Sword Books Ltd incorporates the Imprints of Pen & Sword Books
Archaeology, Atlas, Aviation, Battleground, Discovery, Family History, History,
Maritime, Military, Naval, Politics, Railways, Select, Transport, True Crime,
Fiction, Frontline Books, Leo Cooper, Praetorian Press, Seaforth Publishing,
Wharncliffe and White Owl.

For a complete list of Pen & Sword titles please contact
PEN & SWORD BOOKS LIMITED
47 Church Street, Barnsley, South Yorkshire, S70 2AS, England
E-mail: enquiries@pen-and-sword.co.uk
Website: www.pen-and-sword.co.uk

Or
PEN AND SWORD BOOKS
1950 Lawrence Rd, Havertown, PA 19083, USA
E-mail: Uspen-and-sword@casematepublishers.com
Website: www.penandswordbooks.com

Contents

List of Illustrations

1. *King James II* by an unknown artist (NPG 366)
2. *Queen Mary of Modena* by Willem Wissing c. 1685 (NPG 214)
3. *James Scott Duke of Monmouth and Buccleuch* after Willem Wissing c. 1685 (NPG 151)
4. *King William III* after Willem Wissing c. 1685 (NPG 580)
5. *Queen Mary II* by Jan Verkolje c. 1688 (NPG 606)
6. *Queen Anne and the Duke of Gloucester* studio of Sir Godfrey Kneller c. 1694 (NPG 5227)
7. *Prince James Francis Edward Stuart* studio Alexis Simon Belle c. 1712 (NPG 248)
8. *Prince Charles Edward Stuart* by Hugh Douglas Hamilton c. 1785 (NPG 376)
9. *Chateau de St Germain-en-Laye* (GNU Free Document Licence Wickopedia)
10. *King Louise XIV of France* mezzotint by John Smith (NPG D11965)
11. *William Bentinck 1st Earl of Portland* studio Hyaccinthe Rigaund c. 1699 (NPG 1968)
12. *Thomas Osborne 1st Duke of Leeds* studio of Sir Peter Lely 1680 (NPG 1472)
13. *Robert Spencer 2nd Earl of Sunderland* (Wikimedia)
14. *Henry St John 1st Viscount Bolingbroke* (NPG 593)
15. *Simon Fraser 11th Baron Lovat* by William Hogarth (NPG 216)

Back cover
James II when Duke of York with his first wife Anne Hyde and their children Mary and Anne by Sir Peter Lely.

Acknowledgements

I am indebted to all the authors of the books listed in the bibliography, in particular for the various works of John Callow, Peter Earl, Anna Keary, John Kenyon, Bruce Lenman and Edward Valance. I would also like to thank the National Portrait Gallery for its assistance and agreement to me using their images for illustrations and Wikipedia for their GNU free document licence. Finally I want to thank my wife for her help and support.

Introduction

Treason never prospers
What's the reason?
Why if treason prospers
None dare ever call it treason.

Families can be complicated. Royal families can be more complicated than most. Such was the case of the Stuart royal family in the second half of the seventeenth century. Charles II fathered at least twelve children, most of which were brought up with royal privileges but none could succeed him as they were all illegitimate. On Charles's death the crown passed to his Catholic brother James II, who fathered several bastards but also had two legitimate daughters, Mary and Anne. When James's first wife died he married Mary of Modena, an Italian Catholic. Mary was only slightly older than her husband's two daughters, and they did not take to her. Mary, the eldest of these daughters, was obliged for political reasons to move to Holland and marry her first cousin William of Orange, a dour Dutchman whom she heartily disliked. Mary and Anne's hostility towards their stepmother was such that when she gave birth to a boy they convinced themselves that the child was not hers. These were quite enough complications for any family but there was one overriding issue that was to fracture both the family and the nation: religion.

James was a Catholic, as was his queen, and it was therefore inevitable that the baby Prince of Wales would be brought up as a Catholic, so perpetuating a Catholic monarchy. Both Anne and Mary were devout Anglicans, as were the majority of the country. The prospect of enforced Catholicism led the leading Protestant aristocrats to invite Mary's Lutheran husband William to invade England to preserve the Protestant religion. This he did, and received so much support that James fled, never to return to England. William and Mary were jointly crowned and became rulers of the three kingdoms of England, Ireland and Scotland. For the next hundred years James, then his son and grandson, would try to regain the thrones. In this they were supported by British Jacobites, who regarded them as the legitimate monarchs, and by French aid. The Jacobites and their French backers were to be the main threat to the security of the three kingdoms during the reigns of William and Mary, and then Anne.

This book is about government intelligence in this complex period where some regarded King William as a saviour, others as a usurper. Likewise, King James and his heirs were looked on by some as true sovereigns and others as pretenders. Although espionage and conspiracy are the book's subject matter, its theme is loyalty. James's Catholicism was an excuse for his disloyal nephew Monmouth to lead a rebellion against him. Loyalty to the Crown resulted in that rebellion being savagely put down, but James's continued Catholicisation caused his overthrow by those whose prime loyalty was to the Protestant religion. Foremost of these was William of Orange, his nephew and son-in-law, but it also included his own daughters. In the case of Mary, it meant having to decide between loyalty to her father and to her husband. In religion there was not much room for compromise. With the king's two Protestant daughters turned against him, it became a tragedy of *King Lear* proportions. Indeed the similarity was so strong that performances of Shakespeare's play were banned.

For Catholics, those of the Protestant faith were heretics, and for Protestants, the Catholics were idolaters whose Pope was the Antichrist. To be a member of the opposing faith was to consign your immortal soul to an eternity of damnation in the afterlife. James's loyalty to the Catholic Church not only lost him his crown, but also prevented him negotiating for his son to inherit the throne on condition he was brought up a Protestant. When James died, his son likewise refused the offer of the crown in exchange for converting to Protestantism out of devotion to the Catholic Church. Many Jacobites risked losing their wealth, freedom and even lives out of loyalty to James and his heirs.

The times saw numerous instances of selfless loyalty to monarch or religion, but it also saw another type of loyalty. Adherence to monarch or religion could be trumped by an individual's overriding concern for themselves and their families; in other words, self-interest. John Churchill's sister was a mistress of James, and Churchill owed his rise in fortune entirely to King James. This did not prevent him deserting James to join William, and although remaining apparently loyal to the new regime he kept his options open by sending messages of support to the exiled Jacobite court. There were many like him who did not want to burn their boats and this included Anne's principal minister and secretary of state responsible for intelligence, who plotted to transfer the throne to the Old Pretender on her death. It is no surprise that in dangerous and uncertain times, self-interest was often a greater motivating factor than faithfulness to monarch or religion. As we shall see, this was particularly so in the murky activities of espionage and intrigue, where agents and informants were happy to transfer their allegiance to whoever was likely to pay them most.

The period between 1685 and 1715 spanned just thirty years, but was to lead to the creation of the country as we know it today. As well as ensuring that England remained primarily Protestant in religion and culture, it had other important results. The period saw the foundation of parliamentary democracy with the Bill of Rights, the expansion of trade and commerce with naval supremacy, new overseas territories and with the formation of the Bank of England. Finally, and most importantly, the creation of the United Kingdom of Great Britain by the Act of Union. This work describes how government intelligence played its part in influencing the great events of this fascinating period where conflicting loyalties led to the fracturing of a royal family and the British nation.

God save the King
I mean the Faith's Defender.
God save, no harm in saving,
The Pretender
But who Pretender is and who the King,
God save us all that quite another thing!

Chapter 1

A New King
1685

'The King begins his reign with great expectations, and hopes of much reformation as to the late vices and profaneness of both Court and Country.'

Diary of John Evelyn, entry for 23 April 1685

It was another bitterly cold winter and the Thames in London had frozen over. In the city, there was a general spirit of gloom and uncertainty. Many citizens could be seen weeping as they walked the streets. A feeling had taking hold that something both tragic and momentous was about to take place.

The two brothers had shared the highs and lows of tempestuous times. Their father executed, their birthright removed, then unexpectedly restored, only to be later challenged but finally again restored. Their brother and three sisters had died and they were now the only surviving children of Charles I. It was 4 February 1685 and it had become clear that the two men who had lived through so much together would soon be parted for ever. Charles II lay dying in his bedchamber at the Palace of Whitehall with his brother James, Duke of York, at his side.

During the previous five days the royal physicians had tried the best known medical practices including copious bleeding and placing pigeons at Charles's feet, which seemed to have helped cure the queen when she had been ill a few years earlier, but appeared to have no effect on a male patient. Many other remedies were employed such as shaving the king's head and then applying blistering agents to his skull, and some fifty-eight different drug concoctions were administered, usually with horrific results. These included ingredients such as the spirits of human skull and a bezoar stone from the stomach of a Middle Eastern goat.

Red-hot irons were applied to Charles's head and bare feet, but neither this nor the continued bleeding managed to cure what is now believed to have been chronic granular kidney disease.[1]

James was beside himself with grief and wept openly. It is true that he and Charles had not always seen eye to eye, but there was a deep brotherly bond despite being so different in personality. While Charles was light-hearted, amusing and approachable, James was serious, rather dull and haughty. For all his indolence and pursuit of pleasure, Charles could be shrewd, flexible and politically adept, whereas James was unimaginative, inflexible and unopen to political compromise. There were two things the brothers had in common besides their shared experiences, and that was bravery in military action and exceptionally high levels of promiscuity. But even in the latter there was a difference. Charles's many mistresses were renowned for their beauty and lively personalities, whereas James's were rather plain, dull creatures. This had prompted Charles to jokingly remark that he believed that James had been given his mistresses as a penance by his confessor.

James was of course a Roman Catholic by now. James and Charles's mother, Queen Henrietta Maria, had been a Catholic, and James's first wife, Anne Hyde, had converted to Catholicism in 1660. She had some influence over his secret conversion to Catholicism nine years later. Such was the anti-Catholic feeling in the country, that despite his conversion, he had continued to attend Anglican services for another seven years. Charles may have had Catholic sympathies himself, but was well aware that as king he was head of the Church of England and insisted that James's children were brought up as Anglicans. Anne died of breast cancer in 1671 and their only son, Edgar, died three months later, leaving James with just two surviving children, Mary and Anne, aged 9 and 6 respectively. Charles II had sired numerous bastards such as James, Duke of Monmouth, but never produced a child with his queen, Catharine of Braganza. That meant his brother James was next in line to the throne and after him, James's eldest daughter Mary.

Parliament's concern about growing Catholic influence led to the Test Act of 1673 in which all civil and military office holders were obliged to take an oath denouncing Catholic beliefs. James refused to take the oath and resigned as Lord High Admiral, thus making it clear to all that he had converted to Catholicism. In the same year James decided to remarry in the hopes of producing a male heir. The lady eventually chosen was Princess Mary Beatrice d'Este, daughter of the Duke of Modena in northwest Italy, whom he married by proxy in Modena in a Catholic ceremony.

Mary Beatrice was tall and slim with Mediterranean good looks, was fluent in French as well as her native Italian, and had a good command of Latin. However, at 15 years of age she was twenty-five years younger than James. She had charmed Louis XIV when she visited Versailles on her way to England and he had given her a £6,000 brooch. James was equally charmed by his wife when he first saw her on their wedding day in London. The ceremony was an Anglican one and after it James introduced his daughters to his young wife as 'a new playmate' for them. Mary Beatrice was less than happy when she first met her pockmarked, stuttering, 40-year-old husband and began a somewhat disconcerting habit of bursting into tears whenever she saw him. Fortunately this passed with time and she and James were to become quite devoted to each other.

Charming as she was, Mary Beatrice was a devout Catholic and was not welcomed in Protestant England, where Catholics accounted for only one per cent of the population. Before long many were referring to her as the 'Pope's daughter'. This was no more than standard Protestant prejudice, but parliament was expressing deep concern about James's Catholicism. In an attempt to counter this, Charles decided that James's eldest daughter Mary should marry her Protestant cousin, Prince William of Orange, the *Stadtholder* (leader) of Holland. William was the son of Charles and James's sister, and had become Europe's principal Protestant leader against Catholicism in general, and Louis XIV in particular. Despite this display of support for the Protestant faith, anti-Catholicism not only persisted, but far greater anti-Catholic feeling was to take hold of the country the next year.

1678 saw what became known as the Popish Plot. This was as series of fictitious Catholic plots to kill the king which were fabricated by Titus Oates and other Protestant extremists. The purpose of the supposed plots was to replace Charles with his Catholic brother in order to turn England into a Catholic country. Allegations of complicity in the plot began to be levelled at senior Catholics, including Queen Catharine, Mary Beatrice and various Catholic peers. The country became gripped by an anti-papist hysteria which rampaged for three years with many innocent Catholics being imprisoned and fifteen executed. This then led to the

'Exclusion Crisis' in which the Whigs in parliament, headed by the Earl of Shaftesbury, wanted to exclude James from inheriting the throne for being a Catholic. With so much opposition to James, Charles instructed him and Mary Beatrice to leave England and live first in Brussels and then later in Edinburgh.

In 1680 Charles summoned parliament to royalist Oxford and then dismissed it, thus removing it as a mouthpiece for the Exclusionists. Charles never held another parliament and managed to obtain sufficient funding from subsidies given by his cousin, Louis XIV of France. Deprived of his ability to wield power through parliament, Shaftesbury began considering open rebellion to support the Protestant Duke of Monmouth as the rightful heir to Charles. When Charles had managed to get Tory sheriffs elected in London who could select juries to convict Shaftesbury of high treason, Shaftesbury fled the country and died in Rotterdam in 1682. Meanwhile, the Lord Chief Justice was hearing cases brought against Catholics by Oates, and it became obvious that the evidence of Oates and his fellow accusers was a pack of lies. Oates was imprisoned, there was a public backlash against him and the anti-Popish frenzy died down sufficiently for James and Mary Beatrice to return to London. James then had a great stroke of luck.

In 1683 the Rye House Plot was uncovered to assassinate both Charles and James as they passed a building called Rye House when returning to London after attending Newmarket races. The aim of the plot was to enable a Protestant succession, possibly by putting Monmouth on the throne, but it was not very well developed and much of it was just talk among extremist Whigs. The king was held in great affection by the common people, whose shock at the revelation of the proposed assassination resulted in an upsurge of support for him and even James. Charles played this for all it was worth and in subsequent trials nearly all those implicated in the plot were executed, imprisoned, or escaped abroad. Charles had managed to rid himself of most of the opposition Whig leadership which had tried to prevent James from inheriting the throne.

One prominent person who was probably implicated in the plot was Charles's much loved bastard son, Monmouth. Charles tried hard to get Monmouth to provide evidence against the plotters and return to royal favour, but to the king's sadness he refused and was banished. Monmouth moved to The Hague where he was generously received by his cousin, James's daughter Mary, and her husband William of Orange.

With Monmouth gone, Whig leaders vanquished and no parliament to question the king's actions, Charles had a relaxed and enjoyable final year. He quietly enjoyed the company of his mistresses, dogs, and numerous illegitimate children, with his brother James returning to the Privy Council and taking up responsibilities appropriate to the heir presumptive. This happy state was brought to a sudden end when Charles had a seizure on 2 February which took him to his death bed and the excruciating tortures of his well-meaning physicians.

As Charles lay in pain, falling in and out of consciousness, James took command of the situation. He dispatched messages to lord lieutenants, instructing them to get into a state of readiness in case of any disturbances that might follow the king's death. He had also ordered all ports to be closed so that no messages of Charles's imminent demise could get to Monmouth and be exploited by him. There was one action that had been uppermost in James's mind but was fraught with danger. He needed to save his brother's soul by arranging for him to convert to Catholicism before his life ended. Soon after Charles's first seizure, Queen Catharine had asked Mary Beatrice to request James to arrange for Charles's conversion. James knew how difficult this was, not least because the Archbishop of Canterbury and other bishops, including Durham, London, Ely and Bath and Wells, were constantly in the king's bedchamber trying to provide Charles with Anglican prayer and comfort. James decided he could take no action. The situation was very delicate, Charles had spent his pubic life as an Anglican and would be furious if he recovered and discovered he had joined the Church of Rome.

As Charles became weaker, his principal mistress, the Catholic Louise, Duchess of Portsmouth, got the French Ambassador, Paul Barrillon, to visit James and beg him to arrange a conversion. James realised that time was running out and told Barrillon that 'I would rather risk everything than not do my duty on this occasion.'[2] The decision was made but the problem was how to implement it. Firstly it was necessary to get Charles's consent to conversion and secondly to find a priest. James was the only person who could approach the royal bed on his own authority; he did so as discretely as possible and whispered about conversion in his brother's ear. Charles answered very quietly: 'Yes with all my heart.'

The next step was to find an English speaking Catholic priest, but they were not easy to come by, as being a Popish priest was illegal and risked the death penalty. The queen and Mary Beatrice as foreign royalty had dispensation to have their Catholic chaplains, but they all spoke either Portuguese or Italian. Fortunately, an English priest was found in the queen's household and this was Father John Huddleston. He had been given a position in the queen's household by way of thanks for his part in helping Charles escape after the Battle of Worcester. Huddleston was disguised in a wig and cassock and led from the queen's apartments to a back-stairs closet just off the king's bedchamber which had a concealed communicating door. James told the clerics and courtiers assembled around Charles that the king wished everyone to retire except for the earls of Bath and Feversham who were, respectively, the Groom of the Stole and the Queen's Chamberlain, both Protestants but completely loyal to the crown.

When the bedchamber had been cleared Huddleston was led in and Charles rallied at the sight of him. Huddleston took the king's confession, accepted him into the Catholic Church then administered the Vaticum and Extreme Unction. The king was conscious and accepted the rites wholeheartedly. Huddleston's work completed, he silently left as he had arrived through the secret door. The only people who had seen the king's conversion were James, Barrillon, Bath and Feversham. James had wanted Bath and Feversham to be in the room so they could be Protestant witnesses to the event, if James ever decided to make the conversion public. Having completed his religious duty to his brother, James then recalled all those who had been sent to wait in the antechamber and Charles's prolonged death agonies continued as if nothing had happened.

Charles clung onto life for another two days, prompting the king to apologise to those around his bed for being 'such an unconscionable time a-dying'. Charles then began a series of farewells, firstly to Queen Catharine, then James with Mary Beatrice by his side, and lastly all his illegitimate children, except of course Monmouth. At ten in the morning of 6 February, Charles fell into a coma in which he remained until his death at noon.

News of the king's death resulted in an outpouring of public grief. Queen Catharine received the formal condolences of ambassadors with dignity, and the royal body was placed in the Whitehall's Painted Chamber to lie in state. The funeral took place on 14 February and Charles was interred in the Henry VII Chapel at Westminster Abbey. Much to James's distress, the funeral service had to be an Anglican one, as there was no question that Charles's conversion to Catholicism could be acknowledged. James had done his best to save the soul of his brother, but there was only so far he could go in Protestant dominated England

With Charles dead, James's principal task was to ensure the security of his throne. After all, it had only been a matter of a couple of years previously that the country had been in the grips of anti-papist hysteria and powerful opposition leaders were demanding that he be excluded from inheriting the crown. It was a top priority for James to alleviate fears about him being a papist king of a Protestant country. The day after his brother's death James called his Council and made it clear to them that the country had nothing to fear from him being a Catholic. He included in his speech: 'And I shall make it my endeavours to preserve this government both in Church and state as it is now by law established.' The Council requested that the speech could be published, and following James's agreement copies of it were distributed about the country. James took the further step of reassuring the clergy by summoning Archbishop Sancrof and giving a similar undertaking to protect the Anglican church, adding that he: 'would never give such countenance to Dissenters, knowing it must needs be faction not religion if men could not be content to meet five beside their own family which the law dispense with.'[3]

James's next step was the popular move of summoning parliament, which Charles had been ruling without for the last five years. Following these reassurances to Tories and Anglicans, James received loyal addresses from all parts of his three kingdoms. The City which had been so stridently anti-Catholic during the Popish Plot had even sent a message from the Lord Mayor and Aldermen expressing their duty to James while Charles was still in the process of dying. In fact, so firm was the position of the crown in the last years of Charles's reign, that there appeared to be no opposition to the accession of a Catholic king who had given his word to protect the government and church.

It might be thought that a new sovereign would make widespread changes, but James further demonstrated quiet continuity by making very few. He made some minor appointments in the royal household such as making Colonel John Churchill a gentleman of the Bedchamber. Churchill had shown talent as a soldier and diplomat and had been in James's service for twenty years starting as his page, and James had stood firmly by him during the Exclusion Crisis. It was no surprise that James should want to promote a gifted and personable man who had shown him absolute loyalty. Of more importance were the positions in the Council and these James kept virtually unchanged with the main exception being Laurence Hyde, the Earl of Rochester, who he moved from being Lord President of the Council back to being Lord Treasurer. Rochester had been Lord Treasurer previously but had been removed by Charles when his great rival Lord Halifax accused him of losing £40,000 through mismanagement. Rochester was the brother of James's first wife, Anne Hyde, so was semi-family. On the same basis Rochester's elder brother, Henry Hyde, the Earl of Clarendon, was made first Lord Privy Seal, then Lord Lieutenant of Ireland.

It was entirely understandable that James should give promotion to those who were close to him, but it was a surprise and a relief that he was magnanimous to those ministers who had supported his exclusion. Chief among those was Robert Spencer, Earl of Sunderland, who had voted for the Exclusion Bill, an act Charles described as 'a Kiss of Judas', and immediately dismissed him as Secretary of State for the Northern Department. However, after lobbying from the king's principal mistress, the Duchess of Portsmouth, Charles brought him back into government as Secretary of State for the Southern Department. It should be explained that the inner Council had ministers with particular portfolios such as the Lord Treasurer for finance and the Lord Chancellor for the judiciary, but foreign affairs and general domestic matters were split between two Secretaries of State. The most senior was the one for the Southern Department who covered foreign affairs concerning France and southern Europe. The Secretary of State for the Northern Department covered the United Provinces of the Dutch Republic and Scandinavia. Spencer was nothing if not ambitious, and realised that if he was to keep hold of this important post he would have to exert himself to display exceptional loyalty to the new king. To fail to do so would deprive him of the income he badly needed to pay his gambling debts.

James had, therefore, succeeded to the throne without causing any great alarm about his Catholicism, and demonstrated continuity with the previous reign. The one way in which he was not demonstrating continuity could be regarded as a positive one. That was his own standard of conduct and what he expected of his courtiers. Whereas Charles had been lazy and easily bored by the detailed matters of state, James was hardworking, and unlike his brother, kept a close eye on revenue, scrutinising the accounts of the Exchequer on a weekly basis. As expected, Charles's extravagance had resulted in huge debts and James set about paying them off, devoting over £1 million of revenue to this over the next three years. As part of his reforms he made it clear he would not tolerate corruption or the sale of offices. Naturally such practices were ingrained and did continue, but at least less blatantly than before.

Charles II's court may have been merry and dominated by outrageous but amusing men and grasping but beautiful mistresses, but it was undeniably dissolute. Prior to his conversion, James had joined in with the general amiable decadence, even if he had not possessed his brother's sharp mind to take part in the witty repartee. After his conversion to Catholicism James had become steadily more moral and strait-laced. Now he was king he made it clear that blasphemy, drunkenness and gambling for high stakes were no longer acceptable at court. James drank in moderation and became very abstemious in his tastes. He once told Pepys that he used only one sauce to be served with fish, flesh or fowl, and that was 'made up of some parsley and dry toast beat in a mortar, together with vinegar, salt and a little pepper'.[4] James even decided to set an example by sending away his chief mistress Catherine Smedley. It goes without saying that for someone with James's strong libido this would not last. Before long, ladies of a lesser degree were being smuggled into the king's bedchamber through the same secret door from the back stairs that had been used by Father Huddleston.

James's court lacked the sense of fun that had existed previously, not least because of his own formal and aloof manner. That said, at least it could no longer be accused of open debauchery and extravagance, as had been the case with his brother. James's extra-marital sexual appetite was not public knowledge and was satisfied discreetly. The remorse he felt for such sin actually made him more moral in other ways, for he seems to have expiated his guilt by intensifying his devotions and reinforcing his upright standards. His queen, Mary Beatrice, was also a very devout Catholic and she too insisted on high moral standards and rather sadly lost much of her informal charm by copying her husband's imperious manner. For all that, there was a general feeling, in both the court and the country at large, that James was proving to be a good monarch. The fact that he was calling a parliament was also greatly welcomed for it showed that he had no intention of bringing in absolute government, as was the case of other Catholic rulers such as Louis XIV.

James had summoned the English parliament, but had done so with some trepidation. The last parliament had tried to exclude him from the throne and there was a possibility that a new parliament might bring the return of strident opposition. It could be that the new parliament would refuse to vote him money without him granting unacceptable concessions. To cover this eventuality, James asked the French Ambassador, Barrillon, to request Louis to provide funding so, if necessary, he could to rule without parliament as his brother had done. Louis reluctantly agreed to his cousin having £120,000. The extra cash would be useful, but James did not need to worry about the support he would receive from the new parliament.

Fortunately Charles II had taken steps to ensure that most MPs selected to sit in a future House of Commons would be Tory supporters of the crown. He had done this by the legally doubtful expedient called *quo warranto* (by what warrant?). As the monarch had granted corporations their rights in the first place, the monarch could also remove them if he felt they had been misused. Charles began legal challenges to corporation with the result that thirty-five boroughs and other corporations surrendered their charters. New charters might include new privileges, such as additional markets.

What the new charters did state was that key members of the corporation, such as the mayor and town clerk, had to be approved by the king, which was usually delegated to a loyal member of the local gentry. These key posts in the corporations were able to arrange the selection of juries and the election of MPs. Some 203 boroughs were represented in the House of Commons, and many had two MPs, so as there was a total of 513 seats in the Commons, the *quo warranto* process meant that the king could have a strong representation in the House. On top of this Charles had been removing judges, Lords Lieutenant, Deputy Lords Lieutenant and JPs who had Whig sympathies and replacing them with Tories. The huge extension of royal control over people of influence which had taken place in the last five years of Charles's reign meant that there was every chance that a new House of Commons would be packed with loyal Tories. This proved to be the case, for when parliament opened on 5 May, the Commons was staunchly Tory and Anglican, with only about fifty members who might be regarded as Whig opposition.

Before parliament sat there was the matter of a coronation and that was held on 23 April. It was a splendid affair costing £119,000 and was unusual in that Mary Beatrice was crowned as queen consort alongside James, a practice that had been last carried out at the marriage of

Henry VIII to Catherine of Aragon. James had become the anointed king and despite his private Catholicism he was generally well received throughout his three kingdoms. Most of those who had misgivings had been reassured by the king's promises to support the Anglican faith. They also knew that Mary Beatrice was most unlikely to have any children who would survive beyond a few days. Her health was never strong and her ten pregnancies had taken their toll. Sadly, all of these pregnancies had ended in miscarriages, still births or in two cases, very early infant mortality.

The queen had become convinced that Providence had decided that she would never be able to bear a child strong enough to survive into adulthood. This was the general belief of all, and was a matter of some relief to most. If Mary Beatrice was able to bear a male child, that child would be brought up as a Catholic and become James's heir, thus perpetuating a Popish monarchy. Fortunately this seemed extremely unlikely and James's heir would remain his eldest daughter, the Anglican Princess Mary married to the Calvinist Protestant Prince William of Orange. It was true that Mary had already had three miscarriages, but she was only 23 so could still be expected to produce a Protestant heir. In the unlikely event of Mary not giving birth to an heir, then her sister, the equally strong Protestant Princess Anne, would become heir.

The 20-year-old Anne had been married to the Lutheran Protestant Prince George, who was the younger brother of the king of Denmark and Norway. Prince George moved to England and lived with Anne in the Palace of Whitehall. Anne had one miscarriage but was pregnant again and was expected to produce a Protestant heir if her sister failed to do so. All in all, those who were concerned about James's Catholic faith could feel reasonably confident that his heir would be a Protestant and able to reverse anything that the king might introduce which smacked of Popery.

The day after the coronation, the Scottish parliament sat and showed itself to be fully loyal to James by granting him funding of customs revenues and £260,000 for life. This would set a good example to the English parliament when it sat in May. In short, James's inheritance of the crown had gone surprisingly well, with most of the Whig extremists who had supported his exclusion from the throne safely out of the country. The security of the crown no longer appeared an immediate problem and the ports were soon reopened and the army and militia stood down. The responsibility for security rested largely with the secretaries of state, of whom Sunderland was dominant. It was Sunderland who controlled the government intelligence apparatus. That consisted of covert intelligence gathering through the intercept of correspondence using the General Letter Office and the control of most government agents and informants, as well as overt information such as that provided by ambassadors overseas and Lords lieutenant and magistrates at home. Sunderland had an unusual management style. His main interest was gaming for high stakes. He seldom visited his office and his clerks would bring papers to his house for him to sign at the card table, usually without reading them.

Despite Sunderland's languid manner, he was an astute politician who would burst into energy in the pursuit of anything that might facilitate his advancement. It would soon become necessary for some of his energy to be spent on intelligence matters as a threat to the new king was developing in the Netherlands.

Chapter 2

Conspiracy in the Netherlands 1685

'Such and inundation of fanatics and men of impious principles must needs have caused universal disorder, cruelty, injustice, rapine, sacrilege, and confusion, an unavoidable civil was, and misery without end.'

Diary of John Evelyn, entry for 15 July 1685

The news of the sudden death of Charles II was a major shock to William and Mary in Holland. There was sadness that they had both lost their uncle; less so on William's side as his relations with Charles, although outwardly cordial, had been rather strained. This was largely because Charles had allied himself with William's great enemy, Louis XIV. William's dislike of Louis was for good reason. Louis was a young man seeking fame and military glory by expanding French territory. He seized his opportunity when King Philip IV of Spain died leaving the throne to his 3-year-old, deformed and mentally handicapped son, Carlos II.

Despite having an empire stretching from the Americas to the East Indies, covering 4.7 million square miles, Spain was in decline. The country's finances were in crisis, there were crop failures, economic stagnation and a debilitating war with Portugal. With Spain and its new ruler potentially vulnerable, Louis decided to lay claim to the Spanish Netherlands (now largely Belgium) and invaded it in 1667. During two years of fighting Louis made some gains, but the cost of the war and the increasing number of states coming to the aid of Spain, made him conclude a peace. Louis's ambitions had not gone away. As the United Provinces of the Dutch Republic had been a major part of the alliance against France, Louis decided that he needed to first defeat it, before making a further attempt on the Spanish Netherlands. In 1672 Louis launched an attack on the Dutch Republic, supported by England, Sweden, Munster and Cologne. In time, Spain, Austria and Brandenburg-Prussia came to the aid of the Dutch and formed a Quadruple Alliance to block French aggression.

As hereditary Stadtholder of Holland, William became the military leader of the Dutch Republic and a major figure in the Alliance itself. The war lasted six years and in the final year, under pressure from parliament, Charles II began to support the Dutch Republic, but being Charles, that did not stop him still seeking funding from Louis. During the war French armies occupied a number of Flemish and Burgundian towns and also seized William's own principality of Orange. (An independent territory of 108 square miles on the Banks of the Rhone just north of Avignon). William was, after all, the grandson of William the Silent, who had led the Protestant Dutch revolution against Catholic Spain, and as Stadtholder had inherited the post of commander of the Dutch forces. His family had become the defenders of the United Provinces and champions of the Protestant faith in Europe. As Catholic King Louis laid waste William's family principality and tried to conquer the Dutch Republic, he was William's implacable enemy.

The war finally ended in 1678 with the Treaty of Nijmegen. Louis had been thwarted in his attempt to crush the Dutch but had won battles at Ghent and Ypres, forcing Spain to cede Franche-Comté and a number of Flemish cities to France. Louis's aggression had paid off and he had given ample demonstration that France was a major military power in Europe. William was left in no doubt that the Treaty of Nijmegen was merely a pause in hostilities until Louis felt strong enough to pursue his ambition and once again make an assault on the Low Countries.

The death of Charles II meant that Princess Mary of Orange was now heir presumptive to her father James II. The relationship between Mary and James was good, although as a strong Anglican she greatly disapproved of her father's Catholicism. Mary's relationship with her husband William was polite and practical, but far from loving. Mary was an attractive young woman with a vibrant personality and it had been an unpleasant shock to her when informed that Charles II had decided she would marry her Dutch cousin. She is said to have cried for a day-and-a-half at the news, for she knew what the cold, unsmiling William was like from visits he had made to London. Mary was just 15 years old when she married William, who was twelve years older. They could not be described as a handsome couple. The tall, attractive, outgoing Mary was 4 in taller that her dour and serious husband, with his large hooked nose, blackened teeth, hunched back, spindly legs and chronic asthma. In their early years of marriage, Mary's pregnancy might have brought them closer together, but that had ended in miscarriage. The next year, their relationship was not enhanced by William taking one of her ladies-in-waiting, Elizabeth Villiers, as his mistress.

William and Mary worked together as Prince and Princess of Orange, despite their lukewarm personal relationship. Mary's good looks and friendly manner went down well in Holland and helped to compensate for William being aloof and reserved. The sudden death of Charles and the accession of Mary's father James, had created an embarrassment for them. Both William and Mary had gone to great lengths to make the exiled Duke of Monmouth welcome in Holland. This was because Mary had grown up with her cousin at court and William had known Monmouth when he had been the commander of the English expeditionary force sent to support the United Provinces in the recent war with France. More important than personal reasons, was because they felt that Charles II would have wanted them to treat his wayward son kindly.

Monmouth's remarkable life had, in fact, begun in the Dutch Republic. While in exile on the Continent, the 18-year-old Charles II had an affair with a Lucy Walter. Lucy was strikingly beautiful with long glossy black hair, full lips and a fashionably pale complexion. She also had been free with her affections with several other Royalist exiles. The result of Charles's dalliance was the birth of a baby boy called James, in Rotterdam in 1649. The affair soon cooled and Lucy continued to have a series of other lovers. As time passed her behaviour became increasingly irrational and embarrassing. Lucy was running up debts and making demands on Charles, so some royalists gave her money to return to England. She left with James, and a daughter Mary (whose father was probably Viscount Taaffe, a previous lover) and went to live over a barber's shop in London's Strand. She soon came to the notice of Cromwell's Intelligence Department, was arrested as a suspected spy and committed to the Tower together with James and Mary. It was subsequently decided that she was more of an embarrassment to Charles if she was at liberty, so she was released and deported back to the Low Countries.

Lucy and the children went to Brussels and she continued her extravagant and scandalous lifestyle. In 1658 Charles gave instructions for the then 8-year-old James to be kidnapped from Lucy. After a couple of failed attempts this was achieved by a William Ross, who had visited Lucy's lodgings on some pretext and carried out the abduction when she was distracted in another room. Ross then took James from one place to another for the next few months so that Lucy would be unable to track him down. Charles decided that James should be brought up by his friend, the rich royalist exile, William Crofts. As Charles was penniless, he made Crofts a baron for his trouble. Lord Crofts had a substantial house in Combes, six miles north-west of Paris, which became James's home and where he took Croft's name and posed as a relation. Lucy had not given up searching for James and tracked him down to Paris where she died of venereal disease nine months after she last saw him.

Until his abduction, James had received a chaotic upbringing moving from one place to another as his promiscuous mother changed partners, living in opulence one minute and poverty the next. His education had been virtually non-existent. He had not learned to write his name or even count up to twenty.[1] William Ross became his tutor and found James a willing student. Lord Crofts supervised his education as a gentleman, teaching him to fence, dance and hunt. Crofts, had the style and swagger of a royalist courtier, given to sword fights and seductions. It was this boisterous, generous cavalier that James would learn to emulate and regard as the father figure he had always lacked. James had seen next to nothing of his real father, but very soon would become acquainted with Charles's family.

Charles I's widowed queen, Henrietta Maria, although based in Paris also had a house in Combes and knew Crofts well. As a boy Crofts had been her page and later risen to be captain of her guard. The queen visited Crofts, no doubt curious to see her illegitimate grandson. The French, and many other Continental monarchies, were well used to illegitimate children and accepted them as part of the royal family, but of course debarred from inheriting the crown. The queen was captivated by her grandson and soon become greatly attached to him. Henrietta Maria's daughter, Princess Henrietta Anne, was only five years older than James and she came to regard him very much as a younger brother. In November 1659 Charles visited his mother on his way back from the peace conference at Fuentarrabia and stayed with Lord Crofts where he saw James for the first time. Charles only stayed for two weeks before returning to Brussels, but during that period developed a strong liking for the boy.

With Louis XIV still only 15 years old, France was governed by Cardinal Mazarin who had made a treaty with Cromwell's England and so felt it politic to keep Queen Henrietta Maria and her family at a distance. Once Charles had been invited back to England to reclaim his throne, Mazarin's attitude changed. Queen Henrietta Maria and her daughter were suddenly made particularly welcome at the French court where they were accompanied by James. In the space of just a couple of years James had gone from being the bastard of a disreputable courtesan, to gaining the respect due to an illegitimate son of the king of England. He was now receiving the attentions of his grandmother, sister and French courtiers.

Charles had never hidden the fact that he had an illegitimate son, and after good reports from his mother, decided that James should live with him in England. The Dowager Countess of Buccleuch was having legal problems over her husband's estate and to get the king's support, wrote to Charles suggesting that James should marry her daughter. Charles agreed, and just before he left France, James was duly betrothed to the countess's daughter, Anna. The 13-year-old James soon travelled to England with Queen Henrietta Maria, and then went to Hampton Court to join his father. It had been three years since Charles had seen his son, who had grown to display his mother's good looks and some of his father's charm. Charles was delighted with James and decided to establish him as a recognised and favoured royal bastard.

A few weeks after his arrival, James was made Duke of Monmouth, Earl of Doncaster and Baron Tyndale. A month later he became a Knight of the Garter and a month after that married Anna and was created Duke of Buccleuch with other lesser titles in the Scottish peerage. As Anna's husband he could take control of the richest estate in Scotland. Charles treated Monmouth as a much loved son and James grew up as a thoroughly spoilt major figure at court, constantly by his father's side. As he grew older he began taking part in naval and army operations where he commanded the British Brigade on the Continent with bravery and distinction.

Monmouth continued to receive many other tokens of his father's favour, such as being made Master of Horse, Captain General of the Army and given two lord lieutenant-ships. Unfortunately, Monmouth found himself drawn into the company of power-hungry men such as Shaftesbury. Monmouth was a Protestant and urged on by senior Whigs, became their 'royal' focal point for opposition to Popery and the succession of James, Duke of York. The rumour spread that Charles had secretly married Lucy Walter, and so Monmouth was the rightful heir, rather than Catholic James. In defiance of Charles, Monmouth carried out progresses around the country and received rapturous welcomes with crowds acclaiming him 'A Monmouth – the Protestant Prince!' An angry Charles stripped him of his lucrative appointments and with great sadness eventually banished him for refusing to give evidence against the Whig extremists who had been part of the 1683 Rye House Plot.

Charles had been both saddened and angered that the son he had doted upon had refused to obey him and return to royal favour. For all that, Charles would not have wanted him to have a wretched life of exile, and so William and Mary had done their best to look after him. With Mary's father James suddenly king, this kindness could be interpreted as harbouring one of the main threats to James's crown. Realising this, William at once bent over backwards to recover from this unintended slight to his father-in-law. He told Monmouth and his Whig cronies to leave The Hague and sent an urgent message to James that he had done so. James replied that William and Mary should have no more contact with Monmouth and also that William should dismiss certain officers in the three English and Scottish regiments serving in Holland who James considered unsound. For good measure, James said that as he was now head of the Stuart family, William should follow his directions in his dealings with King Louis.

The relationship between James and his nephew had never been warm, indeed, James had strongly opposed his marriage to Mary, but had been overruled by Charles. James was a Catholic who not only favoured his cousin Louis, but was also receiving money from him. William was an ardent Protestant of the Calvinist tradition who had developed a passionate hatred for Louis. The relationship between the new king of England and the husband of his daughter and heir could hardly have got off to a worse start. Their dealings with each other would remain outwardly cordial, but their relationship would deteriorate further with the accumulation of misunderstandings on both sides. For the present, William agreed to the first of James's demands but was rather vague about the other two, merely giving an assurance that he would do 'nothing against interest' of James.

James was quite right to be concerned about Monmouth. Although his takeover of the crown had gone remarkably smoothly, there was no room for complacency. The Whig opposition had not completely evaporated and violent anti-papist feeling was always just below the surface. Most of the Whig extremists had fled to the United Provinces and included important Presbyterian Scots such as Archibald Campbell, 9th Earl of Argyll, chief of the powerful Clan Campbell, and Sir John Cochrane son of the Earl of Dundonald. The English exiles included the Whig political philosopher and writer John Locke, the Scottish cleric and Whig propagandist Robert Ferguson, and several active Rye Plot Whig conspirators such as Richard Goodenough and Nathaniel Wade. The most prominent of these was Baron Grey of Werke who had escaped from the Tower after being arrested for his part in the plot.

Nor were all the Whig leaders abroad. There were two Whig peers in Cheshire who had been leading supporters of the Exclusion Bill. Charles Gerard, Earl of Macclesfield, and Henry Booth, Baron Delamere. The latter had been condemned to death for involvement in the Rye House Plot but then pardoned by Charles II. There was also a small band of Whig extremists in London, the most influential of whom was the former leader of the Levellers and inveterate schemer, Major John Wildman. In short, despite the general welcome that James had received from his subjects, some significant elements of opposition to him remained. There was thus a need for government intelligence apparatus to monitor the activities of all who might threaten the crown at home and overseas.

The post responsible for identifying and neutralising threats to the crown would normally have been the secretary of state for the Southern Department. The hard-working lawyer Sir Leoline Jenkins had occupied this post with distinction and had uncovered the Rye House Plot. He had also redirected much of the intelligence effort after the Plot against the Whig conspirators who had escaped to the Low Countries and particularly made use of Thomas Chudleigh, English Ambassador to The Hague, to monitor their activities. Chudleigh had achieved one particularly notable success regarding the leading Rye House conspirator Sir Thomas Armstrong, who was living in Amsterdam under the assumed name of 'Henry Lawrence'. Chudleigh discovered Armstrong was going on a journey to Amsterdam and arranged for his agents to kidnap him at Leiden and bundle him onto a ship back to England. On returning to

England, Armstrong appeared before Judge Jeffreys and was hanged, drawn and quartered six days later.

Jenkins's good work came to an end when he retired through ill health in April 1684, and was replaced in the Southern Department by Robert Spencer, 2nd Earl of Sunderland. He had accumulated plenty of experience in his forty-four years. At the age of 3 he had inherited his father's titles when the 1st earl had been killed fighting for the king at the Battle of Newbury. When old enough, he attended Christ Church, Oxford, then joined Prince Rupert's Regiment of Horse, becoming a captain, then in 1665 married Anne Digby the daughter of the Earl of Bristol. This was followed by him being appointed successively as ambassador to Madrid, then Paris, and lastly the United Provinces in a three-year period, after which he returned to court as a Gentleman of the Bedchamber, before being made a Privy Councillor and the secretary for the Northern Department in 1679. As one of Charles II principal ministers he tried to get England in an alliance against France, but given the king's support of Louis this was doomed to failure. He made the big political mistake of voting for the Exclusion Bill for which he was dismissed by a furious Charles, but a year later was back in office replacing Jenkins in the Southern Department and further rewarded by being made a Knight of the Garter.

To all appearances Sunderland seemed a typical product of the Restoration Court: smooth-tongued, self-serving, lazy, extravagant and a high-stakes gambler. However, he was now 43 years old with considerable experience from working at three embassies abroad and at the heart of government, so had developed into an extremely astute politician. Such a man was in many ways ideal for running the Intelligence Department. That said, he was not interested in the boring details of government management so did not bother to take over the Department. Government intelligence and covert activity drifted for a period until August when it was taken over by Charles Middleton, 2nd Earl of Middleton, who had just replaced Lord Godolphin as the Secretary of State for the Northern Department.

Middleton was about ten years younger than Sunderland and had been brought up in a political atmosphere. His father had been a Scottish Royalist general who, at the Restoration, became commander-in-chief of troops in Scotland and Lord High Commissioner of the parliament of Scotland. Middleton himself had been made the envoy at the imperial court in Vienna and then returned to Scotland in 1681, just when James had been sent away to Edinburgh by his brother. James and Mary Beatrice both liked Middleton as a person and the next year made him one of the two secretaries of state for Scotland. When James returned to London, Middleton followed him and through James's new influence with Charles, became a member of the Privy Council and then, as we have seen, secretary of the Northern Department.

Having been a member of the Privy Council, Middleton took over the Intelligence Department, well aware that the main threats to security came from the few remaining extremist Whigs and Scottish Presbyterians. He would have known about prominent Whig leaders such as the Earl of Macclesfield and activists such as John Wildman. He ensured that efforts were resumed to monitor their activities. This would be done directly by agents of the Intelligence Department, or by crown servants such as lords lieutenant and justices of the peace who would report their information to the secretaries of state. To be effective, intelligence gathering and its associated covert activities required funding, and a total of £5,000 a year was allocated for this purpose. Life being what it was in those days, not all government money was used for its correct purpose. Officials would take a rake off and indeed, Charles II had sometimes used the Secret Intelligence Fund to provide for his mistresses. For all that, there was still substantial money available to secretaries of state for intelligence management.

The methods used to attempt to gather such information were various. Some use would be made of static surveillance outside suspect's homes or places they were known to frequent, to report who they were meeting. This was particularly used outside those embassies whose ambassadors might be up to no good. An even better source of intelligence, but more difficult to obtain, was from the infiltration of a subversive group using agents or informants. There were two ways this could be achieved. To try to turn an existing member of an opposition group, or the longer term task of recruiting someone who could gradually win the confidence of the potential conspirators and eventually be accepted into the group. The turning of an existing member would need them to be open to bribery by either direct financial reward or the offer of lucrative appointment, but could also be achieved by offering a pardon for past crimes. The latter was regularly employed after situations like the general roundup of those suspected of involvement of the Rye House Plot. While imprisoned, usually in the Tower, a suspect might be offered release and pardon if they became a government agent. Deciding to become an agent would have the added advantage that they might expect an annual salary of £30–£40 for their information. If the suspect agreed, there was the problem of allowing their release without other members of their group suspecting that they had been turned. A way round this was to engineer their escape from custody so that they could return to their group with the added credentials of being on the run.

Obtaining agents and informants was not just a matter of recruitment by inducement. There were plenty of volunteers. It was known there was money to be had for information and many jumped on the bandwagon, offering information to the authorities in exchange for cash. It is true that much of this was inaccurate or spiteful accusations against enemies, or simply fabricated to obtain money. However, some of these informants did have sufficient access to provide valuable information, and in time the person to whom they reported (their handler), would learn to evaluate the likely veracity of their reports. Added to this were persons who made a profession of being agents. These were often former army officers whose background enabled them to be able to infiltrate a particular subversive group. These agents would be employed on a salary basis and as professionals could be very valuable. They did have the drawback of being mercenaries; some became double agents and were also receiving salaries from the government or organisation they were paid to penetrate.

Middleton and his Intelligence Department would have been receiving reports from this wide variety of human sources, all of which could have serious limitations. A generally more reliable source of intelligence was from the intercept of mail. This was centred on the General Post Office in Lombard Street, which had a near monopoly for the transmission of mail. A highly organised process for intercept had be created under Oliver Cromwell's secretary of state and head of intelligence, John Thurloe. It had then been re-established at the Restoration and brought back to peak efficiency by Charles II's head of intelligence, Sir Joseph Williamson. Charles had dismissed Williamson during the Exclusion Crisis but the intercept apparatus had continued under his successors as secretaries of state, until inherited by Middleton. The process involved covertly opening letters from suspects without breaking their seals, copying them and then resealing them and sending them on their way to the unsuspecting addressee. While the letter was open it would have been checked for any secret ink (usually made from urine or lemon juice) by holding it against a lighted candle. The copy of the letter would be translated, if in a foreign language, and decrypted if it contained ciphertext. This latter process required considerable cryptanalysis skill if the writer had used a complex encryption algorithm. Intercept could provide a very valuable source of intelligence, but could be circumvented if a sender used a private messenger.

Such were the main sources of intelligence available to Middleton and therefore the king. As we have seen, there were pockets of potential Whig extremists in the Midlands and London, but if any serious threat manifested itself it would come from the Whig exiles in the United Provinces. As part of William of Orange's attempt to gain favour with James he had undertaken to provide reports on Monmouth's movements. Naturally, William had his own agents and informants, but he could not operate freely in the United Provinces. William was Stadtholder, but not the country's ruler. The Dutch Republic of the United Provinces consisted of seven independent provinces, the most powerful of which was Holland. Each of the provinces had their own government called 'states' which sent delegates to the Republic's States General, whose most important civil official was the Grand Pensionary of Holland. In time of war a Stadtholder was appointed as military leader who would outrank the Grand Pensionary. In practice the post of Stadtholder had become hereditary to the Prince of Orange, particularly in Holland and Zeeland, but there was constant conflict between Republicans, who supported the Grand Pensionary, and Orangists, who supported the Stadtholder and the House of Orange. In addition, the Republicans largely stood for peaceful trade and were wary that Orangists would drag the country into expensive wars.

William of Orange had been born a few days after his father's death from smallpox in 1650 and the Republicans had used the vacancy of the Stadtholdership to grab power under the Grand Pensionary, Johan de Witt. De Witt effectively ran the Dutch Republic for eighteen years until Louis successfully invaded in 1672. De Witt was blamed for lack of military preparedness, lost his authority, and first Holland and then Zealand declared William as Stadtholder. So unpopular had de Witt become that he was assassinated along with his brother by an Orangist mob. The strength of feeling that could develop between Republicans and Orangists was evident when, after their assassination, the bodies of the de Witts were mutilated, hung up on a gibbet, and their livers roasted and eaten by the mob. Following the assassinations, William became commander of all Dutch forces and managed to create alliances which eventually resulted in French forces withdrawing from the Republic. By 1685 William was secure in his position as Stadtholder, but with the country returned to peace, he once again faced Republican opposition from many in the States General.

William was indeed the de facto ruler of the Dutch Republic but his position depended upon consent, and so he had to tread carefully. Even in the matter of keeping an eye on the activities of Monmouth and Whig activists he was rather at odds with Republicans, many of whom had considerable sympathy for the Protestant Whigs who had tried to exclude Catholic James from the English throne. The responsibility of monitoring the activities of Monmouth and other Whigs also lay with Middleton and his Intelligence Department. There were a few English agents in the United Provinces and they were reporting back, normally via a fictitious address which would be known to the intelligence team in the General Post Office and passed on to their handler in the Intelligence Department. The intelligence team in the General Post Office were of course intercepting all mail going to or from the Netherlands between known Whig extremists. Perhaps the most important source of intelligence could be expected to come from the English Ambassador at The Hague. Any ambassador would be running their own agents and informants and reporting the information received back to London.

The United Provinces fell into the responsibilities of the Secretary of the Northern Department, the Earl of Middleton, and so the ambassador would send his reports back to him. This fitted well with Middleton's oversight of Intelligence. In March 1685 Bevil Skelton had been appointed Ambassador to The Hague. He was an experienced diplomat but it was in some ways an unfortunate choice. Skelton had served for two years as a lieutenant colonel in the English Royal Regiment in France and was rabidly pro-French. He was also well known for his intense dislike of the Dutch. He was hardly the sort of person to win the confidence of William of Orange or the Dutch generally. It remained to be seen whether the occupant of this key post could provide the necessary quality of intelligence on the exiled Whig extremists.

But what, if anything, were Monmouth and other Whig exiles getting up to? Back in 1683 Monmouth had gone into exile leaving behind his wife Anna and five children (also at least seven other children by his mistresses – there could be no doubt he was the son of Charles II !)[2] He was accompanied by Lady Henrietta Wentworth who had become the genuine love of his life. Although Monmouth retained his exuberance, he seemed to have become more settled. He hoped to obtain a senior position in a Continental army and settle down to a new life with Henrietta. Although banished by his father, he had lived in hope that he might be forgiven and wanted to do nothing to prejudice his situation. The Whig exiles on the Continent had made repeated efforts to get him to join them in continued resistance, but much to their frustration, had made it clear that he would have no dealings with them and their conspiracies.

Monmouth and Henrietta had been made very welcome by William and Mary at their Honselaardyk Palace in The Hague, and in November 1684 he received the news he had been hoping for. The Marquis of Halifax, Lord President of the Council, asked him to discreetly return to England for secret talks about his future.[3] The upshot of this brief visit was that Monmouth had been assured that in the next few weeks, Charles was likely to allow him to return to England and royal favour. When Monmouth returned to The Hague in December he told William about this in confidence. The Christmas period became a very happy one filled with balls, private theatricals, skating and general merriment enlivened by the jovial Monmouth. This blissful period for Monmouth and Henrietta came to an abrupt end when the news of Charles II's death shattered their dreams of the future.

As we have seen, William was obliged to send Monmouth away and he went with Henrietta to his house in Brussels seeking employment in a Continental army. William now knew Monmouth well and rightly believed that he was not interested in conspiracies and posed no threat to his father-in-law, James II. In addition Monmouth had given William his word that he would never consider making a claim for the English crown. While in Brussels, Whig exiles began contacting Monmouth asking for his support, but he replied: 'I am now so much in love with a retir'd Life, that I am never like to be fond of making a Bustle in the World again'.[4] Then, following pressure from James II, the governor of the Spanish Netherlands told Monmouth to leave his territory; two weeks later, he and Henrietta were back in the United Provinces and stayed in Rotterdam, where most of the Whig exiles had converged. Here he met Argyll, Grey and Ferguson, who began to persuade him to lead an invasion to restore Protestantism.

Bevil Skelton had only arrived at The Hague a couple of weeks before Monmouth had left for Rotterdam. He had to act quickly to gather intelligence. His informants had already told him that the main Whig exiles had gathered in Rotterdam and had been joined by Monmouth.

An agent then correctly reported that the Whig exiles were, 'very ill satisfyd with the Duke of Monmouth's conduct.'[5] It looked as though Monmouth would continue to shun their advances and the conspiracy fizzle out. However, during the next few days of that fateful April in Rotterdam, Monmouth would be persuaded reluctantly to change his mind. Lord Grey, the Earl of Argyll, and the smooth-tongued Ferguson, set about convincing Monmouth that he was honour-bound to lead an uprising to restore the Protestant faith. They were entirely confident of success and presented a plan for a two pronged invasion. Argyll would sail to Scotland to raise his clan, and Scottish Presbyterians and Monmouth would land in the West Country, where he had received so much popularity during his progress there in 1682. In order for the uprisings to be as simultaneous as possible, Monmouth would depart Amsterdam as soon as possible after Argyll. The king's army would have to divide to counter both threats, and so could be overcome in battle once the rebels had received reinforcements raised by the Earl of Macclesfield in the north, and John Wildman in London.

Ferguson produced a 'Mr Smith', who brought a message from Wildman that London would rise in rebellion and that he would arrange 'any reasonable sum' to equip an army. What Monmouth did not know was that the message was a fabrication and 'Mr Smith' was in the pay of Ferguson. A messenger to Monmouth from Walter Disney, a Whig publisher in London, advising Monmouth not to think of coming was waylaid by Grey. Under so much pressure, and with Henrietta away in The Hague, Monmouth finally agreed to the plan by the end of April.

During these secret debates information was leaked and one of Skelton's agents reported that he had heard that Monmouth would take part in a rebellion. On 10 April, Skelton sent a letter to Middleton saying, 'it is whispered that Monmouth intends to passe over to England and land in the west part of the kingdom and that Matthews and those who are gone before are sent to prepare his reception.'[6] On receiving the information, Middleton immediately issued an arrest warrant for Captain Edward Matthews, but was unable to locate him. Skelton's agent's information was premature, but turned out to be correct. Unfortunately, the situation became rather muddied by other reports that Monmouth and Argyll were planning to go to Scotland or Northern Ireland. However, Middleton and James II were now aware that an insurrection was being planned.

Suddenly things began moving fast. There were strong rumours that Argyll had obtained three ships and was loading them with weapons. Although this rumour was true, it was hard to verify. Argyll had shrewdly assembled his ships off the Island of Texel at the mouth of the Zuyder Zee, and therefore outside the jurisdiction of Amsterdam, which was itself outside the jurisdiction of William of Orange. He had also bribed the port officials to turn a blind eye to his activities. As the relations between the burgers of Amsterdam and William were strained, they were not prepared to provide him with any information about English exiles, even if they knew it. Skelton got Henry Bull, the English consul in Amsterdam, to request the States General to authorise a search of Argyll's ships. Bull eventually received the States General's permission and presented it to the Amsterdam Admiralty, who merely said they had no ships available to carry out the task. Bull was by all accounts a timid man, but gamely hired a yacht and took customs officials out to board Argyll's ships. Once on board, the customs men discovered that the ships were indeed carrying arms, but that duty had been paid on them and the paperwork showed they were bound for Konigsberg and Danzig. Bull could do nothing but to sail back to Amsterdam and report the situation to Skelton.

Bull's visit had made Argyll impatient to leave and so he set sail on 2 May and it was only on that day that either William or Skelton knew he had departed. The big question was whether Monmouth was on board as well. There were reports that he had been seen boarding in a seaman's jacket, but then there were other reports that he had been seen in Liege on 11 May. Skelton sent an assessment to Middleton that 'Most people here think that he (Monmouth) has gone to England or Scotland'[7] Finding out precisely where Monmouth was, and what he was doing, became an intelligence priority of the highest importance for William and Shelton.

As it turned out, Argyll's uprising was to be of little consequence as it deteriorated into a farce. He had set off with just 300 men, but stopped at Orkney where his secretary was landed to discover the latest news. The secretary was arrested by the Bishop of Orkney, and was interrogated. In England interrogation was called 'examination' and was a judicial process in which the subject would be questioned and their answers recorded. Naturally, inducements and threats might take place which would not be recorded, but there was no torture. Torture was a royal prerogative and Charles II had never given approval for its use. In Scotland torture was perfectly legal and widely used. The most common method of torture was the boot. For this, a special boot was put on the subject's foot and wooden wedges driven into the sides. Argyll's secretary was tortured, probably with the boot; a thumb screw could possibly have been used, but it was a fairly recent Russian invention which might not have reached Orkney. Whatever the method used it was successful, and the secretary not only provided all the information he knew about Argyll's expedition, but also gave the code to decipher Argyll's intercepted letters.

Argyll's plan to land on the west coast of Scotland was immediately sent to the Edinburgh authorities, with the code dispatched south to Secretary of State Middleton and on to the decryption team. The government in Edinburgh called out the 12,000-strong militia and sent a force of 300 regulars to meet Argyll, who was known to be heading for his clan territory. Argyll landed first in Kintyre near Campbeltown, then moved to Tarbert, and raised about 1,000 of his clansmen. He tried to capture his family home, Inveraray Castle, but failed, then blundered on into Dunbartonshire hoping to go south to recruit Lowland Presbyterians. In this he had no success. During his advance all his ships were captured by the English fleet and he began taking losses from attacks by the militia. Knowing they would soon be facing regular government troops, Argyll's force of 2,000 had reduced to 400, then melted away completely. Argyll found himself alone except for one major. He disguised himself as a peasant hoping to get back into the Highlands, but was captured by some militiamen near Erskine having drawn attention to himself as a result of falling in a river during a brawl with a drunk. The dishevelled and bedraggled Argyll now had a full beard and was not at first recognised by his captors. Once his identity was realised he was taken to Edinburgh Castle where he was put in irons and interrogated by the council; he refused to give any information.

Under normal circumstance he would then have been tortured with the boot, indeed the council threatened him with torture, but did not carry it out, probably because of his rank. Although this was a missed intelligence opportunity, it turned out not to make much difference. As Argyll had already been convicted on the trumped-up charge of treason back in 1681, there was no need for further delay and he was executed on 30 June. The method of execution was the 'maiden', Scotland's early form of guillotine, the same method that had been used on his father twenty-four years earlier. This feeble attempt at rebellion in the Highlands was soon forgotten – apart from the unusual incident that when Argyll's head was struck off, his body briefly convulsed into a standing position.

The intelligence of Argyll's departure and then his landing in Scotland reached James just as he was opening the English parliament. In his speech James gave parliament his usual assurances about supporting the Church of England, then asked them to vote for revenues, and at the end said that the Earl of Argyll had landed in Scotland. At this there were general shouts of 'God save the King!' James could not have hoped for a more compliant parliament because it soon afterwards voted the king the traditional royal revenues, and agreed additional customs dues to pay off Charles II's debts and refurbish the fleet.

The outcome of Argyll's expedition was that it not only resulted in the removal of the main leader of Presbyterian opposition in Scotland, but actually boosted support for James in England. The question now was whether Monmouth would mount his own expedition and if so, how much of a threat that would pose to James.

Chapter 3

King Monmouth
1685

'God be thanked, here is an end of all troubles in such a
manner as that we may never hope to see the like again as
long as we live.'

Letter from Queen Mary of Modena to
William of Orange on 19 July 1685

It was not immediately clear what Monmouth was doing. Rotterdam
was the second largest town in the United Provinces and although
the English community had settled mainly in the Nieuwehaven and
Haringvliet districts, they were a mass of alleyways, making surveillance
difficult. Skelton had been receiving his best information on Whig
conspirators from an agent in Utrecht, a Frenchman called Massell;
those involved in Whig conspiracies often stayed in his house. Massell
passed his information back to Skelton using a husband and wife team
as intermediaries.[1] The information was usually accurate, but took a bit
of time to arrive. Skelton had another well-placed agent, Dr Covel, in
William of Orange's court, but he was not able to shed any light on
Monmouth's activities, largely because William himself was still trying
to find out. Skelton began making use of a shady Irishman called
Edmund Everard.

Back in 1681 Everard had been involved in a particularly murky
Catholic entrapment plot and, in exchange for a pardon, had offered his
services as a spy. Middleton had directed him to go to the Netherlands
to penetrate the Whig and Nonconformist exiles. He had the right
credentials for this task, having once been employed as a junior secretary
to Monmouth. In time, Everard established himself in Holland as a
reasonably prosperous merchant, who was well integrated with the exile

community, but dishonesty seems to have led to him being dropped as a source. Skelton had been reluctant to employ a man he believed to be a thoroughly unreliable scoundrel, but lack of alternatives made him reactivate Everard as an agent to get information on Monmouth.

Monmouth was having second thoughts. A little before Argyll had sailed, Monmouth had sent two agents, Edward Matthews and John Battiscombe, to England to make preparations for the uprising. They were to contact two Cheshire peers, Macclesfield and Delamere, and ask them to get word to Whig leaders in the South West. Also to contact Wildman in London to make arrangements about the financing of the uprising. Matthews and Bettiscombe later returned to Rotterdam reporting that they had only received vague and evasive answers from English Whigs. Monmouth's misgivings multiplied, but he felt it a matter of honour to hold his agreement with Argyll and set about raising money for his expedition. He pawned the contents of his house in Brussels, sold most of his clothes – including his garter robes – and got Henrietta to sell her jewellery, raising about £9,000. This, and donations of £1,500 from Whig supporters in Rotterdam, was sufficient to buy a 32-gun warship, three small sloops and weapons and breastplates for 1,500 men. On 17 May he was ready to sail, but gales prevented him leaving till 1 June. Already time was slipping by to achieve the simultaneous uprising with Argyll.

The pawning of Monmouth's gold and silver in Brussels could hardly have gone unnoticed, as it raised £4,000, let alone the recruitment of men and the fitting out of a small fleet. Historians have blamed Skelton for not obtaining timely intelligence, but the truth is he was doing the best he could in a difficult situation. He was encountering the same problems as before regarding the lack of cooperation of the Amsterdam authorities. Skelton heard that Monmouth was having ships loaded and made the mistake of informing the Amsterdam authorities and not the States General. It was only on 23 May that he discovered he needed a special order from the States General to detain the ships. He did not receive the special order until 28 May, and when it came it only covered one ship, not all four. Following bureaucratic delays and confusion, a Dutch frigate was sent to intercept Monmouth's ships, but they had already gone. The States General issued an order for Monmouth's arrest on the very day that he had departed. Skelton was new to the United Provinces and had been faced with an intelligence emergency in his first weeks; despite some frantic efforts on his part, he had presided over what was regarded as a major intelligence failure.

Although Skelton had not provided Middleton with detailed information of Monmouth's plans, he had at least given warning that rebellion was about to take place. On 22 May he had reported:

> I have informations from Amsterdam that there hath been of
> late bills drawne upon from Amserdam and that there hath
> been late bills drawne upon from mostlv merchants of that
> citty for vast summs and that from most parts of the world,
> and all for use of His Majesties rebellious subjects.[2]

On receiving this, Middleton informed the king, who authorised the issue of warrants for the arrest of a long list of those who were believed to have been involved in the Rye House Plot, but had not been prosecuted through lack of evidence. The two secretaries of state also sent messages to mayors and deputy lieutenants to disarm 'all dangerous and suspect persons', especially in the West Country and the North West.

If Skelton's agents had not produced details of Monmouth's plans, the same could be said of William of Orange, who at first found it hard to believe that Monmouth would act in such a way. William tried to regain the initiative by sending his close friend and chief minister, Willem Bentinck, over to James with the news that Monmouth had set sail, and providing whatever information about the uprising he was able to gather. William naturally had no wish for Monmouth to try to take the throne, to which his wife Mary was the heir. As a token of goodwill, Bentinck also said that if James needed assistance, William himself would bring over the three English and Scottish regiments in the Dutch service to fight against Monmouth. James replied that William was not required, but that he would be glad of the regiments. Middleton and his Intelligence Department were not clear where Monmouth intended to land. Then, on 30 May, two letters from London were seized, one in Taunton and one in Ilminster; they read: 'friend … These are to advise thee that honest Protestants forthwith prepare and make themselves very ready … for they have notice here at Court that a certaine person will appear in the West'[3] This looked pretty definite, but there were other conflicting reports and, as late as 12 June, James wrote to William saying that he thought Monmouth would land in Scotland, Lancashire or Cheshire.

Despite James's views, Middleton thought the West Country was Monmouth's most likely destination, and Sunderland gave orders for the mayors and justices in the west to search all posts, coaches and carriers and check out all strangers. Militia units were dispatched to Exeter and Taunton to keep the peace. There were some stories coming in from the west about parties of horsemen being seen at night, but these just turned out to be rumours. Apart from this, the West was quiet. As Monmouth was known to have set sail on 1 June, it should not have taken him more than a few days to reach the West Country, so it looked as though he must have gone to Scotland or the North of England. On 4 June the militia were stood down. What was not known was that Monmouth had been delayed by adverse winds. On 6 June Skelton at last received a report from Massell in Utrecht, who wrote that, 'the duke purposeth to land and set up his standard at Lyme'.[4] Skelton immediately sent this information back to Middleton, but his letter was delayed by the same west wind that was delaying Monmouth, so James and his government in London were still no wiser about Monmouth's movements.

Adverse winds meant that it had taken a fortnight after leaving Holland before Monmouth and his flotilla completed the 400-mile journey to the Dorset coast. There he landed two scouts at the village of Saston to discover whether royal forces had been alerted. Local fishermen told them that the only news was that the Earl of Argyll had landed in Scotland and the Duke of Monmouth was leading an invasion somewhere in England. James was relieved by the intelligence that his landing would be unopposed and, on 11 June, he disembarked eighty-three men at Lyme Regis. There he received a welcome from the ordinary people, but not from the mayor. The mayor of Lyme was Gregory Alford, a royal appointee under the *quo warranto* system and chosen for his dislike of dissenters. He saw the disembarkation and immediately rode to Exeter to give the alarm, and then to the Duke of Albermarle (George Monck's son) who, as lord lieutenant of Devon, commanded the militia.

In addition, two customs officials who also witnessed the landing rode to Crewkerne to spread the news and then, with several changes of horses, rode on to London and arrived at the house of their local MP at 4 am on Saturday 13 June. This was just thirty-six hours after Monmouth's landing. By coincidence, the MP for Lyme was Sir Winston Churchill and his son John, Brigadier Lord Churchill, was staying with him. Sir Winston and Lord Churchill immediately took the two customs men to the Palace of Whitehall. As Lord Churchill was a gentleman of the bedchamber he had ready access to the royal bedroom and woke the king in the early hours of the morning. There the king was briefed by the customs men who were given £20 each for their trouble.

The situation had clarified, but James still did not know how successful Argyll would be in raising the Highlands against him. He could assume that Argyll would be held back, and hopefully defeated by royal troops in Scotland, but what if he broke through into England? James's army numbered 10,000, but was scattered about the country in various garrisons. He only had about 6,000 troops immediately to hand. He did not want to divide his army to cover the threats of both Scotland and the West Country and decided to concentrate on the latter. Lyme was 150 miles from London and infantry could cover only fifteen miles a day on long marches, so there was no time to lose. James was an experienced soldier and acted decisively. He immediately ordered Churchill to ride westwards to command an advanced guard, taking four troops of the Oxford Blues and four of his own regiment of dragoons. He also gave orders for Churchill to be followed as soon as possible by Colonel Kirke with five companies of his Queen's Regiment, recently back from Tangiers.[5] It would take some time for the king to make full preparations for countering Monmouth, but he put the immediate defence in the hands of someone he could trust implicitly: Churchill.

Churchill had spent nearly his whole life serving James. His sister, Arabella, had been maid of honour to James's first wife, Anne Hyde, and subsequently became his mistress for ten years, bearing him four children. John had become James's page at the age of 15 and later joined the army, serving with James at the naval Battle of Solebay, then took part in various operations on the Continent, rising to colonel before returning to court. There, he fell in love with, and subsequently married, Sarah Jennings, one of the ladies of James's subsequent wife, Mary Beatrice. He was sent on various diplomatic missions and returned at the time of the Exclusion Crisis, where he demonstrated complete loyalty to James and accompanied him and Mary Beatrice on their semi-exile by Charles II to the Continent and Scotland. When Charles II felt it was safe for James to return to London, Churchill accompanied him and was rewarded by being made a baron in the Scottish peerage. When James's daughter Anne married Prince George of Denmark, she chose Sarah, her childhood friend, to be her maid of honour. John Churchill was tied to James through long service, close relations with his family, and gratitude for advancement.

When news of Monmouth's landing reached London, parliament gave its resounding support to the king and voted through a supply bill of extra taxes on linen, silk and spirits for five years to finance the crushing of Monmouth's rebellion. They also passed an act of attainder against Monmouth, meaning that he was condemned to death for treason without trial, and his lands and titles were forfeit to the crown. At James's instigation, parliament also agreed to renew authority for the royal censorship of the press, which had lapsed. This powerful weapon for propaganda had been used very successfully by the crown in the past and was now again at royal disposal.

In the next few days James made detailed military plans. He ordered some companies to deploy to the north and east of London to defend the city and decided that the rest of his troops should follow Churchill to the West Country to seek out and destroy Monmouth's force. The additional troops consisted of battalions of foot guards under Monmouth's half-brother, the Duke of Grafton, together with some cavalry, dragoons and an artillery train. Once this force caught up with Churchill's advanced guard the royalist army would total 3,500. James felt this was too large a force to remain under the command of Churchill who was a brigadier, so placed it under a man of higher rank and birth, Lieutenant General Louis Duras, Earl of Feversham, a man he could trust completely. Feversham was a French Huguenot nobleman and a professional soldier who had come to England in James's train back in 1663. Since then he had proved himself as a diplomat, officer of the House Guards and central figure at court. Feversham was one of the two men James had trusted to be present at Charles II's deathbed conversion. He was a totally loyal servant and a reasonably competent, but not gifted, general.

James knew that little could be expected of the county militias, which seldom trained and were poorly equipped. Nevertheless, he ordered the Duke of Bedford, who was the greatest landowner in the west, to take the Gloucester, Hereford and Monmouth militia to defend Bristol from any attack by Monmouth. The king also ordered the navy to retake Lyme and gave orders for the general arrest of 'All disaffected and suspicious persons, particularly all Nonconformist ministers and such persons as served against our royal father and late royal brother.'[6] The secretaries of state, particularly Middleton, had their work cut out producing lists of potential suspects. Several hundred arrests took place in London, and there were so many people rounded up that the halls of the livery companies had to be used to accommodate them.

All the actions that James had taken in response to Monmouth were sound, as might be expected of someone who was an experienced soldier and military leader. He had, after all, fought in a number of campaigns under the great French general, Turenne, including the siege of Arras, then later against France at the Battle of the Dunes and latterly, as Lord High Admiral, had let the navy at the battles of Lowestoft and Southwold Bay. James had done all he could to secure his throne, it was now up to Feversham and Churchill to defeat Monmouth.

Meanwhile, Monmouth had recruited well in Lyme. He was taking an active part in raising volunteers and his affable, approachable style, coupled with good looks and princely bearing, immediately won people over. His numbers had risen to about a 1,000 as he set off for Taunton amid cheering cries of 'A Monmouth!' marching behind his blue flags emblazoned with 'For God, Freedom and Religion'. The Devon and Somerset militias had turned out but pulled back from attacking the rebels, probably because their commanders were conscious of Monmouth's popularity among their ranks. It all seemed a promising start. The rebel recruits were made up of weavers, shopkeepers, miners and farm labourers, but Monmouth used his military expertise to organise them into a manageable force and give them intensive training in drill and military service. He divided his army into regiments, each given a colour. For example, the Green Regiment was led by the old Cromwellian colonel, Abraham Holmes, and the red Regiment was under Nathaniel Wade, a Bristol lawyer who had been one of the Rye House conspirators, but had no previous military experience.

Although he had recruited enthusiastic amateurs eager to learn how to be soldiers, no member of the gentry had yet to join him. This not only meant that Monmouth was not getting the high-level support he needed to demonstrate wide approval for his cause, but he was missing their financial backing and most importantly, their good horses to use as cavalry. Monmouth had put Grey in command of the cavalry, which consisted of men unused to moving in formation, mounted on less than forty rather scruffy horses more suited to the farmyard than the field of battle.

Ferguson advised Monmouth that lack of support from the gentry would be resolved if he declared himself king, and so those following him would consider themselves not traitors but fighting for the lawful king. Monmouth knew he would be breaking promises he had made to William and others, but eventually agreed. On entering Taunton he was declared 'King Monmouth' at the market cross. (He could hardly call himself 'King James' as he would be confused with James II.) The common people might be content to believe that Charles II had married Lucy Walter, but not so the gentry. To them, Monmouth's declaration of kingship turned him from being a rather naive champion of Protestantism and parliament, into a treasonous adventurer. Still, Taunton was a Whig and Nonconformist stronghold, so Monmouth's charisma brought good recruitment. The number of cavalry rose to about 500, and he was able to march onwards with a rather rag-tag force now totalling 4,000.

The king had dispatched an army to the west, but the government in London did not know where Monmouth and his rebels had reached, or what their next objective was. Monmouth had, in fact, decided to conduct a surprise attack on Bristol; James had anticipated this and ordered Feversham and his force to join the Duke of Bedford in defending the city. Feversham had not yet reached Bristol but sent out cavalry reconnaissance for over a week, before a group under Colonel Oglethorpe encountered some of Monmouth's troops at Keynsham, and a minor skirmish took place. Oglethorpe was pushed back with some losses and leaving behind a few prisoners. The action would have been of little consequence had it not been for the intelligence it brought to both sides. Oglethorpe was able to report back that he had located Monmouth's army. The prisoners taken by Monmouth's men said that the king's army was over 4,000 strong and close by in Bristol. The figure of 4,000 was an exaggeration, but word of so strong a force about to bear down upon them hit the morale of Monmouth's men. It made Monmouth's own morale even lower because he knew of the poor quality of his little army compared with that of the royal army, which he knew exceptionally well having served in it himself for seven years, four of which as its captain general.

In fact the royalist main body was some way off, so Monmouth might still have been able to launch a surprise attack on Bristol and so take the second largest city in England as a firm base for the rebellion. However, the inaccurate intelligence from the captives persuaded him to retreat south. This was a major disappointment for Monmouth, but he was to be made even more disappointed when news reached him of the failure of Argyll's expedition, and then the realisation that he would get no support from Wildman in London or Macclesfield in Cheshire. Clearly not only was an attack on Bristol now out of the question, there seemed no hope for the rebellion. He began to believe that his only option was to give up his attempt for the throne and return to the Continent and his beloved Henrietta. Sadly, Grey and Ferguson convinced him that he could not, with honour, abandon his troops, and so he began withdrawing to Bath. He had hoped to raise spirits by getting Bath to surrender, but when his herald appeared before the city he was killed by a lucky shot from the ramparts and the gates closed.

Monmouth continued to retreat to Bridgewater, with Feversham now in close pursuit. Feversham camped his 2,000 infantry in the open marshland of Sedgemoor and billeted the bulk of his cavalry and most of the officers in the village of Westonzoyland, half a mile away. The royalist army was just seven miles from Monmouth at Bridgewater. Feversham was confident that Monmouth would realise he was about to be beaten and that his only hope was to attempt an escape by making a break for it to the north. As a result, Feversham did not order defences to be dug round the infantry camp and only deployed a minimum number of sentries and cavalry scouts under Colonel Oglethorpe. Feversham's feeling was held by the majority of his force who felt they could relax in the knowledge that the rebels would either run away or be brought to battle and be easily beaten. Able to relax, it is understood that all ranks enjoyed large quantities of local cider.

Monmouth had indeed been thinking of breaking out to the north, but this changed when a local farmer called Benjamin Godfrey was brought to him and said that Feversham's infantry camp was in open ground with no defences prepared. Godfrey explained that there were deep drainage ditches called 'rhines' in the Sedgemoor area, but that it would be possible to navigate round them and for the royalist picket sentries to attack the vulnerable enemy position. Godfrey probably also explained that Feversham's infantry was camped about 100 yards behind the 12 ft wide ditch of the Bussex Rhine. Monmouth was fully aware that his untrained force would not stand a chance against professional royalist troops in a formal daylight battle. He therefore decided upon a last throw of the dice: he would mount a night attack. The plan was for Grey and the cavalry to be led by Godfrey in an indirect way avoiding Feversham's pickets and navigating over the rhine bridges to get behind the royalist infantry. The infantry would follow the cavalry but deploy along the Bussex Rhine. Grey would attack the sleeping infantry in their tents and when they ran out they would be shot by the infantry lining the rhine. This would result in the destruction of most of the royalist army before Feversham and the cavalry arrived from Westonzoyland. It was a good plan, and Monmouth had the military experience to carry it off.

At 11 pm on 5 July, Monmouth set off with his men walking silently in file and with rags tied around the horses' hooves. Amazingly, Monmouth's long advance with 4,000 men was not noticed by any of Oglethorpe's scouts. Cider may have played a part in this. After about two hours Monmouth's men were getting over one of the ditches when someone accidently discharged his pistol. Monmouth's attack was no longer a surprise and they were still 1½ miles from the enemy. A royalist trooper heard the shot and galloped back to the camp. Knowing that soon the alarm would be raised and drums would be beating 'stand to', Monmouth decided to attack with all speed, sending Grey with the cavalry to launch the assault. When Grey arrived near the government camp it was misty and Godfrey was unable to find the bridge across one of the rhines. Grey and his men desperately rode up and down the rhine trying in vain to find a bridge, not realising that the water in the ditch was only about a foot deep and could have been crossed easily. Feversham had retired to bed at Westonzoyland leaving Churchill as the officer of the day; in effect, the army's temporary commander. Churchill was at the infantry camp and on hearing the alarm he had begun mustering the infantry and had them firing at Grey's cavalry as they rode up and down the rhine. Grey then saw a troop of royalist dragoons approaching and fled to a nearby village.

Monmouth and his infantry arrived at the rhine to find the cavalry had fled, but they still had a faint chance of overcoming the unprepared royalist infantry. Monmouth's leading infantry battalion, under Nathaniel Wade, managed to move into position along the Bussex Rhine ready for an assault over the ditch and onto the still drowsy camp. Unfortunately, he had not moved up far enough and the battalion following began opening fire at the royalists, which would have meant Wade's assault would have gone straight into friendly fire. The assault never happened. Monmouth's infantry at last deployed along the rhine and the next hour-and-a-half consisted of both sides firing at each other across the rhine. It was not an even contest, with Monmouth's brave but mostly civilian followers pitted against Churchill's disciplined and well equipped soldiers. Monmouth had brought three cannon with him which were having a serious effect, with the royalist right flank already receiving the main rebel fire. Churchill responded by redeploying some of his left flank battalions over to the right and managing to bring up artillery for their support. Now it was Monmouth's men who were in receipt of devastating musket and cannon fire. Despite this royalist onslaught, Monmouth was bravely standing shoulder-to-shoulder with his men, pike in hand, shouting encouragement.

At daybreak, Feversham and the body of horse arrived. Feversham split the cavalry in two and sent them over the north and south crossings of the rhine to prepare to attack Monmouth from the flanks. Grey had by then returned to join Monmouth and they both now realised that they were about to be encircled by enemy cavalry. It was clear the day was lost, so Monmouth, accompanied by Grey and a few others, made their escape on exhausted horses. Monmouth stopped briefly on a nearby hill and looked back to see his army out of ammunition and Feversham ordering the final assault, with the royalist infantry crossing the rhine as the cavalry charged. He did not remain to see the remnants of his army fighting on bravely with the butt-ends of their muskets and their scythes until there was no option but to flee.

Feversham had been slow to join the battle, but brought energy and enthusiasm into a merciless pursuit of Monmouth's fleeing followers. The bloody pursuit continued for the rest of the day and about 1,000 of Monmouth's men cut down by Oglethorpe's cavalry as they fled, stumbling into the rhine to be butchered, despite pleading for quarter. By the end of the day the cornfields round Sedgemoor were red with blood; a total of 1,400 rebels had been killed in the fighting and pursuit. However, some were able to surrender and they were stripped of their possessions and clothes of any value, and imprisoned in makeshift gaols; 238 were crammed into Westonzoyland church to await the king's justice for rebels.[7]

Monmouth was now a fugitive with a £500 price on his head; government officials and bounty hunters alike were urgently searching for him. He and Grey hoped to get to the coast and find a ship to take them to the Continent. Hungry, scared and very weary, they eventually made it to the Ringwood area, just ten miles from the coast. It was decided that Grey should go ahead with three others, but on 8 July he was recognised by a government patrol near the Dorset village of Horton, and arrested.

Grey immediately informed his captives the likely location of Monmouth, and a detailed search of that area was conducted with dogs. Eventually a man was found hiding in a ditch covered over with bracken. It was hard to believe this was the handsome, dashing Monmouth. He had swapped clothes with a shepherd, was filthy, bedraggled and emaciated, with several days' beard growth. Monmouth's capturers gave him food, washing water, and clean clothes, then dispatched him to London. By 12 July, Monmouth found himself in the Tower of London where he had last been a prisoner with his mother as a 7-year-old boy back in 1656.

As soon as he was captured, Monmouth sent a letter to the king begging for his life. He had, after all, disobeyed his father Charles II more than once and been forgiven, surely his uncle would be moved by his plea for forgiveness. Monmouth's hopes rose when James granted him an audience which was attended by just the king, Queen Mary Beatrice and the two secretaries, Sunderland and Middleton. James's purpose in seeing Monmouth was to receive an apology, not to grant a pardon. Monmouth got on his knees to beg for his life and promised to do anything to be pardoned, including converting to Catholicism. James was unmoved and Monmouth was taken away, but not before he was berated at length for his disloyalty in highly unladylike tones by the queen.

Monmouth had been captured, but as he had claimed to be king, his children might make the same claim once he was executed. For this reason, his two sons and daughter were also removed to the Tower and their mother, Anna, accompanied them. Anna had been allowed to have a short meeting with her husband, but it had not gone well; she was understandably very angry about his relations with Henrietta and his treason. Monmouth had much longer sessions with two bishops sent to extract confessions from him. Monmouth confessed to his parents being unmarried and his bad conduct in life, but would not ask forgiveness for his relationship with Henrietta. As a result, the clerics refused to give him a final communion. The next day was set for his execution, which the king had commuted from being hanged drawn and quartered to public beheading on Tower Green.

On 15 July, the morning of his execution, the 35-year-old Monmouth was smartly dressed in grey. He was calm, dignified and at peace. He saw Anna briefly, declared that she had no knowledge of his rebellion and asked for her forgiveness. Anna's heart melted and she flung herself weeping at his feet. He was then taken by coach the short distance to Tower Hill where he was awaited by a sad and expectant crowd. Monmouth read out a short speech he had written in which he confessed he had no rights to the crown and that his wife was completely innocent. Despite continued harassment from the bishops on the scaffold, he refused to express loyalty to the king, only to the Protestant religion. He then knelt down and rested his head on the block; the first stroke of the axe did not sever his neck and he remained alive. A second and then a third blow also missed their targets, leaving Monmouth writhing on the scaffold. The public executioner, Jack Ketch, threw down his axe in exasperation. The crowd were now going wild and the sheriffs ordered Ketch to continue. Two more blows were made but Ketch had to use his knife to cut the final sinews of the neck.[8] The Monmouth rebellion was at last well and truly over.

Although Monmouth's rebellion had been swiftly put down, the effects were longer lasting. The impact of the rebellion would be felt not only by Monmouth's family and followers, but would also affect the government and the king's standing. At a personal level, Henrietta Wentworth never recovered from the loss of her great love. She returned to England having given what wealth she had to equipping Monmouth's expedition. A broken person, she became ill and died the next spring; she was 25. Monmouth's wife Anna fared better. She and the children were released from the Tower; although Monmouth's titles were revoked, she was allowed to keep her Buccleuch estate. She recovered from the trauma of her husband's execution and three years later married Baron Cornwallis.

For the victors there was some glory. Although playing little part in the main battle, Feversham was made a Knight of the Garter. Nevertheless, it was Churchill who received the main acclaim for the victory from the London public and the rumour spread that Feversham, being a Frenchman, had spent so long dressing and insisting on a good breakfast, that he arrived only when the battle was nearly over. This tells us more about the English deep dislike of Frenchmen than it does about Feversham. He was indeed fat and lazy, but also a competent, if not energetic general, and a particularly loyal servant of the crown who had lived in England for twenty years and was a naturalised Englishman,

Feversham and Churchill had departed Bridgewater with the army the day after the battle but had left Colonel Percy Kirk with 500 men of his two Tangiers' regiments to capture rebel fugitives, guard the prisoners and bury the dead. Kirke, and what were called his 'lambs' after the Agnus Dei emblem on their colours, conducted their work with maximum brutality. They hanged a hundred rebels without trial on the first day. This was reasonable enough, as Sunderland wrote to Kirke that the king had been advised by lawyers that those who had proclaimed Monmouth as king could be hanged without trial. Sunderland added that the king 'would have some of them made an example of as a terror to the rest'.[9] The prisoners were manacled and marched to Taunton, where six were hanged on arrival. During the next six weeks there was a general round-up of suspects, and constables of each parish were ordered to produce lists of anyone suspected of being involved. The scope for dishonesty was huge and Kirke and his men made the most of it by taking bribes from those who could pay enough to be released.

Kirke and his men treated the West Country as if it was defeated enemy territory. The soldiers were billeted on families without payment, and the men paid for food, or anything else they wanted, only if they felt like it – which was seldom. It goes without saying that many rapes took place, especially of Nonconformist girls. Kirke has always been rightly condemned for these actions, but it must be said they were not unusual. When the Lambs were replaced in August by Dunbarton's regiment of dragoons, they behaved the same. In their own way, Kirke and the rest were doing what they were told. They had certainly struck terror and, despite the hangings and releases resulting from bribes, they had sought out most of those in hiding and gathered together 1,400 prisoners to await trial in the Kings Courts. Of course, the conditions in which the prisoners were held were unimaginably appalling. The gaols were filthy with no sanitary arrangements, prisoners' wounds were left undressed, and they were virtually starved with only 3½d a day per prisoner being spent on their food and maintenance. Overcrowding was so bad that the 400 prisoners squeezed into Ilchester gaol did not have enough room to lie down at night. It was almost a relief to be brought out into a courtroom.

The man tasked with conducting the trials was Lord Chief Justice Sir George Jeffreys, a man of sharp intellect whose career had been built on demonstrating total loyalty to royal interests. Jeffrey's was also known for his hectoring of prisoners, drunkenness and appalling temper, made no better by being in regular pain from a gallstone. He had a lot of work to get through in a short time. On his way west he stopped at Winchester to try a Dame Alice Lisle, who had given food and shelter to two rebels fleeing the battle. As harbouring rebels was a treasonable offence, she was sentenced to be burned at the stake, the penalty for female traitors. Fortunately, after petitioning to the king, this was commuted to beheading, on the grounds that she was 70-years-old and 'dim-witted'.

Passing through Salisbury, Jeffreys had six men fined and savagely whipped around the town for saying seditious words then, on 5 September, he reached Dorchester to start his main trials. On the first day he tried and sentenced 540 prisoners. He let it be known that anyone pleading guilty would be shown mercy. Those that did were then found guilty of 'waging war against the king', and sometimes executed anyway, but usually sentenced to transportation to the West Indies and sold into ten years of slavery. Planters would pay between £10 and £15 for buying an indentured labourer, so there was money to be made. For those sentenced to execution, Jeffreys was a traditionalist and ordered them to be hanged, drawn and quartered, and arranged for Jack Ketch and a butcher to travel down from London for the work.

It is worth being reminded what being hanged drawn and quartered entailed. In Jeffrey's own words of sentence it was:

> That you be conveyed from hence to a place from whence you came, and that you be conveyed from there on hurdles to a place of execution, where you are to be hanged by the neck; that you be cut down alive, that your privy members be cut off, your bowels taken out and burned in your view; that your head be severed from your body; that your body be divided into four quarters, to be disposed of at the king's pleasure; and the god of infinite mercy have mercy on your soul.[10]

The heads and quartered limbs of the executed were boiled in hot water and tarred to preserve them, then paraded and hung up in the different towns and villages of the West Country. Jeffreys and his Assize moved on from Dorchester to Exeter, Wells, Taunton and other towns. By the time he had completed his task he had sentenced 250 people to be hanged, drawn and quartered, and 850 to be transported into ten years servitude. Jeffreys left behind the ubiquitous dangling body parts and returned to London via Windsor. There he saw the king who appointed him to the recently vacant post of Lord Chancellor and a little later elevated him to the peerage as Baron Jeffreys. After arriving in London, he continued his commitment to bringing rebels to justice by hearing the case of a woman called Elizabeth Gaunt, a tallow chandler. She was accused helping a suspect in the Rye House Plot to get passage to escape. He sentenced her to being burned at the stake while still alive, rather than the usual procedure of having her neck broken first. Elizabeth had the distinction of being the last person to be burned at the stake in England.

At the time, the brutality of Kirk and his men after Sedgemoor, and the merciless judgements of Jeffreys in what became known as 'the Bloody Assizes', were seen as perfectly acceptable. There was a great outpouring of public support for James and condemnation of Monmouth as a traitorous opportunist. Those who tried to overthrow the legitimate king and government were traitors and should get their just deserts. It was quite right that the West Country had been taught a harsh lesson for its revolt and any other potential rebels in the rest of the realm could learn the fate awaiting traitors. It was only later when James lost popularity that the harsh actions he had condoned were regarded as proof of a tyrannical nature. In time also, Monmouth would be remembered by some as the handsome, popular prince who had both fought and died bravely as a protestant martyr. For the moment, public sympathy was firmly with the king. Someone whose star had risen for his part in successfully countering the rebellion was Sunderland. Middleton had provided intelligence and helped keep parliament on side, but Sunderland had been directing activities in the South West by giving instructions to lords lieutenant, Kirke and Jeffreys. He had succeeded winning the king's trust that he had lost when supporting the Exclusion Bill.

Thanks partially to Sunderland, James was now in a very strong position. Monmouth was defeated, his followers dealt with or escaped abroad and the king's popularity had markedly risen. More importantly, he had a very supportive parliament who Middleton had ensured rallied to its sovereign at his time of need. Middleton although a Scottish peer was also MP for Winchelsea and so was not only able to offer royal patronage to MPs in exchange for their loyalty to the crown, but sit among them to see they held their side of the unwritten bargain.

Parliament had granted James a revenue which would have been the envy of his Stuart predecessors. In addition they had voted to cover the expenses of putting down the rebellion. James could rule without having to go cap in hand to a parliament unprepared to grant funds without a reciprocal reduction in royal power. As a further demonstration of support for James, parliament drafted a bill extending treason to cover acts 'to incite or stir up the people to hatred or dislike of the person of his majesty or the established government', but added rather ominously that it would be lawful 'to defend the Church of England's doctrine against Popery'. James soon ended the session.

By late summer 1685 the king was enjoying a wave of popularity, the support of parliament and had got most town councils under his control through the *quo warranto* procedure. In addition, the judiciary was headed by a Lord Chancellor who was an ardent royalist and the lords lieutenant – and therefore the magistrates appointed by them – were loyal royalist appointments. There was no likelihood of further rebellion, as the extreme Whigs and Covenanters had been dealt with or were on the run. Their future activities would be very seriously limited because of the large amount of intelligence gathered as a result of captured rebels offering to give evidence against their associates in return for a pardon.

Chapter 4

Dissident Survivors
1685–6

'All engines being brought at work to bring Popery, which
God in mercy prevent!'
                    Diary of John Evelyn, entry for 5 May 1686

As we have seen, most of those involved in Monmouth's rebellion had
been executed or transported. There were also a few who managed to
escape abroad, and others who saved themselves by offering to give
evidence against their fellow conspirators. Large amounts of information
about the uprising eventually made its way to the secretaries of state
from magistrates, gaolers and informants. Indeed, information so
inundated the secretaries that they made a particular point of writing
to the various West Country authorities thanking them for their many
reports. However, useful though it was, the great bulk of this information
was low level. It came for the most part from individual rebel soldiers
and their friends who could only report what they had seen and heard
for themselves. They were seldom able to provide the information which
was particularly sought by the government. This was about prominent
people who had supported or condoned the rebellion and so needed to
be arrested and brought to trial. To achieve this intelligence requirement,
a more formal interrogation, or 'examination' as it was called, needed to
be conducted on the rebel officers captured after the battle.

Of all the people arrested, those best placed to provide such information
were Republicans like the Old Ironsides officer, Colonel Holmes. He had
helped Argyll get to the Netherlands after he had escaped from Edinburgh
Castle and been the earl's agent in London, liaising with the Rye House
plotters, before himself getting away to Holland. Holmes had joined
Monmouth's expedition as colonel of the Green Regiment and captured

on the Sedgemoor battlefield. He had led his men bravely, despite losing his son and having his left arm shattered in a small engagement three days before the main battle. After capture, he was taken to a local JP for questioning; he refused to provide any information that was not already public knowledge. It is an indication of the strength of character of this man that he amputated his injured arm with his own penknife while waiting in the JP's kitchen. After a brief appearance before Judge Jeffreys on 12 September, he was taken for execution to the beach at Lyme Regis where Monmouth had landed. At the end he was shown a little kindness as someone helped him up the ladder to the scaffold, because he was unable to climb it with only one arm.[1]

Another senior rebel interrogated was Captain Battiscombe, an officer in Monmouth's Red Regiment. He was a young Dorset lawyer who had previously been arrested for suspected involvement in the Rye House Plot but had managed to talk his way out of the accusations and been released. He had been travelling back and forth to the Netherlands keeping contact with the Whig exiles. Battiscombe was one of the men Monmouth had used to sound out support in the West Country just prior to the expedition. He would have been a very useful source of information to the government on Whigs in the West Country who had not come out in support of Monmouth but were sympathetic to his cause. Unfortunately for government intelligence, he refused to provide any information of value and was executed with Holmes on Lyme Regis beach.

Despite some disappointments regarding the examination of prisoners, government intelligence did have three significant breakthroughs. Foremost of which was Lord Grey, the very man who, more than any other, had urged Monmouth to not only lead the rebellion, but to proclaim himself king. After capture, Grey was taken, together with Monmouth, to the Tower; unlike Monmouth however, he was seen to be in high spirits, chatting to those around him about racing. It could well be that his cheerfulness was because he had already made a deal to save his life. On the face of it, Grey had absolutely no hope of mercy. He had encouraged Titus Oates to make his false accusations against the queen, been a close associate of Shaftesbury and the Whig exclusionists and had been deeply involved in the Rye House Plot. He had been arrested as a conspirator, but later managed to escape and then flee to the United Provinces with £500 on his head. In his absence, he had been indicted for treason, and now he was captured again, having taken a leading part in the Monmouth rebellion.

Despite this catalogue of crimes, Grey held two good cards. The first was that he had a powerful person to intervene on his behalf. This was the Earl of Rochester, who was not only Lord High Treasurer, but also the king's brother-in-law. Grey owed Rochester £16,000 to be repaid over twenty-one years. As the debt would be cancelled on Grey's death, the last thing Rochester wanted was to have him executed for treason.[2] The other card was that Grey's nefarious past meant that he was in the perfect position to provide the government with full details of all opposition activity over the previous eight years. While in the Tower, Grey traded his information for a pardon. He provided a full account of both Monmouth's and Argyll's uprisings, naming all those implicated. In addition, he was able to provide information about some of those involved in the Rye House Plot who had not already been brought to justice. Middleton and his Intelligence Department already had a great deal of information on Whig and Covenanter suspects, but Grey was able to either confirm their existing information or fill in any gaps. He was an invaluable source.

Other lesser leaders also decided to betray their friends to save their lives. Nathaniel Wade, the colonel of Monmouth's Red Regiment, almost got away. Realising the battle was lost he took fifty of his men to Bridgewater, then collected horses and rode to Ilfracombe. There they seized a coastal ship, and took it to sea, but were intercepted by two government frigates which were patrolling the coast and were forced ashore. Wade fled into the woods and then made his way north of the edge of Exmoor to the village of Bradon, just south of Lynmouth where he hid in a remote cottage for two weeks. Wade was unfortunate that the rector of Brandon, one Richard Powell, was a robust Anglican who, as soon as he had heard of Monmouth leading a largely Nonconformist rebel army, had bought two pistols intending to join the fight against him. Powell had been disappointed to hear that Monmouth had been defeated before he had time to take up arms, but a second chance came when he learned of Wade's whereabouts. Powell took two parishioners with him to arrest Wade at his cottage hiding place. Wade tried to make an escape but was shot as he fled and captured.[3]

The wounded Wade was taken to Windsor Castle where, as soon as he was examined, made it clear that he would cooperate fully in exchange for a pardon. Wade was the son of a major in Cromwell's New Model Army who had spent most of his life associating with extremist Whigs. He had been involved in the Rye House Plot before fleeing to Holland where he then began conspiring with the Whig and Covenanter expatriate community. He was responsible for the purchase of most of the provisions, weapons and equipment for Monmouth's expedition and so could provide information on the Dutch traders who had dealings with British rebels. Having been one of Monmouth's colonels, he had been deeply involved in all aspects of the rebellion and so was in a good position to provide corroboration of the information provided by Grey.

The third cooperative captive was Richard Goodenough. He had been one of Wade's captains in the Red Regiment, had fled with him, and shared the experience of being in the stolen ship, which was forced aground. He was captured, sent to the Tower to be examined and immediately tried to bargain for his life. Goodenough was able to provide detailed information of subjects that had been only partially provided by others. He was a barrister and former undersheriff of London, removed from his appointment because of his opposition to the government. He became one of the principal Whig conspirators in London and had undertaken to arrange uprisings in twenty different London districts if the Rye House assassinations had been successful. He had fled to the United Provinces on discovery of the Plot, and became an active figure in the Whig expatriate community. Goodenough was a valuable source of information on not only the Whigs and Presbyterians in the Netherlands, but also about extremist Whigs in the City of London.

The testimonies of Grey, Wade and Goodenough, together with previously gathered intelligence, meant that there was very little Middleton did not know about those who had been enemies of the crown. However, what was of equal value to the government was for the turncoats to be prepared to give evidence in court against the few remaining prominent members of the opposition. Grey agreed to go to court and give evidence against Baron Delamere and the Earl of Macclesfield's eldest son, Lord Brandon, for their connection to Monmouth's rebellion; and also against John Hampden, (grandson of John Hampden of Ship Money fame) for involvement with the Rye House Plot. Wade and Goodenough also agreed to provide supporting evidence, and Goodenough to give direct evidence against Alderman Cornish.

It has to be said that, although those accused had wanted to exclude James from the throne because of his Catholicism, none had been engaged in actual treason. Delamere had been an MP and part of Shaftesbury's group pressing for the exclusion of James. He had indeed made some injudicious contacts with Monmouth before his rebellion, but never took part in it. Indeed he had been arrested and imprisoned in Chester Castle as part of the general round up of potential suspects. The Earl of Macclesfield had also been a close associate of Shaftesbury and in defiance to Charles II had entertained Monmouth at his home in Cheshire when Monmouth had been on one of his semi-royal progresses. His son, Lord Brandon, had been an MP and a close associate of the conspirators in the Rye House Plot, but had been pardoned by Charles II. John Hampden was also an MP who had supported James's exclusion and in the same group of leading Whigs involved in the Rye House Plot. He too had been pardoned, on payment of £6,000, but as he had been unable to raise the money, remained in gaol.

Alderman Cornish was a Whig who had opposed the application of *quo warranto* on the City of London Corporation and had been the Whig party's choice for Lord Mayor. He had failed in both, but was regarded by the government as a troublemaker. Cornish had antagonised Goodenough by not making him deputy-sheriff in 1680. Goodenough now had the opportunity for revenge, so he fabricated evidence that Cornish had been involved in both the Rye house Plot and the Monmouth rebellion. Cornish was arrested, committed to Newgate prison, charged with treason, briefly tried at the Old Bailey, convicted, then hanged, drawn and quartered at Cheapside, in sight of his own house. Another potential irritant to the government had been removed.

There was less success over the trials of Delamere, Brandon and Hampden. Brandon and Hampden were tried at the Old Bailey for alleged involvement in the Rye House Plot with evidence given by Grey, Wade and Goodenough. They were found guilty, but as Grey had stipulated that their lives should be spared, they were merely given heavy fines. Delamere was a peer and as the House of Lords was not sitting, he had to be tried in a special court of peers with a Lord High Steward as judge. Things looked less than promising for the accused when Jeffreys was chosen as Lord High Steward and personally selected the jury consisting of thirty loyal Tory peers. Six years earlier, when Jeffreys had been Lord Chief Justice of Cheshire, Delamere had criticised him saying that Jeffreys's behaviour was not befitting a judge but more 'a drunken jackpudding.'[4]

No one likes to be called a 'jackpudding', and Jeffreys had not forgotten such an insult. The trial took place in January 1686 and Grey made his accusations against Delamere, but despite Jeffrey's normal bullying court tactics, it was clear that there was insufficient evidence for a treason conviction. As Lord Churchill was the junior peer on the jury, he was asked to give his verdict first. He declared not guilty and the others peers followed. Jeffreys was furious, and the king was less than pleased with his protégé, Churchill. It was disappointing for the crown that Delamere, Brandon and Hampden were freed, but they posed little threat and returned to their estates for a quiet life.

Despite this slight set back, the government had been able to demonstrate that anyone suspected of treasonable acts could expect to be brought before the law to answer for their crimes. Charging these additional significant figures following the executions of Argyll and Monmouth, together with the Blood Assizes, sent a very strong message to anyone considering dabbling in treason. Also, those who had turned king's evidence were seen to prosper. As Grey had been indicted for high treason in the past, he had to be pardoned first before he was able to give evidence in a court. He was released in early November and about a year later his title and estate at Up Park in Sussex were restored to him. Wade was sufficiently rehabilitated to be asked to accompany the king as guide on a battlefield tour of Sedgemore and later was appointed town clerk of Bristol. It took rather longer for Goodenough to be released, but he too obtained his freedom and settled in Ireland as an attorney.

Something had changed between the beginning of Jeffreys's Bloody Assizes in August 1685 and the not guilty verdict on Delamere in January the next year. In October, Louis XIV passed the Edict of Fontainebleau revoking the 1598 Edict of Nantes allowing French Huguenots to practise their religion without persecution by the state. The Huguenots were French Calvinist Protestants numbering 8–900,000. Louis had already begun persecuting them by billeting dragoons without payment on leading Protestant families. With the Revocation, their churches were now destroyed and schools closed. The dragoons were implicitly authorised to abuse the Protestant population, stealing their possessions and generally terrorising them to force them to convert to Catholicism. Life in France for Huguenots who refused to convert became intolerable, indeed, 1,500 were made galley slaves. During the next ten years, most Huguenots fled from France and about, 50–80,000 settled in England.

It was during the end of 1685 that the first Huguenots began arriving in England, bringing terrible tales of persecution. What Louis had done in France was every Protestant Englishman's nightmare. Now Catholic James was on the throne, the old fears returned that he might impose Popery on the nation. However, sensible people noted that James had given many assurances that the Church of England would be safe in his hands. Indeed James publicly condemned the revocation of the edict and contributed to the relief of Huguenot refugees. Despite this, the fear remained that a Catholic king of England might follow his cousin in France to impose Popery.

Monmouth's rebellion had been swiftly put down, but that might not have been the case. In some ways, Monmouth had failed through faulty intelligence. Had he not received the inaccurate information about the strength and proximity of the royalist army at Keynsham, he might well have been able to implement his plan of taking Bristol. Had he captured Bristol, the second city in the kingdom, it would have given confidence to his dormant Whig supporters and resulted in the local gentry coming to his support and uprisings in London. Had there been better intelligence on the Sedgemoor ditches, Grey would have found the crossing bridge and been able to attack the royalist camp from the rear before the infantry fully deployed. If Monmouth's plan had worked, he would have defeated the royalist infantry before Feversham eventually arrived with the cavalry. James was an experienced enough soldier to know that the defeat of Monmouth had not been a completely forgone conclusion. The poorly trained and badly equipped county militias had proved next to useless, and although the standing army was an effective professional force, the king had only been able to put about 4,000 of them into the field against Monmouth's force of similar numbers. James concluded that a larger standing army was vital to guard against any future uprisings.

James decided to ask parliament to provide funding for a larger standing army when it met again on 9 November. Following Monmouth's rebellion this appeared a most reasonable proposal, especially as it was to put to a very compliant, Tory dominated, parliament. However, traditionally English parliaments had been very wary of having standing armies at all, let alone large ones. It was fine for the monarch to have household guards and sufficient forces to garrison the main forts, or outposts such as Tangiers, but the monarch could use any home-based force larger than this to overawe parliament. It was felt that the militia should be the principal means for providing the nation's military force. For these reasons, James's proposal was not well received, especially as it was accompanied by something even more potentially sinister. Prior to the parliament meeting, James had told his council that he wanted parliament to repeal the Test and Habeas Corpus Acts.

The Test Act was a major discrimination against Catholics and Nonconformists whereby they were barred from holding civil or military public office unless they swore to conform to the rights of the Church of England. Habeas Corpus prevented indefinite imprisonment by the crown as it gave a prisoner the right of trial before a court. The Test Act was unjust, but regarded as a Protestant nation's essential bulwark against papists gaining power in the country. Habeas Corpus was equally regarded as defence against arbitrary government by the monarch. When Lord Halifax, the Lord President of the Council, heard of James's intention he argued against it, and said that he could not support such a motion. The king reluctantly dismissed him from his post and in doing so, turned him into a potential focus for parliamentary opposition. Undeterred, James put his proposals for an increased standing army and the repeal of the two acts to a bewildered parliament. Nether the Commons nor the Lords wanted to antagonise the king and were prepared to vote some extra funds for the army, but could not bring themselves to repeal the Test and Habeas Corpus Acts. Despite a prolonged period of negotiations, neither king nor parliament would give way and James prorogued parliament for three months. As it happened, parliament would be repeatedly prorogued and never meet again during his reign.

It was a pity that James had fallen out with what had been an exceptionally supportive parliament, but he could rule without them, as his brother had done before him. In some ways, he was in an enviable position. Thanks to his first session of parliament, he had been granted funding for life and so, with the additional customs duties that had been voted subsequently, he had enough revenue to rule without further parliamentary funding. What was more, he had sufficient revenue to enlarge the regular army and began to double its size to 9,000 men, redirecting funds from the militia to the army. James also began to devote a significant amount of his time to personally overseeing the expansion of the army and supervising its training. This expansion and training resulted in a royal army well capable of swiftly dealing with any future uprisings. Such uprisings were, of course, extremely unlikely with Monmouth and his rebels eliminated and the great majority of Whigs and Republicans who might have favoured his cause dead, cowed into submission, or fled to exile in the Netherlands.

Although they posed little risk, it was to the Netherland's exiles that Middleton and his Intelligence Department turned their main attention. Some prominent Whigs, such as John Locke, had not joined Argyll or Monmouth expeditions and had remained in the Low Countries; a few who had escaped after Sedgemoor managed to make it to the Netherlands. Ferguson was one of these and on 28 July, Skelton reported him having arrived in Amsterdam in an open boat with sixteen other fugitives. Ferguson was more than the Chaplain General to Monmouth's army because, with Grey, he had been his main adviser. He had a long record as a conspirator. Ferguson had joined Shaftesbury to become the Whig's principal pamphleteer for exclusion, then fled to the Continent with Shaftesbury. On Shaftesbury's death Ferguson had returned to England to be active in the Rye House Plot. He had been declared an outlaw and fled back to the United Provinces where he had joined Argyll in his intrigues, before helping to organise his and Monmouth's expeditions.

Ferguson was now top of the government wanted list, but sadly for Skelton was to vanish from view. The inveterate schemer was thought to have gone to Holland's province of Friesland, where he could expect support from the Scottish Covenanter clergy who had sought sanctuary there. Ferguson was by now 48 years old, but there was no likelihood that he would quietly retire and desist from his subversive activities. Skelton therefore tasked agents to try to locate him with a view to arranging his kidnap and return to England for trial. As this was probably too ambitious an operation, a more convenient alternative was to arrange his assassination. Ferguson was fully aware that he was a target for government agents, but was sufficiently wily to always keep one step ahead of his assailants.

As well as the members of Monmouth's army who made it to the United Provinces, there were also a few who had fled because they were deemed to have been accomplices. Most notable of these were Charles Gerard, the Earl of Macclesfield, and John Wildman. Macclesfield was a staunch Royalist who had fought for Charles I in some of the major battles of the Civil War and then followed Charles II into exile. At the Restoration, he had been made Captain of the Life Guards and had led Charles II's procession into London. He continued in royal service becoming a Gentleman of the Bedchamber and then in 1679, Earl of Macclesfield. However, being strongly antipapist, he believed in the exclusion of James from the throne, joined Shaftesbury's Whig group and supported Monmouth. Although he had taken no part in Monmouth's rising he was regarded as a conspirator and when, on 7 September, a royal proclamation was issued for his apprehension, he fled to the Continent, after which a sentence of outlawry was passed against him. Macclesfield then spent his time keeping a low profile as an exile in Germany and the United Provinces.

Wildman was a lawyer from Norfolk who became a major in the New Model Army and leader of the Levellers. He was an MP during the Commonwealth, but being a strong Republican he schemed to overthrow Cromwell, including entering into plots with the exiled Royalists. He was imprisoned but later released and continued his Republican plotting, first for, and then against, the rule of the Army Council which had replaced Richard Cromwell. During Charles II's reign he began plotting against the king and was imprisoned for six years after which he returned to his subversive ways and fell in with Shaftesbury's Whigs and made preparations for an armed uprising. He was arrested for involvement in the Rye House Plot, but later released through lack of evidence. On the accession of James II, he had been in contact with Grey, Argyll and other Whig exiles and had given assurances that he would provide funding for Monmouth's cause and organise an uprising in London to be launched as soon as the royalist army had left London. He then appears to have had cold feet and did neither of these things. This was probably because it dawned on Wildman that Monmouth was making a bid for the crown which, being a Republican, he could not support. As a well-known dissident, a warrant was issued for his arrest on 19 May, but he evaded capture and by October had joined John Locke in Cleves, before moving on to Utrecht.

The defeat of Monmouth and the savage retribution served out to his followers had not made the life of Bevil Skelton any easier as ambassador to The Hague. He organised two firework displays to celebrate Monmouth's defeat, but they were a flop in terms of boosting the popularity of King James or Skelton himself. William of Orange had no time for him and the English government remained as unpopular as ever with both the States General and the Dutch population as a whole. Amsterdam was receiving significant numbers of political refugees, both those fleeing from prosecution for suspected involvement with Monmouth and the Rye House plot, together with those whom the government was now cracking down on for being former witnesses in the Popish Plot. In addition, Monmouth was beginning to be regarded by some as a protestant martyr and various people jumped on the bandwagon. Imposters muddied the waters by claiming to be Monmouth's son, or one of his daughters, and Whig extremist groups attempting to exploit them as a focus for further resistance against popery.

The States General had issued a proclamation banning all rebels from its territory but, this was not enforced. Skelton tried very hard to have the proclamation implemented, but without any success. Indeed, the former Monmouth supporters or suspects, together with exclusionists and prosecution witnesses in the Popish Plot were joined by a number of ordinary Protestant West Countrymen, who found the appalling action of the troops intolerable. Amsterdam began teeming with expatriates, making it very difficult for Skelton to monitor their activities. In November, Ezekiel Everest, Skelton's main agent in Amsterdam was reporting: 'There are so many strangers' faces here of our english fugitives … this town is become a kinde of purgatory to moderate and peacably inclined men.'[5] For ordinary Englishmen without a private income, the problem of fleeing to the United Provinces was having enough money to live on. Some who were soldiers or had taken to military life after their brief service with Monmouth, decided to enlist in continental armies. The great majority of those who had supported Monmouth in the West Country were weavers, who were resigning themselves to being unemployed.

Joseph Tiley, one of the richer exiles, had a solution. He was a Bristol clothier who had proclaimed Monmouth as king in Taunton. He decided to make use of the weavers' expertise and began negotiations with the estates of Friesland to establish a cloth production business in Leeuwarden. The estates were very enthusiastic about creating their own cloth industry rather than having to purchase cloth from England, and offered Tiley an exceptionally advantageous business opportunity. The final agreement included providing premises large enough for sixty looms rent free, the state to build a fulling mill, exemption from taxes for twenty years, and 300 child labourers over the age of 10 at no cost for the first year then 10*d* a week, per child thereafter. All Tiley had to supply was skilled weavers and the working capital. Tiley agreed the deal and obtained the financial backing of many of the richer exiles. The model was so attractive that the Prince of Luneburg made a similar deal with Joseph Hilliard, an Exeter clothier.[6]

By February 1686 virtually all the exiled weavers had moved from Amsterdam to Leeuwarden or Luneberg, and plans were being made for a further 500 families of West Country serge workers to be shipped over to join them. On top of this, a Major Manley began establishing a third cloth-production centre in Groningen. The whole enterprise was a resounding success and the cloth produced was sold in Amsterdam 15 per cent cheaper than the English product, and with much reduced transport cost. As the sale of cloth was an essential part of the English economy and a major source of taxation, the rival production on the Continent was a serious concern. Skelton had used his main agents, Everest and Captain Slater, to gather information on this unexpected threat from the rebel expatriate community and was keeping Middleton and the government informed. Whether or not because of this economic challenge, the king issued a general pardon to all rebels except for the ringleaders. This made not a bit of difference. The entrepreneurs financing the schemes spread the rumour that if anyone returned to England, their pardon would be revoked and they could expect little mercy from a legal system under Lord Chancellor Jeffreys.

Skelton tasked Everard to hire a lawyer, called Mr Hunt, to counter the propaganda by visiting the cloth factories and explaining to the weavers that the pardon was legally binding. This produced no results, as Hunt's presence was not welcomed by the weavers and still less by their financial backers. Captain Slater wrote to Skelton on 29 April to say that he felt the only remedy was for the king to grant specific pardons to those who were financing the workshops. Skelton relayed this back to England and the king was persuaded to grant pardons to those exiled weaver financiers who had been exempt from the general pardon. The first of these was issued on 5 May for Christopher Cooke, which granted a pardon on condition that he: 'forthwith breake of his designes, and return himself, with his estate and servants and mechanics to England.'[7] The pardon succeeded and Cooke did return to England with his workforce. Other pardons were issued and the recipients also returned, but James was reluctant to grant pardons to those he regarded as principal offenders such as Tiley and Hilliard. As a result, much of the cloth production continued.

Eventually, and very reluctantly, the king realised that he had to grant pardons to Joseph Tiley and the other main miscreants if he wished to put an end to economic competition. They were pardoned, disbanded their businesses and returned home with their 'servants and mechanics'. By the end of July, Everest visited the Leeuwarden factory and discovered that its doors were locked, the workers gone, and the estates of Friesland had seized Tiley's goods for breach of contract. The Netherland's competition to the English cloth trade was at an end.

The large scale return of refugees following the general pardon made life much easier for Skelton and his agents, and at the same time caused little problem back in England, as the great majority of those returning posed no threat to the crown. Skelton could now concentrate on those who were left in the United Provinces. These were people like Wildman, who had been specifically excluded from the pardon and others, such as John Locke, who despite the pardon were content to remain abroad. Skelton continued to gather intelligence on Whig activists but as most had gone to ground, he had little to report.

Although major troublemakers like Ferguson, Wildman and Peyton were a potential cause for concern, they remained inactive. This was not because they had lost their ardour for conspiracy, but because there was no focus for their subversive energies. Argyll and Monmouth had been leaders who might have been able to gather support for rebellion in Scotland and England, but now they were gone, no one of that status remained. There would be no support for a rebellion against King James led by someone of the likes of Ferguson or Wildman. Indeed, after the dismal failures of Argyll and Monmouth's rebellions, few would consider attempting to mount another. The only realistic operation that was left was to somehow organise the assassination of James, which would result in him being replaced by his Protestant daughter. There is no record of a plot of this sort being considered, not least because it would be extremely difficult to organise an assassination from the distance of the Netherlands. The rebel exiles in Holland had become of little or no threat to James.

Although we can see that the existing rebel exiles posed no immediate threat, this was not a view shared by the government in England. Skelton and his informants remained busy trying to monitor their activities. To this was added the need to keep an eye on a few new arrivals, the most prominent of which were Rev. Gilbert Burnet and Sir Robert Peyton. Burnet was the son of a Scottish judge who had become ordained in the Church of Scotland and eventually moved to London to join his brother, who was one of Charles II's physicians at court. The intelligent and personable Burnet soon attracted the notice of Charles and despite his Whig sympathies joined the king's circle of courtiers. He made his name academically by writing *The History of the Reformation of the Church of England*, which chronicled the Anglican's Church's triumph over Popery. For this, he was awarded a Doctorate by Oxford University, but fell from the favour of James, then the Duke of York. Burnet had not been involved in the Rye House Plot, but was a potential suspect, as he knew some of the leaders. As soon as he heard of Argyll's expedition he feared he would be arrested, so fled to France. He then travelled to Italy and Switzerland, ending up in Utrecht in May 1686, from where he was invited to the Stadtholder's court at The Hague. In a short time, Burnet had gained the confidence of both William and Mary, particularly the latter to whom he became devoted, and used as her advisor on the workings of the English court, from which she had been away for the last eight years.

The other newly arrived exile was Sir Robert Peyton, a colourful, hot-headed character given to physical attacks and duels with those he disliked. He been an Examiner in Chancery under Cromwell, but lost his appointment at the Restoration. Under Charles II he had become a prominent Whig MP associating with Shaftesbury and supporting James's exclusion. This led to him being charged with high treason, and sent to the Tower for a spell, but later having the charges dropped. Possibly to make peace with James, he had been involved in the 'Meal Tub Plot' to discredit the Whigs, in which a false letter describing a Whig plot to murder the king was found in a meal tub. He became generally disliked by all sides, but was one of those arrested for complicity in the Rye House Plot. He was released through lack of evidence, but Lord Grey and Goodenough obligingly helped the government to remove this long standing irritant. As part of their accusations, Grey and Goodenough gave evidence that Peyton had undertaken to organise a rising in the city as soon as Monmouth had landed. Peyton heard of the accusations and fled to the United Provinces. He was outlawed for high treason in his absence.

James had a particular dislike for both Peyton and Burnet and requested the States General to extradite them both to England. This request was refused and Skelton was left with the continued presence of two men who might have posed very little threat, but who were considered the king's enemies. Of course, Skelton had received no help from William of Orange in his efforts to persuade the Dutch authorities to take action against Peyton, Burnet or any other English and Scottish rebels. William had a strong distaste for Skelton and regarded him as a dangerous Francophile and the two hardly ever met. It was probably a relief to both men when Skelton's frustrating period in the United Provinces ended. In October, he was recalled to England in preparation for his promotion to Envoy Extraordinary to France, and one of the royal yachts was sent to take him back.

Skelton realised that his return transport offered an opportunity to at last resolve the Peyton problem. He decided to kidnap Peyton and bundle him back to England in the royal yacht to face trial. With this in mind, Skelton recruited some English officers serving with the Dutch forces for the operation. Peyton had meanwhile become a burgher of Amsterdam, and as such a Dutch citizen, which complicated matters. Skelton decided that the kidnap should take place when Peyton was visiting Rotterdam. The operation began smoothly with Peyton appearing as expected and the English officers grabbing him, but it then all went wrong. Those citizens who witnessed the kidnap immediately gave the alarm and within moments, a mob of irate Dutchmen appeared demanding the release of a fellow citizen. The English officers let go of Peyton but were themselves taken by the mob to the Rotterdam authorities. News of the attempted kidnapping did not go down well with the States General. James sent word that he had not authorised the kidnapping and requested the officers' release. The States General disregarded James, cashiered the officers, and sent them back to England. James was furious at this snub, which further soured his relations with the United Provinces and did nothing to improve understanding with his nephew William, who he felt could have been more supportive.

Unfortunately, during the course of 1686 relations between James and William had been deteriorating. Much of the reason was misunderstanding on both sides, which built into mistrust and then animosity. The two men had very different agendas. James wanted to fulfil his duty as God's anointed king by doing all he could to encourage the spread of Catholicism in his three kingdoms. William of Orange focused on two issues: securing his own principality of Orange, and protecting the United Provinces against the threat of Louis XIV and Catholicism. James was disappointed that his own nephew had not done more to use his influence with the States General to support the extradition of English and Scottish rebels from Dutch soil. He even began to think that William was tacitly sympathising with the rebels. This feeling increased when Skelton reported to James on his return from the United Provinces. Skelton made little of William's constitutional inability as Stadtholder to dictate to the various estates and implied that William actually favoured the rebels.

William regarded himself as the principal Protestant leader in Europe and was naturally apprehensive about James's Catholicism, but could live with that in the knowledge that as James had no sons, Mary would inherit the throne and could undo any Popish mischief that had occurred. Of more immediate concern was that contrary to the treaty of Nijmegen, Louis was occupying his principality of Orange and persecuting its Protestant population. In 1685, William had asked James to intervene with his cousin Louis and persuade him to withdraw from Orange territories. James did, in fact, try hard to persuade Louis, much to the French king's annoyance, but found he could not be budged. By February 1686, William realised that James had failed to move Louis. Instead of crediting James with risking his own relations with Louis by continuing to pester on a matter Louis regarded as a gross impertinence, he blamed James for not trying harder. William also wrongly believed that James might be forming a secret treaty with Louis. This fear had arisen at the end of 1685 when a French envoy, de Bonrepaud, was sent to England for secret talks. Unknown to William the talks had just been about trying to avoid the outbreaks of hostilities which occurred between English and French settlers in North America.

William was obsessed about Louis preparing for another war in the Low Countries, whereas James felt that Louis wanted to continue a period of peace to recover from the costs of the recent Franco Dutch War. James also felt that the French navy was not up to another war, having lost its Huguenot sailors. In the spring of 1686, there had been an incident between French and Dutch ships off Cadiz which convinced William that Louis was preparing his navy for war. William made alliances with Sweden and Brandenburg as a defensive measure. He also liaised with a number of German princes who formed the League of Augsburg. Louis became concerned about this European build up against him, especially as it seemed likely that Austria would join the League now the emperor had successfully dealt with the Turkish threat to Hungary. Louis took the precaution of reinforcing his forts on his eastern frontier, which merely provided proof to William and the League of Augsburg that France was preparing to launch another attack on the Rhine and Low Countries. Both sides were escalating for groundless reasons. Had there been better intelligence on both sides, then future conflict might have been avoided, or at least postponed. That said, it is notoriously difficult in intelligence to become sure of the intentions of opposing leaders, and given Louis's pursuit of grandeur, another attempt to enlarge his kingdom was a likely outcome.

There were a number of minor areas of friction between James and William in 1686, some of which stemmed from the beginnings of James's attempts to promote the Catholic Church. In May, James appointed an Irish Catholic, the Earl of Carlingford, to command one of the English regiments serving in Holland. William informed James that a Catholic would not be acceptable to the Holland estates. James was furious and decided to leave the post vacant in protest. Despite James and William's conflicting interests and occasional clashes, relations remained cordial, at least on the surface. As far as the close family was concerned, Princess Mary was on good terms with her father and her mother-in-law, Mary Beatrice. The Stuart family were holding together, but the manifestations of James and his wife's ever deepening Catholic faith were making Anglican Mary and her sister Anne back in England, distinctly uneasy.

Chapter 5

Sleepwalking over the Edge
1687

'A young prince was born, which will cause disputes.'
Diary of John Evelyn, entry for 10 June 1688

The year 1687 began with James having every reason to be confident. He had defeated Monmouth and delivered harsh retribution to the rebels. His healthy supply of revenue meant that it was sufficient to run his government, maintain the court and provide a strong standing army. Much of the civil administration was now under his influence through crown appointments. To cap it all, his three kingdoms were stable and at peace, as was most of Europe, so his subjects could enjoy a period of commercial prosperity free from the taxation and trade disruption that accompanied war. It would be reasonable for him to feel that he had the means to do as he liked as God's anointed monarch. What he wished to do above all things was to serve God by encouraging his subjects to return to the Catholic faith.

The only unsatisfactory aspect of James's life was that he lacked the male heir he had always wanted. Of course he had his daughters Mary and Anne by Anne Hyde as an heir and spare, but neither Anne Hyde nor Mary Beatrice had given birth to a surviving male child. For Mary Beatrice the situation was even worse; after thirteen years of marriage she had no surviving children. She was by no means barren, as she had given birth to her first child Catherine Laura in 1675 who had sadly died, then Isabella, who reached the age of 3 before dying in 1681, and lastly Charlotte May, who died shortly after her birth the next year. This was a personal tragedy for Mary Beatrice and she turned to her Catholic faith for both consolation and to answer her prayers for a healthy child. Mary Beatrice's devotion sometimes bordered on religious mania and her unhappy state was not improved by the fact that James had brought Catherine Sedley back as his mistress. Fortunately this did not last long because as Sedley was a Protestant, James was persuaded to banish her from court by his Catholic confessor and he reverted to casual sexual liaisons.

James may have had a dispirited wife, but at least he knew she fully supported his aim to bring his kingdoms to the Church of Rome. James had no intention of following his cousin Louis and forcing Catholicism on his Protestant subjects. He genuinely felt that there was little difference between High Anglicanism and Roman Catholicism and that many Anglicans would return to the Mother Church if the restrictions on membership were lifted. In other words, if all the legislations discriminating against Catholics were removed to allow them freedom of worship and to be appointed to public office.

James's parliament had not been prepared to repeal the Test Act, but he got round this by using his royal powers of dispensation to override the provisions of acts of parliament for three month periods. By the end of the first year of his reign he had used these powers to commission some hundred Catholic officers into his enlarged army. As there were few Catholics in England, the majority of those commissioned were Irish. This was greeted with great concern. Since Charles I's time there had been a fear that an army of Catholic Irish would be brought over to subdue England. The king was also taking a variety of other small measures to promote Catholicism which were causing Protestant alarm. Catholics were encouraged to worship openly despite prohibition, and Anglican clergy who decried popery from their pulpits were ordered to remain silent.

James used his dispensing powers to appoint Catholics to many civil public offices including making a Catholic the Dean of Christ Church College, Oxford. As Catholics were banned from even attending university, giving a Catholic a top university appointment was greeted with amazement. The list of Catholic appointments just kept growing. All of these changes were seen as undermining the Anglican faith but encountered little outward resistance other than a fracas around a Catholic chapel which had opened in Lime Street and had been ransacked by an angry London mob. When James had made his intentions of establishing religious toleration for Catholics known to his council, Halifax voiced his opposition and resigned, but there were still powerful members with deep reservations.

James made it clear that he required his councillors to wholeheartedly support his Catholic emancipation initiative and began replacing those from whom it was not forthcoming. He went to considerable lengths to encourage his ministers to join the Catholic faith, particularly his brother-in-law, Laurence Hyde, Earl of Rochester. Despite Catholic priests spending hours attempting to convert him, Rochester refused and was dismissed as Lord Treasurer in January 1687. The Treasury was put into commission under Baron John Belasyse, a Catholic. Rochester's brother, Henry Hyde, Earl of Clarendon, was Lord Lieutenant of Ireland and had not cooperated with the appointment of Catholics into civil and military positions, so he too was dismissed. The important post of Lord Lieutenant of Ireland was given to a Catholic Irish soldier, Richard Talbot. He had fought for the Royalists in the Civil War, joined James's household, and when James became king was made Earl of Tyrconnell and commander-in-chief of Irish Forces. The post of Lord Privy Seal, vacated by Clarendon, was given to Baron Arundel, another Catholic.

One member of the council had seen the writing on the wall from the start and decided to further his career by throwing himself behind James's Catholic policy. This was the Earl of Sunderland, whose eagerness to please had helped him to supplant his main rival, Rochester, as the king's principal adviser. His enthusiasm for implementing the king's wishes had been recognised by him being made Lord President of the Council after the fall of Halifax, while still remaining secretary of state for the Southern Department. After Rochester's dismissal, Sunderland was universally recognised as James's premier-minister. A little later he cemented his position by privately converting to Catholicism and was rewarded with the Garter.

It was the all-powerful Sunderland who had directed that Bevil Skelton should be recalled from the United Provinces and sent as ambassador to France. Sunderland had chosen Skelton as he was a known Francophile and Sunderland was now distinctly pro-France, despite having tried to build a Protestant alliance against Louis XIV when he had been Charles II's secretary of state. The reason for this conversion, like his religious one, was plain self-interest. As Rochester had supported good relations with the United Provinces, Sunderland, his rival, had supported France. This was a sensible move as James admired his Catholic cousin Louis, even if they did not always see eye to eye. Lastly, and probably most important of all, was because Sunderland was in receipt of a French pension.

In fact the appointment of Skelton to Paris was something of a non-event. Louis was pleased to receive a Francophile ambassador but disregarded him for nearly all communications with James. Communications were almost exclusively through France's long serving ambassador in London, Paul Barrillon. James had a high opinion of Barrillon and it will be remembered that Barrillon was one of the three people James had wanted present for Charles II's death-bed conversion. James had been removing Protestant council members and replacing them with Catholics, but three men had come to the fore as encouraging him in his mission to bring Catholicism back to his kingdoms. These were Sunderland as his principal minister, Barrillon as adviser and conduit to Louis, and Sir Edward Petrie as his Jesuit chaplain and spiritual mentor.

Catholics were pleased that James was placing them in positions of responsibility and trying to end the Test Acts and Penal Laws. However, they only accounted for a tiny proportion of an overwhelmingly Protestant country. Sunderland advised James to seek wider support for the introduction of religious toleration by extending it to Nonconformists. Nonconformists were discriminated against in much the same way as Catholics, thanks to the Penal Laws of Charles II's Cavalier parliament. If the whole band of Nonconformists, that is Baptists, Presbyterians, Congregationalists, Independents and Quakers, were offered religious toleration then the policy might attract the backing of about quarter of the population. Nonconformists hated Catholicism and were pleased to see them discriminated against in the Penal Laws and Test Acts, but could become allies for repealing those acts if that was what was necessary to win freedom of worship for themselves.

James was hard to convince on this as he had always regarded Nonconformists as Whig activists and little better than rebels. William Penn had been back in England to see the king about a land dispute concerning his Quaker landholding in North America called Pennsylvania. James took a liking to Penn and, accepting that Quakers were pacifists, had agreed to release a number of them from prison in 1686. Sunderland built on this and eventually convinced James to offer religious toleration to all. Once the king had made this decision, he used Penn as his righthand man to sell the idea of total religious freedom to Nonconformists. James then used his royal prerogative to dispense with parliament's Penal Laws and Test Acts. Royal proclamations were issued to this effect, first in Scotland in February 1687, and then in England on

4 April, in what was called *The Declaration of Indulgence*. This dramatic turn of events was received with horror by most Anglicans. They hated papists but were not too keen on Nonconformists; however, Anglicans and Tories were instinctively loyal to the crown. They felt hurt and let down but there were no riots, and as parliament was not sitting there was no formal means for expressing discontent.

James and Sunderland were now confident that they could develop Catholicisation further. They believed that most of the king's normal opposition, the Nonconformists would be full of gratitude for their religious freedom and that traditional Anglican loyalty could be relied upon, despite their feathers being ruffled. Catholics continued to be placed in more and more crown appointments, but soon an event occurred that was to cause even greater concern than the appointments of papists. James had invited the Pope to send a nuncio to England. Ferdinando d'Adda had been chosen as nuncio and the Pope made him titular Archbishop of Amasia. He was consecrated archbishop on 1 May in a full Catholic ceremony in the royal chapel at St James's Palace. This was bad enough, but during the ceremony James decided to prostrate himself before d'Adda. For an English king to prostrate themselves before anyone was outrageous, but to do so before a papist representative of the Antichrist was beyond belief.

Sunderland was dominating government, but Middleton was still secretary of state for the north with responsibility for intelligence on Northern Europe. However, Sunderland, in a typical power grab, obtained the king's agreement that all intelligence reports from ambassadors should be sent to him, irrespective of which department they came from. Middleton was left with responsibility for intelligence in England but had little to do; despite the deep disquiet over the king's Catholic policies, there was as yet no meaningful subversive opposition to the crown. Middleton would have continued to be focused on the exiled Whigs and Republicans in the Netherlands but had been rather usurped by Sunderland. It was Sunderland who had decided that Bevil Skelton should be replaced as ambassador to the United Provinces by a Irish Catholic, Ignatius White, Marquis of Alberville.

White was the eldest son of Dominick White, mayor of Limerick, who had gone to the Continent after Cromwell's conquest of Ireland. Dominic White and Ignatius had taken service with Leopold I of Austria and been granted the Holy Roman Empire title of marquis for success as diplomats. In fact their diplomatic skills were secondary to their success as intelligence gatherers. During his espionage career Ignatius had spied first for Spain, then France, after that the English Republic followed by the United Provinces, then back to Spain and finally Austria. Dominic's two other sons, Andrew and Richard, also gained employment as spies. They became agents for France, but were sent to the Bastille by Cardinal Mazarin when he discovered they were double agents for Spain. On release they were recruited by the English Protectorate's spy Joseph Bamfield to collect intelligence in Italy and Madrid respectively. Espionage was a family business for the Whites.

On the one hand, Alberville's espionage experience made him an ideal choice for keeping an eye on Netherlands dissidents, but as a Catholic adventurer he was anathema to both William of Orange and the States General. Alberville was still less welcome, as he had been tasked to persuade William and Mary to support James's freedom of worship initiative and the repeal of the Test Acts. James had sent William Penn to The Hague a few months earlier on the same mission but had met with only partial success. William politely replied to James that he and Mary agreed with granting freedom of religion but could not support the repeal of the Test Acts. When Alberville put the same case to William and Mary, he received the same reply. James blamed Burnet's influence for this refusal, especially as Burnet had just published his *Reasons against Repealing the acts...Concerning the Test.* James was quite right that William and Mary had consulted Burnet over the Test and received his strong confirmation of their own views. Burnet had become increasingly close to William and Mary and did much to bring the two together as a married couple. One aspect of this was that William had been annoyed at the prospect of being subordinate to Mary when she inherited the English throne from her father James. He made it clear that he had no wish to being merely regarded as 'his wife's gentleman usher'. Burnet got Mary to tell William that even when she inherited the throne, she would always be commanded by her husband.

Burnet became James's bête noire because of his influence on his daughter and son-in-law and the king became even more annoyed to hear that Burnet was about to become a rich man as a result of marrying Scottish heiress Mary Scott. James decided to charge Burnet with high treason in Scotland for supposed correspondence with the Earl of Argyll. As Burnet failed to appear in court a sentence of outlaw was passed which allowed Alberville to apply to the States General for Burnet's extradition. As Burnet had been rapidly granted Dutch citizenship, the States General refused. All James could now do was to request William to ban Burnet from his court. As usual, William did not want to offend his uncle and dismissed Burnet from his court. However, Burnet remained in The Hague and William and Mary used the faithful Willem Bentinck, to act as a go-between.

Despite Alberville's espionage experience, intelligence dried up on any subversive activities by Whig and Republican exiles in the Netherlands. The principal reason was that men like Wildman and Ferguson were continuing to lie low and Alberville was receiving next to no support or information from William or the Dutch authorities. Alberville was also unfortunate that he had lost the services of two of Skelton's best agents. These were Monsieur Massell in Utrecht, and Edmund Everard in Amsterdam. Massell's house was a longstanding meeting place for radical conspirators, which enabled Mansell to obtain high quality intelligence. Somehow his spying activities became compromised and retribution followed. John Wildman was living in Utrecht, as was another London conspirator and former Ironside, Colonel Henry Danvers, who like Wildman had fled to Utrecht after the failure of Monmouth's rebellion. It is likely that Wildman and Danvers arranged for Mansell to receive a severe beating.

Massell lost an eye and was 'in danger of being deprived of his senses through the many blows he received on his head.'[1] When Skelton had tried to get the Dutch authorities to investigate the incident, they merely took Massell to court and fined him 300 guilders for being a spy! As a result of Massell's unhappy experience, Edmund Everard became nervous of continuing as an agent. He had decided to retire to England when Skelton left the United Provinces and requested that a well-paid job was given to him in the Custom's House for his past services. In short, the secretaries of state were therefore receiving little intelligence from Alberville on ex-patriot dissidents or the intentions of William of Orange.

William, on the other hand, had long had good quality spies in James's kingdoms organised by Gaspar Fagal, the Grand Pensionary of the Province of Holland, who also assumed the role of William's principal minister. Fagal had largely recruited agents from the Scottish Covenanter exiles in Holland such as William Carstares and James Stewart, who had a long record of conspiring against James, whether it was with Argyll,

Monmouth, or the Rye House plots. As well as these, the United Province's ambassador to England, Aernout van Citters was the focus for Dutch intelligence gathering, but he was appointed by States General, and so was not William's man. William wanted someone to begin assessing the strength of dissatisfaction with James's Catholicisation among Protestant peers. Earlier in the year he had sent a diplomat, Everhard van Weede Dijkvet, to London to dissuade James from any French alliance. Dijkvet also took the opportunity to make it generally known that although William was a Calvinist, he would support the Church of England but not persecute either Catholics or Nonconformists. In other words, dissident peers could look to William for support against James's Catholicisation.

Dijkvet had returned to The Hague in May having had a reassurance from James about not making an alliance with France. William now needed to build on Dijkvet's subversive work but required an excuse to send over another emissary. Fortunately, William was presented with an opportunity in July when the death was announced of Duchess Laura of Modena, Queen Mary Beatrice's mother. He selected his trusted cousin and army companion, Count Zylestein, to visit England to relay his condolences on the duchess's death. The real purpose of the visit was for Zylestein to find out how the Protestant nobility were reacting to James's Catholic policies and the recent decision to dissolve parliament and call a new one for November the next year.

Zylestein was a charming and good-looking courtier, able to mingle with the aristocracy with ease. Having relayed his condolences to Mary Beatrice he began a series of private meetings with powerful Whig aristocrats such as Charles Talbot, Earl of Shrewsbury, who were likely to be disenchanted with their monarch. He also met disaffected Tories, the most important of whom was Thomas Osborne, Earl of Danby, a staunch Anglican and the leading Tory in the House of Lords. Danby had been Charles II's Lord Treasurer and principal minister, who was pro-Dutch and had proposed the marriage between William and Mary. Powerful though he was, he had been brought down following a series of false accusations. These accusations had been largely orchestrated and paid for by Barrillon the French ambassador because Danby had pressed for an alliance with the Dutch against Louis. This led to Danby's impeachment and detention for almost five years in the Tower until he was released in 1684 and returned to the House of Lords. The proud, ambitious, ruthless and cold-blooded Danby was almost universally disliked as a person. Nevertheless, he was a highly experienced politician and party manager who had the ability to rally others to his views.

Zylestine's conversations with Danby and Shrewsbury, and several other magnates left him in no doubt about the mounting concern they had over the king's actions. To them, James was on a path to impose Catholicism on the country. He had left the archbishopric of York vacant and used the revenue to set up four Catholic bishops in England as a rival episcopate under the Papal Legate. As part of this policy, Anglicans were being removed from power and replaced by Catholics. This was happening in the Privy Council, the judiciary, the army and universities. Ireland was now under the Catholic Tyrconnell, and Scotland was under the two Drummond brothers: John, Earl of Melfort, the Scottish Secretary, and James, Earl of Perth, the Lord Chancellor, both of whom had recently converted to Catholicism. The Tories were the traditional supporters of the crown, but instead of receiving royal preferment they were being frozen out of the lucrative and influential government positions. On top of everything, the king was likely to use his patronage to ensure that the members of next parliament were sufficiently obedient to repeal the Test Acts.

The discussions with Zylestein prompted Danby to write to William of Orange about the general dissatisfaction of Tory peers. Understandably the letter was worded cautiously but it left the reader in no doubt that Danby and several other magnates would look to William as their saviour if England's Protestantism was at stake. As part of his official visit to England, Zylestein would have called on Princess Anne and her husband, Prince George of Denmark. Anne and George were living in the Cockpit in Whitehall (the site of which is now occupied by the Cabinet Office) and an informal opposition group was gathering around them. Anne loved her father, but being a strong Anglican, was pained to see his promotion of Catholicism. Anne had never been fond of her stepmother Mary Beatrice, but sadly they had drifted even further apart. Anne was now 22 years old and Mary Beatrice 27. When Mary Beatrice had married James, Anne was just 8, and unlike her elder sister Mary, took a dislike to her new mother. Mary Beatrice was a friendly, fun-loving girl and went out of her way to play with Anne and win her friendship. This had worked up to a point, but Mary Beatrice had changed over the years. After becoming queen she became more formal and distant and her failure to produce a healthy heir brought depression and religious devotion bordering on mania.

To all outward appearances the relationship between Anne and the queen remained cordial, but Anne had come to hate Mary Beatrice, whom she blamed for encouraging her father in his headlong support of Catholicism. As early as May that year Anne had written to her sister, Princess Mary of Orange, expressing her dislike of their father's wife, saying,

> one thing I must say of the queen, which is that she is the most hated in the world of all sorts of people; for everyone believes that she pressed the king to be more violent than he would be of himself; which is not unlikely, for she is a very great bigot in her way and one who may see by her that she hates all protestants.[2]

Mary of Orange had been quite close to Mary Beatrice before she had left for married life in Holland, but receiving letters like this from Anne must have helped to sour the former relationship with her stepmother.

Anne was devoted to her husband Prince George, but the latter sought a quiet life away from politics and intrigue. Anne's dislike of both the queen and popery were reinforced by her very close confidante, Sarah, wife of Baron John Churchill. Sarah was genuinely fond of Anne but was also very ambitious for herself and her husband. As a result Churchill became Anne's principal male adviser. Churchill remained close to James, as he was a Lord of the Bedchamber, member of the Privy Council and a senior general, but had been unwise enough to advise the king that his pro-Catholic policies were becoming deeply unpopular in the country. This honesty had not gone down well with James who had become accustomed to receiving unquestioning agreement from Sunderland and his mainly Catholic advisers. Churchill owed his advancement in life to James, but the king's Catholicism, and Churchill's refusal to convert, was putting their long relationship under strain. Churchill was becoming less inclined to help patch up the difficult relationship between Anne and her father and stepmother.

There was no formal opposition to the king's pro-Catholic policies, but with Mary of Orange overseas, Anne, as second in line to the throne, became something of a focus for Anglican discontent. Some of those who had tried to defy the king began to frequent her little household in the Cockpit. Most prominent of these was Henry Compton, a younger son of the Earl of Northampton who had been made Bishop of London and Dean of the Chapel Royal by Charles II in 1674. He had also been made responsible for the education of Mary and Anne and had not only become close to them, but helped instil his own strong Anglicanism and detestation of Catholicism. On becoming king, James removed Compton from the Privy Council and the Chapel Royal and then had him suspended as Bishop of London for refusing to dismiss a London rector for preaching against Catholicism. James was less than pleased that his daughter was associating with his religious enemies.

When Zylestein returned to The Hague to report back to William, it is unlikely that he brought any new information about Princess Anne and her Anglican circle, because she and Mary were in regular correspondence. Indeed earlier in the year Churchill had written to William on Anne's behalf:

> ...she [Anne] has resolved, by the assistance of God, to suffer all extremities, even unto death itself, rather than be brought to change her religion.

Then adding about himself:

> ...my place in the king's favour I set at nought, in comparison of being true to my religion. In all things but this the King may command me, and I call God to witness, that even with joy I should expose my life for his service, so sensible am I of his favours.[3]

What Zylestein was able to report was that a number of both Whig and Tory magnates were feeling that their loyalty was being stretched too far and were looking to William, as the husband of James's heir, to be prepared to save the country from Catholicism.

With Zylestein returned to The Hague, William used Henry Sidney, a son of the Earl of Leicester, to promote his secret interests in England. Sidney had been a senior courtier and colonel of one of the English regiments in Flanders, but had been dismissed after James came to the throne, probably James had not forgiven him for flirting with his first wife, Anne Hyde. William had come to trust Sidney during his time in the Netherlands and found him an ideal secret representative in England, not only because of his shared dislike of James, but also because his pleasant manner and good looks made him welcome among his own aristocratic class.

Sidney was dedicated, energetic and efficient but needed additional help for this the major task of subversion. It was decided to send James Johnston to England – foremost to act as a spy, but also to assist Sidney in propaganda and the general organisation of rebellion. Johnson was a Scotsman who had fled to the Netherlands back in 1663 after his father Lord Warriston had been executed for his Presbyterian opposition to Charles II. He had attended Utrecht University and been selected for the role of agent, having shown his ability as secretary for William's close friend and confidante, Willem Bentinck. Johnston turned out to be one of the foremost agents of his generation. He was a cousin of Burnet and used his connections to obtain valuable information from disaffected Anglican clergy. In a short period of time he built up well-placed informants, including one of Mary Beatrice's bedchamber women and someone with access to the proceedings of the Privy Council.

Johnston sent back high quality intelligence reports at least twice a week, but as this was too often to be carried by private courier he devised his own system for using the Royal Mail in a way which overcame the otherwise highly effective government intercept service. He wrote ostensibly business letters using the name 'Mr Rivers', and added the secret content in cipher in invisible ink which became visible when soaked in a solution devised by another exiled Covenanter, Dr Hutton, William's principal physician. Normally urine or lemon juice was used for invisible ink and the intercept office would check suspect mail for this by holding letters up to a candle. Johnston's method of communication meant that his excellent intelligence was delivered undetected, via Huguenot accommodation addresses in the Netherlands, back to Bentinck until he left in August the next year.[4]

The next few months were to reveal what the Anglicans had expected and dreaded. The two secretaries of state were directed to use all means to ensure that the king had a majority for repealing the Test Acts and penal laws in the November 1668 parliament. The main person they used to implement this task was Sir Nicholas Butler. Lords Lieutenant were instructed to ask all their deputies and magistrates whether they would assist in nominating parliamentary candidates who, if elected, would vote to repeal the Test Acts. When these replies came in, the secretaries could see exactly who could not be relied upon to support the crown. As a separate initiative the king had also sent commissioners around the country to identify those influential post holders who might not endorse crown candidates for election and to note suitable others who could replace them. As if this was not enough to cause alarm among the Anglicans, the king sent commissioners and three troops of cavalry to Oxford to install a Catholic as President of Magdalen College and dismissed the fellows who had refused to elect him.

James Stewart was a Scottish Covenanter exile who had been allowed to return from the Netherlands, having been asked by William Penn to help to encourage Presbyterians in Scotland to agree James's offer of toleration. He had been made a member of the Scottish Privy Council with responsibility for getting agreement to the Indulgence, but was still sending reports back to William Carstares in The Hague. It was decided to publish extracts from Stewart's letters saying that James was intent on establishing Catholicism rather than liberty of conscience, and at the same time publish a document written by Gaspar Fagal and George Burnet called *Their Highnesses the Prince and Princess of Orange's Opinion about a General Liberty of Conscience.* This document announced that William and Mary supported for liberty of conscience and the repeal of the Penal Laws, but desire to keep Anglican monopoly of power through the retention of the Test Acts. It was published in November and over the next few weeks 50,000 copies were printed and distributed in England and Scotland. This pamphlet received massive readership and made it clear to all where William stood on religion compared with the king. This was a major setback for James, but the year of 1687 ended on a happier note with the announcement that the queen was pregnant.

The news of Mary Beatrice's pregnancy was received with disbelief. She had suffered many miscarriages, her health was poor and it was five years since her last confinement. The Earl of Clarendon wrote: "'tis strange to see, how the Queen's great belly is ever where ridiculed, as if scarce anybody believed it to be true; good god help us'.[5] Anne certainly did not believe that her stepmother was pregnant and wrote to her sister Mary: 'There is much reason to believe in a false belly. For me thinks, if it were not, there being so many stories and jests about it, she should to convince the world, make either me or one of my friends, feel the belly.'[6] Anne's dislike of Mary Beatrice and the prospect of losing her position in line to the throne, led her to convince herself that the pregnancy was false and

Mary came to the same conclusion. For all that, William and Mary showed outward loyalty to James. Alberville reported back that the royal chapel at The Hague were having daily prayers for the safe delivery of a boy.

The new year of 1688 found James in high spirits. By God's grace, his wife was at last pregnant and there was now the prospect of having a male heir to continue his Catholicisation of the nation. Also, things were looking promising for packing the new parliament with government supporters. Those deputy lieutenants and magistrates who would not support candidates prepared to repeal the Test Acts had been removed and replaced by Catholics, Nonconformists or the religiously compliant. For the boroughs, the *quo warranto* procedure had worked well and 1,200 members of town corporations had been turned out and replaced by government nominees. Two thirds of the members of corporations were Catholics. One thing not working so well for James was that many Nonconformists had proved suspicious of the king's policy of toleration through dispensing with the Tests and Penal Laws. They wanted religious toleration, but not at the expense of letting in Popery. James decided that his Declaration of Indulgence of the previous year required greater publicity and support. In February he directed that it be reissued and that all Church of Scotland ministers in Scotland should read it from the pulpits in a Sunday service. In April he gave the same instruction to Anglican clergy in England.

For Anglican clergy to be ordered to endorse the Declaration of Indulgence was stretching their loyalty to breaking point. The Archbishop of Canterbury and six other bishops petitioned the king to be excused from reading the Declaration. James was furious at this insolence and had them indicted for seditious libel and sent to the Tower. There was an outpouring of public sympathy for the bishops, but James would not back down and in June they were put on trial. An even more important event occurred on 10 June: Mary Beatrice gave birth to a baby boy. The child at once became heir to the thrones of England, Scotland and Ireland and ensured a continuing Catholic dynasty. As was the custom, many courtiers attended the birth, but they were almost all Catholic. The Archbishop of Canterbury was in the Tower, Mary and Anne's Protestant uncles Clarendon and Rochester were not invited, nor was the Dutch Ambassador. On the advice of Sarah Churchill, Anne had gone to Bath – supposedly to take the waters for a pretended pregnancy. This was all to prove most unfortunate, because it allowed those whose interest it was to disbelieve the birth to spread the rumour that the baby had been smuggled into the bedchamber in a warming pan.

Anne wrote to her sister Mary:

> I shall never now be satisfied whether the child be true or false. Maybe 'tis our brother ... Where one believes it, a thousand do not. For my part, unless they do give a very clear demonstration... I shall ever be of the number of unbelievers.[7]

The unlikely story of the warming pan was spreading through the country and would be accepted as fact by growing numbers. James Johnston, William's brilliant agent in London, had accurately reported back to The Hague that Mary had been genuinely pregnant, but that unwelcome item of intelligence was quietly lost in the archives.

James and Mary Beatrice were of course overjoyed at the birth, as were their Catholic entourage. The boy was named James Francis Edward and became Prince of Wales. A Catholic succession now looked certain. Sunderland was so confident of the future that he publicly announced his conversion to Catholicism. Bonfires and fireworks were ordered to celebrate the happy event. Catholics might rejoice, but for Anglicans it was an end to the hope that Mary's succession would reverse her father's efforts to return the country to Rome. Eight days after the birth seven prominent Anglicans wrote to William to say that they would raise support for him if he landed a force in England. Their invitation had been drafted by Henry Sidney, who had arranged for the seven to make the undertaking and wrote the covering letter. They had been in secret communication with William for some time and mainly through Sidney and using Admiral Edward Russell as a courier. In April, William told Russell that he would be prepared to invade England to restore Protestantism if he was invited by powerful peers and was assured of them raising sufficient support. The time had come for the invitation to be made. Suddenly private grumbling and theoretical armed opposition was transformed into high treason.

The men who 'signed' the letter were the Duke of Devonshire, the earls of Danby, Oxford, and Shrewsbury, Viscount Lumley, Henry Compton the Bishop of London, and Edward Russell, grandson of the Duke of Bedford. They did not actually sign the letter, but wrote the cypher numbers allocated to them for their name. The fact that they had all been given a cypher indicates that they had all been in contact with William for some time and probably had secret meetings with Zylestein on his English visit. The highly efficient intercept office in the Post Office was a victim of its own success and as a result, those engaged in covert activity never corresponded through the Royal Mail. The invitation to William was therefore taken by Arthur Herbert disguised as a common seaman. Herbert had been a rear admiral and Master of the Wardrobe until dismissed by the king for refusing to support the repeal of the Test Acts.

Had Mary Beatrice been delivered of a girl, James's daughters and sons-in-law would probably have been genuinely happy for her. For some time William had been planning a possible invasion of England, but a boy heir now made that imperative. William naturally wanted to support his wife's claim to the throne but more importantly he wanted to seize the opportunity of bringing the three kingdoms of Britain as allies into the looming war against his arch-enemy Louis XIV, who was showing every sign of preparing to resume hostilities. Also the opposition to James was becoming so strong that there was a danger that there might be a rebellion without him and the three kingdoms would dissolve into civil war and be unable to ally against France. One difficulty for William might have been persuading his wife Mary that armed action should be taken against her father. Mary was a dutiful daughter, but also a dutiful wife and devout Protestant and so supported William, particularly as she believed the royal baby to be a fraud. Indeed Mary's decision to back her husband over her father brought the couple closer together and developed into a belated love match. William could now put all his energies into the difficult task of organising both an external invasion and internal uprising in England – without alerting his father-in-law.

The letter of invitation was received by William on 30 June, the day of the verdict in the trial of the seven bishops. Despite James's efforts to select compliant judges and jury, the verdict had been 'not guilty'. News of the acquittal brought widespread rejoicing throughout London and the Anglican bishops received a level of popularity they had never experienced before (nor since), with people kneeling before them to kiss their hand, bonfires lit, church bells rung, and even the many soldiers of the royal army in Hounslow drank to their health. James was furious, dismissed the disobedient judges and had those known to have lit bonfires publicly whipped.

For Sunderland the public response to the bishops' trial had been a shocking revelation. He had advised the king against prosecuting the bishops, but he had not foreseen just how unpopular it would be. Sunderland had been called to give evidence for the prosecution and travelled by sedan chair to the trial at Westminster Hall. He had been amazed to see at close quarters the massive crowds who had come to protest about the bishops' trial. People were shouting 'Papist dog!' at him as he passed and it was noted that by the time he arrived he was visibly shaken. The widespread jubilation over the bishops' release further proved to Sunderland that the king's policy of Catholicisation, which he had supported so avidly, had gone too far, and a very dangerous reaction had set in. From then on he would be pressing James to pull back on the policies that had become so obnoxious to the majority of his subjects.

William, for his part, now had many problems to overcome. He had to raise a strong enough force, then transport it and its equipment, ordnance and supplies to a suitable landing site in England. In doing so he needed to raise a large amount of money and also to get the backing of the various states of the United Provinces, particularly the powerful burgomasters of Amsterdam who distrusted William and were opposed to war. He also had to ensure that his invasion in the name of Protestantism did not lose him his important alliance of Catholic Spain, the Holy Roman Empire and Italian states against Louis. On top of it all, he had to ensure that he had sufficient armed backing and public approval in England to rally to his invasion.

William took the opportunity of James Edward's birth to send the urbane Count Zylestein, back to England to formally congratulate the king and queen on the birth. Naturally he used the occasion to contact the grandees who had come out in support of the invasion and try to bring others to the cause. Sunderland and Middleton were so relaxed about Zylestein's visit that they did not consider putting him under surveillance. Zylestein remained in England without suspicion till the end of July and was even given a ring by James valued at £300 when he departed. As well as the ring, Zylestein returned to The Hague taking with him secret letters to William from Halifax, Shrewsbury, Nottingham and Compton. Unknown to James and his secretaries, the planning for invasion and armed uprising was developing well.

Chapter 6

A Protestant Wind
1688–9

'It brought people to so desperate a pass that they seemed passionately to long for and desire the landing of that Prince, whom they looked on to be their deliverer from Popish tyranny, praying incessantly for an east wind, which was said to be the only hindrance of his expedition.'
Diary of John Evelyn, entry for 7 October 1688.

William decided to build on the success of Fagal's pamphlet and make extensive use of propaganda. There had been strict censorship in England since the re-imposition of the Licencing Act at the start of his reign. However, there were more than enough dissident propagandists, in the Netherlands, such as Ferguson, to write pamphlets attacking James and popery, and many Dutch printing presses happy to produce them. William put Willem Bentinck, in charge of the propaganda offensive, and very effective it was. Before long, large quantities of propaganda material were regularly smuggled across the North Sea and distributed across England, Wales and up to Scotland, to taverns, coffee houses and the porches of private houses. This was a major operation, largely coordinated by James Johnston with up to 30,000 copies of a single pamphlet at a time being smuggled in and distributed. The propaganda not only attacked the king, but in contrast portrayed William as a true Stuart, yet blessedly free from the usual Stuart vices of crypto-Catholicism, absolutism, and debauchery.

Most importantly, the pamphlets emphasised the belief that Prince James Francis Edward was not the king's son. The suggestion was that either the queen was never pregnant, or if she was, had had a still birth; in either case, papists had smuggled the baby into the birthing chamber in a warming pan. In normal circumstances few people with any knowledge of new-born children would be convinced by the warming pan story, but these were not normal times. Protestants believed what they wanted to believe.

James was annoyed by the onslaught of Dutch propaganda and had counter propaganda pamphlets produced in response, but did not recognise it as an act of aggression by his son-in-law. Nor did he appear concerned that William began expanding his navy by commissioning twenty-four additional men-of-war. William's pretext for this was that it was defence against Algerian corsairs operating off the Dutch coast. More difficult to explain was William's concentration of regiments and military equipment at Nijmegen. Alberville had been back in England in April and May, but the spies of Avaux, the French ambassador to the United Provinces, had noted this military build-up. Avaux's informants had also noted that a fast packet boat had been going back and fro between England and Rotterdam carrying mysterious English visitors who would then be closeted with the Prince of Orange. Some, like Admiral Edward Russell, were identified frequently making the journey. Avaux reported that in his view, William was preparing to invade England. This assessment was passed to Barrillon, the French ambassador in London, who in turn warned James. The king dismissed the assessment and was convinced that William was merely gathering forces as part of the League of Augsburg's defensive measures against an expected French invasion.

Sunderland agreed with James that William was getting ready for war with France. He and Middleton appeared blissfully unaware that powerful peers were now actively plotting William's invasion. Of course they knew that many senior Whigs opposed the king and that there had been meetings between them and Count Zylestein, and that other disaffected peers had visited The Hague. Of course, this could all be explained by the fact that it was perfectly reasonable to 'pay their duty' to the king's son-in-law and his daughter, who still remained second in line to the throne. Indeed, little Prince James Francis Edward had been seriously ill in July and then in August, so could yet die, making Mary once more heir to the crown. As early as April, Sunderland received information that William was planning to invade. A magistrate at the Somerset Quarter Sessions called William Coward wrote to Sunderland reporting one Elias Bragge, who had been sent to gaol for treasonously saying there was to be an invasion from Holland.

Sunderland and Middleton both completely discounted the possibility of William invading his father-in-law's kingdoms and so took no trouble to gather intelligence on the activities of those peers such as Halifax and Danby who were known to be leading opponents of the king's Catholicisation. With the king and his government in denial of the threat and the urgent need to monitor the activities of known opponents, the only hope was that Alberville and his spies in the Netherlands could establish exactly what William was intending to do with his great fleet and awaiting army. Through his informants, Alberville was well aware of William's naval and military activity. He had probably heard about William raising the large sums of money needed to fund a war, and that special envoys were being sent to Leopold I, the Holy Roman Emperor, and a number of German rulers in the League of Augsburg. Of course, all of this could be explained by William and his allies preparing to defend themselves against Louis's next military adventure. Louis wanted to put his own candidate in the vacant post of elector bishop of the state of Cologne and so take control of strategic fortresses on the Rhine. This had been resisted by Pope Innocent XI who wanted his own candidate to defend the Rhineland against French aggression.

The situation had reached crisis point and there could be little doubt that Louis would soon attack. The only question was whether he would first send an army to sweep though Flanders to neutralise William's Dutch forces, or send all his armies to attack the Rhineland. What Alberville did not know was that William's secret envoys had persuaded his allies to given their support to him invading England. William accomplished this by spreading the rumour that James had made a secret alliance with Louis and so an attack on England would prevent it coming into the war against the League of Augsburg. This was accepted even by the Catholic members of the League of Augsburg, including the Emperor Leopold, the Pope and their allies among the Italian states.

Although William was preparing for the invasion with the utmost secrecy, Alberville was extremely negligent not to have picked up on the warning signs earlier. It is true that he had been putting much of his diplomatic efforts into James's request that the six English regiments on loan to the United Provinces should be returned, and also that Gilbert Burnet should be extradited to England. However, even in this he did not see the signs of rupture between William and James. The States General refused to return the English regiments, but after long and rather acrimonious negotiations, finally agreed to let those officers and soldiers who wished to, return to England. This did William a favour, as it purged the regiments of personnel who might not have been prepared to follow him in his invasion. As far as Burnet was concerned, not only was there no question of agreeing his extradition, but William actually stood as godfather at the Christening of Burnet's first children. More ominously, it was noted that the prayers for the English royal family in William's chapel now omitted little Prince James Francis Edward.

During the summer of 1688 more and more English nobles were visiting The Hague and some, such as the sons of the Earl of Halifax and the Marquis of Winchester, together with Lord Lorne, son of the Earl of Argyll, took up residence. By September, dissident exiles such as Wildman and Ferguson also appeared. Middleton, who was nominally responsible for intelligence, had been side-lined by Sunderland and Alberville was sending his dispatches to him. Sunderland did not believe William was planning to invade and did not pass any of the dispatches on to the king, whom he knew completely discounted the possibility that William might be preparing action against him.

Alberville and Sunderland had failed to identify the intelligence indicators of an invasion, but not Avaux, the French ambassador to the United Provinces. In May he informed Louis that an invasion was being prepared, and Louis did his best to convince James through his ambassador Barrillon. Having failed to get James to recognise the threat from William, Louis decided to take action himself by getting Skelton the English Ambassador in Paris and his own ambassador, Avaux, in The Hague to issue a joint statement to the States General that France would regard any Dutch attack on England as an attack upon France. This did not in fact help because it because it merely seemed to confirm William's propaganda that England and France were in an alliance. The result was that the Republican burgers of Amsterdam in the States General who had opposed William's preparations for war began to support it. James was annoyed at Louis intervention and not only publicly repudiated a French alliance but recalled Skelton and sent him to the Tower. About this time Alberville seems to have realised that William might be preparing to invade and sent the following report to Sunderland: 'The talk at the Hague is that people of England and even the Army are on the point of revolution and it is openly said that if the Prince of Orange were to show himself in England the whole nation would declare for him.'[1]

Neither Sunderland nor the king had much confidence in Alberville and his report was disregarded. Sunderland wrote: 'The country was never less [in] danger of rebellion.'[2]

On 25 August Louis sent the Marquis de Bonrepaus as a special envoy in a last effort to warn James and to again offer the French fleet to defend against the invasion. James was annoyed with Louis for having sent the ultimatum to the States General and promptly disavowed it, so proudly dismissing Louis's offer of military assistance. Bonrepaus was told by James that he did not believe that William was preparing to invade, and that in any case, it was too late in the year for the sea to be calm enough to bring over flat-bottomed troop transport ships. When this was reported back to Louis he was highly irritated that James had disavowed the ultimatum to the States General, rejected the intelligence of the imminent invasion and spurned his offer of assistance. Louis decided that he would leave James to fend for himself and prepared to attack the Rhineland with his whole force. As we shall see, James's meeting with Bonrepaus was the critical event which enabled the Glorious Revolution, completely changing the course of British history and causing reverberations around Europe for the next hundred years. This failure to accept intelligence came at a time when the invasion was was virtually common knowledge, as is shown by the entry in John Evelyn's diary for 10 August: 'Dr Tension now told me there would be suddenly be some great thing discovered. This was the prince of Orange to come over.'

Following the 25 August meeting it was too late to stop the inevitable. Nevertheless, warnings of William's invasion continued unheeded. On 4 September, Louis made a final effort to make James realise the threat from William and sent Bonrepaus back to London with a renewed offer of naval help. This was again spurned by James. In The Hague, Alberville had at last realised that William was to invade and so travelled to England intending to bring positive information from one of Skelton's informants from Paris. On arrival, he was immediately sent back by Sunderland and rebuked for leaving his post. The Papal Nuncio, Ferdinand d'Adda formally warned James about William's intentions, but was likewise disregarded. So much was James's disbelief in an impending invasion that on the same day as the nuncio's warning he was writing cordially to William, 'this place itself affords little news, what news from your side of the water?[3]

William's great fleet of 700 ships was ready, as was his 15,000 strong army composed of the Dutch soldiers, the six English regiments and contingents from various German states from the League of Augsburg. William and Bentinck had made meticulous preparations for the force with its 8,000 horse, so that it had sufficient supplies, ordnance and equipment to be self-sufficient on landing. This went into the detail of having sufficient spare boots and even tobacco and rum. Sidney and Johnson had just returned from England and brought with them the plans made with those magnates who had pledged to support the uprising. All was poised for launching the invasion. However, there were two fundamental issues to be resolved before William could proceed. He needed the agreement of the States General to used Dutch ships and soldiers in the expedition and he had to be certain that the United Provinces would not be attached by France while its forces were in England. Fortunately for William, Louis had been antagonising the States General for almost a year by imposing damaging commercial sanctions, first on the import of Dutch herrings and then on other goods. He had also annoyed them by threatening them with attack if they invaded England. It looked promising that the States General would support the invasion, but their agreement was not quite in the bag yet.

On 15 September, Louis's armies began besieging Philipsburg, 200 miles from the Dutch border. This meant that the United Province would be not be vulnerable to attack if its forces were taken away for the invasion. Having recalled Bevil Skelton from Paris and placed him in the Tower, news of the attack did not reach James and Sunderland for some time and they continued to remain in denial about an invasion. Indeed, on 17 September James wrote a friendly private letter to William endorsed: 'for my son the Prince of Orange'. That very day Sunderland received a letter from Alberville that William would be embarking in a week's time. At last, Sunderland was convinced that an invasion would take place and informed James, who finally accepted the situation when Alberville sent a copy of the manifesto William had just published.

The manifesto stated that many peers and bishops had asked William to intervene by force to save Protestantism. It did not say that William was seeking to overthrow James, indeed it did not attack the king as such, but rather 'his councillors'. However, it did emphasise that Mary was James's true heir to the throne and it referred to Prince James Francis Edward as 'the pretended prince', but stated that William himself had no

1. King James II of England &
VII of Scotland.

2. Queen Mary of Modena,
second wife of James II.

3. James Scott, Duke of Monmouth, rebellious spoilt illegitimate son of Charles II.

4. William of Orange, astute Stadtholder of Holland and King of England, who was determined to stop Louis XIV's French expansion.

5. Queen Mary II, daughter of James II and joint monarch with her husband William.

6. Queen Anne with her only surviving child, the Duke of Gloucester, who died aged 11 and was the last of the Protestant Stuart royal line.

7. Prince James Francis Edward Stuart, son of James II known as the 'Old Pretender'.

8. Prince Charles Edward Stuart, 'Bonnie Prince Charlie', the 'Young Pretender', aged 65 with all hopes of gaining the throne gone.

Above: 9. Chateau de St Germain-en-Laye, Jacobite court in exile outside Paris.

Right: 10. King Louise XIV of France who supported his cousin James II's attempts to regain the crown.

Lewis XIIII King of France & Navarre.
I.Smith ex:

11. William Bentinck 1st Earl of Portland, William of Orange's right-hand man and expert in covert activity.

12. Thomas Osborne 1st Duke of Leeds, a powerful politician adept at intrigue and espionage.

13. Robert Spencer 2nd Earl of Sunderland, James II's Secretary of State and self-serving survivor.

14. Henry St John, 1st Viscount Bolingbroke, Queen Anne's Secretary of State who conspired with the Jacobites.

Simon Lord Lovat
Drawn from the Life and Etch'd in Aquafortis by Will.ᵐ Hogarth.
Price 1 Shilling.
Publish'd according to Act of Parliament. August 25.ᵗʰ 1746.

15. Simon Fraser, 11th Baron Lovat, double agent and rogue.

other design but to 'have a free and lawful parliament assembled'. It was only be a matter of time before William's propaganda machine ensured large quantities of the manifesto would be distributed throughout the three kingdoms.

Sunderland realised that the king's best course was to look to the defence of his kingdoms and put all unpopular policies into sharp reverse. James agreed, and much to the anguish of his close Catholic advisers began undoing all the Catholicisation of his reign. The king issued writs for a new parliament, announced that Catholics would be excluded from the Commons, restored the deputy lords lieutenants and magistrates who had been dismissed and allowed boroughs to nominate their own officers by restoring their old charters, which had been removed by under the *quo warranto* procedure. And so the back-peddling went on, with the fellows of Magdalen College being restored and the Catholics removed from crown appointments. The king even got some forty-two people who had been present at the birth of Prince James Francis Edward to give depositions that the birth was genuine, but as most were Catholic this did not dispel the 'warming pan' story. None of these efforts improved James's popularity with the majority of Protestants who simply felt that despite his public assurances to protect the Anglican Church, he remained intent on Catholicisation. The king had summoned his bishops and they had advised taking all the measures which he and Sunderland were frantically implementing. Despite James's taking their advice, they prevaricated when asked to publish a document condemning William and his impending invasion.

It would seem that James's close Catholic advisers, such as Sir Edward Petre, began to regain their influence over him because on 24 October, Sunderland was unexpectedly dismissed. The Catholic councillors had opposed Sunderland's dismantling of the Catholicisation programme and they may have persuaded James that he was now a traitor. Indeed, that might have been the case. Sunderland's uncle was William's principal conspirator, Henry Sydney, who was also very close to Sunderland's wife (unkind people said she was his mistress). It would be totally in character for the ambitious Sunderland to have contacted Sydney to tell William that he had transformed his loyalties to him. On the other hand, James may have felt that it would be politic to dismiss the unpopular Catholic convert Sunderland and replace him as senior secretary of state with the Protestant Earl of Middleton and have Middleton's post of Secretary of the Northern Department filed by the Protestant, Viscount Preston. Whichever way it happened, James lost the services of an experienced politician at a critical time.

On 25 September news reached The Hague that Louis had launched his total force of 70,000 men into the Rhineland; safely away from the United Provinces. More English grandees appeared in The Hague, including the Earl of Shrewsbury, who had sold up his estate and brought over £40,000 for William's war chest. William had appointed Admiral Herbert as commander of the invasion fleet, and the Duke of Brandenburg had sent him the very experienced general, Marshal Schonberg, to be his second in command. The final preparations were completed, all in the greatest secrecy. Plans were only discussed with Williams trusted circle of Bentinck, Schonberg, Herbert, Sidney and the ailing Fagal who was in the process of dying with cancer. George Burnet was even left out of the planning group because he was prone to gossiping. On 4 October, William extended the circle by briefing the States General on his invasion in a secret session. As just over a week earlier Louis had carried out the hostile act of impounding all Dutch ships in French ports (some 100 of them), the States General now fully supported war against France and its supposed English ally. William still retained the tightest security of his plans, although he knew his father-in-law was fully aware of the impending invasion. Indeed, on 9 October James had written to Mary saying that he could not believe that his own daughter had given her blessing to rebellion against him.[4] This was to be his last letter to her and was to remain unanswered. The Stuart family were now irreconcilably divided.

Herbert had wanted to send ships to scout out the British fleet and possibly make contact with disaffected naval officers. William had turned this down on grounds of security, but did decide to collect more land intelligence. Citters, the United Provinces' envoy in London, had been recalled to The Hague in July and given a briefing by the States General on the possibility of an invasion. When he returned to London he therefore began gathering intelligence of direct value to William. Building on the fact that Citters was now on side, William had Jacob van Leeuwen sent out to him as his assistant secretary on 11 September. Van Leeuwen was an experienced intelligence operator and replaced James Johnson as William's main agent in England. He made contact with key conspirators such as Danby, Russell and Delamere to organise the coordination of uprisings once William invaded. Van Leeuwen also sent back valuable military intelligence. Although he slightly overestimated the fleet as being forty-four ships, his information on the strengths and commanders of the garrisons was largely accurate.

This was all useful, but in October William decided to send his trusted Zylestein secretly to England to provide a final intelligence assessment prior to the invasion. All was now ready. After taking leave of the States General, William made a touching farewell to Mary, then joined the invasion fleet which sailed on 20 October. Security had been maintained to the end; soldiers and sailors were not informed that their destination was England until they were actually on board, prior to that it had been put out that they would be landed in Flanders. William's huge fleet, four times the size of the famous Spanish Armada, set sail but was driven back by a north-west gale. James was able to rejoice that a benign Providence had saved him from invasion. However, on 29 October, the storm abated and the wind turned to the east – what was to be called the 'Protestant wind', allowing William's fleet to proceed down the Channel and at the same time leaving James's fleet under Lord Dartmouth trapped in the Thames estuary, unable to get out to engage them.

William's armada was under way, but where was it going? Again, keeping tight security, William had not announced a final decision until the last minute. One possibility had been to land on the north east-coast of England, indeed Danby and William's supporters in Yorkshire had been expecting this. Another possibility was to land on the West coast of England and this has been anticipated by William's supporters in Cheshire. In fact, Zylestein had completed his intelligence mission and joined William on his ship, the *Brill*, to report back. He provided very accurate information of James's troop deployments and garrison strengths, and recommended that William land in Devon or Dorset. Based on this intelligence, William headed for the Devon coast and made an unopposed landing at Torbay near Brixham on 5 November, the great Protestant commemoration of discovering the Catholic Gunpowder Plot. Such had been William's security that Alberville had been unable to inform London of the intended landing site prior to William's departure, and the reconnaissance ships of James's admiral, Dartmouth, had been confused by William first sailing north towards Harwich before then turning south into the Channel.

Once James was finally convinced that there was to be an invasion, he was not idle. He had immediately ordered mobilisation and summoned reinforcements from Scotland and Ireland. His total army was 53,000 strong, greater than the one Cromwell had to win the Civil War, and considerably lager that William's invasion force of 15,000. Once it was clear that William would probably be heading for the south west, the king had received incorrect intelligence that William would be landing small forces in different places along the coast to raise false alarms. Middleton therefore instructed the Earl of Bath, who was lord lieutenant of Devon and Cornwall, to have the militia keep watch and remove all horses, cattle and oxen twenty miles inland in the event of a landing. The royal forces were deployed along the coast with the main force concentrated in the villages of Salisbury Plain.

Although James had removed most of the recently appointed Catholics from civil offices, that was not the case with his armed forces. The navy was under the Catholic Dartmouth, the army was still commanded by Feversham, key garrisons such as Portsmouth and Dover were placed under Catholics and even Bevil Skelton found his position in the Tower changed from prisoner to lieutenant governor. James was an experienced general and admiral who had put a considerable amount of his time into the training of both services. It would be reasonable for him to assume that his close interest and support would be repaid by loyalty. However, that was not the case as the great majority of soldiers and sailors were Protestant, and there was considerable resentment at the appointment of Catholic officers and their open celebration of the Mass.

William, for his part, had spent three days disembarking his force without opposition and then set off to Exeter where he was well received. As William's army consisted of many overseas contingents, he was aware they might appear to the local English population as a group of foreign plunderers. As with everything in his planning, William was meticulous in ensuring that this force did not forage, but bought any supplies it required with hard cash. He gave a public demonstration of army discipline by having two soldiers hanged for stealing a chicken. Although William's army received a polite welcome, he was disappointed that the local gentry were not rallying to his standard. It is probable that the locals had not forgotten the savage reprisals on Monmouth's followers. While William was receiving only limited local support, the king was receiving even less. Middleton was desperately trying to get intelligence on William's forces and the progress of the rebellion, but was receiving next to nothing. He noted that the reason 'we have so little intelligence is that none of the gentry of this or adjacent counties come near the court and the common [folk] are spies to the enemy.'[5]

Following the news of William's landing, Danby and other conspirator lords began to discreetly raise forces in the north. However, for the first few weeks of November most of the kingdom lay in confusion with people carefully avoiding taking sides, neither rallying behind the king nor welcoming William. There were some anti-papist riots in London, but once these were under control, James decided to advance against William by taking his main force of 19,000 to rendezvous with his troops on Salisbury Plain. Accompanying James were Feversham, his commander; the Duke of Grafton (one of Charles II's illegitimate children); his son-in-law, Anne's husband, Prince George of Demark; John Churchill and the Duke of Berwick (James's illegitimate son by Churchill's sister). Just before departing from Windsor, James had received the disconcerting news that his brother-in-law, Clarendon's son and heir Lord Cornbury, had gone over to William. It could have been worse as Cornbury would have taken three regiments of horse with him had he not been intercepted by a force led by the 18-year-old Berwick. Nevertheless, it unnerved James to find he was being deserted by someone close to him who was in his daughter Anne's protestant circle.

James was wary of others in Anne's circle, including her husband Prince George and more importantly Churchill, whom he had recently promoted to lieutenant general. James had become suspicious of Churchill and had even considered arresting him, but did not want to take any action that might further destabilise an already unstable situation. As it happened, James had every reason to be suspicious of Churchill. As early as five months previously Churchill had declared his support for William in the following letter carried by Sidney:

> Mr Sidney will let you know how I intend to behave myself: I think it is what I owe to God and my country. My honour I take leave to put into your Highness's hands, in which I think it is safe. If you think there is anything else that I ought to do, you only have to command me and I shall pay an entire obedience to it, being resolved to die in that religion that it had pleased God to give you both the will and power to protect.[6]

Having arrived in Salisbury, James held a council of war on the evening of 23 November. Intelligence on the strength of William's force and the northern rebels was seriously lacking. Middleton bemoaned the fact that his agents were taking his money, but then went over to join William. In the absence of hard intelligence James was having to rely on rumours of William's strength, often exaggerated, which did not fill him with confidence. At the meeting, Churchill and Grafton had advocated an advance against William, but Feversham insisted on retreat. James was being gnawed away by distrust and anxiety and had begun having fainting fits and nose bleeds. He decided not to go forward in case it was a plot by Churchill to hand him over to William, and so decided upon retreat. It is hard to tell what Churchill would have done if James had decided to advance, but his advice having been rejected, Churchill and Grafton stole away from the camp and rode through the night to join William. They took with them some 400 troopers.

This event was to alter the whole situation. William had now been joined by Cornbury, Churchill and Grafton, and a day later would be joined by Prince George of Denmark and the Duke of Ormond. Then there was Danby's rising in Yorkshire, with others by the earls of Devonshire in Derbyshire and Delamere in Cheshire. The trickle of notables rallying to William's standard now started to became a flood. What was more, some of the royal army had defected and it was likely that many others might be considering following Churchill's lead. James had been aware of disloyalty in the army since September, but for some reason had not arrested the officers involved. Had he done so, there was still a chance he could have brought his purged army to face William's smaller force and either achieved a victory, or at least negotiated an accommodation with his son-in-law, who was, after all, only saying that he invaded for no other reason but to have a free parliament. As it was, James lad lost the initiative and began returning to London with his dispirited army leaving the rest of the country for William to advance through unopposed.

James was having something of a breakdown, with continued nose bleeds and fainting fits. He could see he was being deserted on all sides, but things are never so bad that they can't get a great deal worse. When the king returned to London he did receive some cheers from the crowd, but there was anti-papist rioting in the city which the trained bands were unable to control, indeed the door of the Lord Mayor's house had been broken down, at which he had suffered a stroke and died. Rumours were swirling around of Catholic massacres of Protestants, and the city was in foment. A far greater blow than these was for James to discover that his daughter Anne had forsaken him. She had secretly fled at night with Sarah Churchill in a plan arranged by Henry Compton, the Bishop of London. Compton, in buff coat and armed with sword and pistols, took her first to his own house in the City, then by a circuitous route to avoid her father's returning army, she was escorted to Nottingham where she given an enthusiastic welcome. The Earl of Devonshire joined her with several hundred horse which he had raised, the townsfolk trooped out to see her and there was a public banquet that night. Princess Anne was safely among Protestant friends.

A dispirited James summoned such lords spiritual and temporal he could get hold of for their advice. The result of the meeting was to send a delegation to William to negotiate. It was eventually agreed that the king should offer free elections and a general amnesty for rebels. The king dispatched Halifax and Godolphin to negotiate with William, who had then reached Hungerford. By this time James had decided to escape. The anti-papist riots had spread from London to nearly all towns and cities, including Bristol, York, Cambridge, Dover and Hereford. James used the negotiations to play for time to allow Queen Mary Beatrice and the Prince James Francis Edward to escape to France on 9/10 December. With his queen and son safely away in one of the royal yachts, James began his own escape the next night. Before leaving he had given orders to Feversham and Dartmouth to disband the army and navy and burned the writs he had issued for a new parliament. He then boarded a small skiff and sailed down the Thames throwing the Great Seal overboard on the way, before joining a larger vessel to take him to France. His intention was of bringing government to a halt and produce anarchy in his absence. James's escape did not go well. When his ship stopped to take on ballast near Sheerness he was seized by Kentish fishermen who thought him a Popish priest. They brought him to Faversham and took him to the Queen's Arms Inn. There he was stripped, generally abused, robbed of his money, and his treasured piece of 'the true cross' was prised from his crucifix and thrown away.

After two days, word got back to London of the king's whereabouts and a dirty, hungry and dishevelled James was rescued and returned to London, escorted by 120 of his Life Guards. It was a London convulsed by the anarchy he had instigated. On the night James had escaped there had been riots and looting of the houses of Catholic families and several foreign embassies, together with the burning of Catholic chapels. The following night, mass panic had spread through the city following a false rumour that Catholic Irish soldiers were about to attack and slaughter Protestants. In fact, these Irish soldiers had already been disbanded and, fearful of a Protestant backlash, were streaming back to the North West to return to Ireland. In the absence of proper information, fear-fuelled rumour filled the vacuum and a mob of over 100,000 assembled to defend the city, while others scoured the streets in search of Irish papists.

Strangely enough, many London citizens came on to the streets to cheer the returning king who had been the cause of so much trouble. They had been so alarmed by the anarchy that they welcomed their sovereign in the hopes that his presence would help restore order and bring about some accommodation with William of Orange. There now followed a surreal situation. James resumed his position as king and, as though nothing had happened, held a meeting with his depleted Privy Council; he even held a ceremony to touch a group of poor people for the 'King's Evil'. All this, despite having disbanded his army and navy and thrown away the great seal, without which no parliament could be legally summoned. With a return of confidence, James then dispatched Feversham to William, who was then at Windsor Castle, to arrange a face-to-face meeting to carry out negotiations. This was a hopeless mission. William placed Feversham under arrest.

Unknown to virtually everyone, William had long decided that he would take his uncle's throne. He sent James's commissioners back to him to say that he could no longer guarantee the king's wellbeing and that for his own safety he should leave London. By this time Dartmouth had surrendered the fleet to William and most members of James's bewildered, disbanded army were enlisting with William's force. As the king still had the support of his Life Guards and three companies of the Coldstream Guards in Whitehall, William gave orders for them to depart twenty miles outside London, and his own forces entered the capital on 17 December. That night Lords Delamere, Halifax and Shrewsbury woke the king from his opiate-induced sleep and told him William wanted him to retire from London for his own safety. A bleary-eyed king agreed to move to Rochester and for his own guards to be replaced by the Dutch Blue Guards. The next day he left London and travelled to Rochester by boat under the protection of the Dutch Guards. William entered London as James left and was welcomed by cheering crowds, many wearing orange ribbons or waving oranges in the air.

William moved into Whitehall Palace and called on his aunt, Catherine of Braganza, the dowager queen, at Somerset House. When he enquired how she was, she said that she was content but missing having Feversham as a partner at piquet. William gave orders for Feversham's immediate release, such was his confidence that he was in total command of the situation. The next day was another family reunion when William visited Anne and Prince George, both of whom had returned to the Cockpit. One member of the family that William had no intention of seeing was his uncle and father-in-law; the last thing William had wanted was to come into open conflict with James. Fortunately, although there had been a couple of skirmishes at Wincanton and Reading between elements of the invading troops at the royal army, no significant battle had taken place. William had managed to avoid the embarrassment of a meeting with James and had persuaded him to leave the capital.

At Rochester, James was becoming very worried that he would suffer his father's fate and William did nothing to reassure him. James was out of the capital but was still king, and there was a growing mood that he had been treated badly; indeed, a small court was forming about him, which included former advisors such as Sowcroft, the Archbishop of Canterbury. Middleton and others including Sowcroft were begging him not to consider flight, but to force William into some agreement. William had to get James to leave the country in order to be able to take the crown. He therefore did everything he could to convince James his life was in danger and assist his 'escape'. It was made clear to the guards in Rochester that they should do nothing to prevent the king's departure and ensure that doors and gates to the river were left unlocked.

Letters of support to the king were suppressed and he was only allowed to see those advising him to escape to save his life. James, with mounting fear for his safety, received a letter from Mary Beatrice begging him to join her under the protection of Louis XIV in France. On the night of 23 December, James, with his son Berwick and two gentleman, went through the unlocked doors leading to the garden that backed on to the river, where a rowing boat was waiting. Despite adverse wind and tides, the king and his group eventually boarded a fishing boat and after being blown off course arrived on Christmas Day in the small French harbour of Ambleteuse. James set foot in France in high spirits, he was now safe and his people would soon be calling for his return to the throne. It was also exhilarating to know that he had managed to escape the clutches of his nephew. He was unaware that William's agents had not only ensured that those organising the escape were unhindered, but even obligingly facilitated passports for the group.

William was in control of England and could achieve his objective of bringing the country into the war against France. Louis had by now declared war on the United Provinces and one of William's first acts was to give Barrillon, the French ambassador, twenty-four hours to leave the country. He had achieved control of the country with his own forces without needing to rely on the uprising of the northern earls, Danby and Delamere etc. The English navy and most of the disbanded army had declared for him and he was the power in the land. But what next? The overwhelmingly Protestant English had welcomed him as their saviour from Popery, but who was to govern the country? On 28 December the peers appointed William to head a provisional government and called a parliament composed of the surviving members of Charles II's last parliament. This parliament met and called a Convention Parliament which convened on 22 January and began considering the future of the monarchy.

James had left the country, but could he return as king with William acting as regent to protect Protestant interests? This was an idea put forward by many Tories. Another was for it to be assumed that the throne was now vacant and the crown should go to William's wife, Mary. To the surprise of most, William insisted that he should take the crown. He was only fourth in line to the throne, and a Dutchman at that, but he held all the cards. After much wrangling a compromise was reached that William and Mary should be joint monarchs, with William as the senior partner. Mary was still in The Hague, having been unable to join William because of bad weather, but had let it be known that she fully supported this settlement. Part of the bargain for William being given the crown was his agreement to the Bill of Rights which placed limitations on royal power, such as making it illegal to suspend legislation passed by parliament, or raise taxation, or have a standing army in peacetime, without parliamentary approval, and that parliament must meet frequently. These, and the other provisions, form the basis for many of the freedoms in the Britain's unwritten constitution.

On 12 February, Mary at last arrived join William in London, and the next day received members of both houses of parliament in the Whitehall Banqueting House. *The Declaration of Right* was read by the clerk of the House of Lords and Halifax formally asked William and Mary to be joint sovereigns. Following their agreement they were proclaimed king and queen of England. The coronation was not to be until early April, but William and Mary had become the official rulers of the three kingdoms, although still not in control of Scotland and Ireland. The de facto situation of William's bloodless conquest of England had brought about a fudged compromise for future government. The highly doubtful constitutional theory behind it was that James had voluntarily vacated the throne and as the little Prince of Wales was not royal, his daughter Mary should succeed with her husband. It was a neat solution to a constitutional conundrum, but whether this glib interpretation of events would be accepted by all, remained to be seen.

Chapter 7

A Precarious dual Monarchy
1689–90

'The French fleet rides in our channel, ours not daring to
interpose and the enemy threatening to land.'
Diary of John Evelyn, entry for 14 June 1690

After Queen Mary Beatrice had arrived in France with the little Prince
of Wales, she at first stayed in Normandy, anxiously awaiting news of
her husband. Louis invited her to Paris and sent a squadron of dragoons
to escort her through the winter snow. It was during this journey she
received word of James's escape. As she neared Paris, Louis and the
whole court came out of Versailles to welcome her and her son. Now
30 years old and in poor health, Mary had retained her good looks and
charmed Louis and the court with her dignity and grace. In a particularly
generous gesture, Louis put his fine chateau of St Germain-en-Lage at
her disposal and provided the funding for its upkeep. St Germain was
a suitably regal residence, having been Louis's own principal palace
until 1682 when he began building Versailles. After James landed at
Ambleteuse he was given an escort to reach St Germain where his wife
was then in residence. Louis was there to meet James on his arrival
and the cousins embraced with genuine affection before Louis led
James through to Mary Beatrice's apartments where the couple had an
emotional reunion.

William and Mary had been proclaimed joint sovereigns but James
was the anointed king, had his own court at St Germain and was being
treated by Louis as if he still ruled his three kingdoms. How did this
extraordinary state of affairs come about? The quick answer is that
powerful Protestant nobles had had enough of James's Catholicisation
and invited William of Orange to restore Protestantism. William landed,

James was deserted by his followers and fled to France, leaving the throne vacant for William. This is all true, but as we have seen there was more to it than that. In particular there was the organising ability, political acumen and sheer willpower of William. It was he who secretly raised the money, men and ships necessary for the invasion and whose brilliant use of agents brought Protestant magnates to his cause and carried out such successful propaganda that the population would side with him against their king.

Despite James's folly and William's brilliance, the outcome was not inevitable. When William landed, James had by far the larger army. The majority of English people despised Popery but were instinctively loyal to the king. The lack of immediate support for William after he had landed showed the population's reluctance to oppose their monarch. Many Londoners rallied to cheer James as he returned after his first escape, and even when a prisoner in Rochester, several leaders wanted him to remain king, including the Archbishop of Canterbury.

William began seriously planning to invade in April 1689. Had James appreciated this and begun reversing his Catholicisation policies in May, June, July or even August, William would have had little or no support for his invasion. As it was the sharp reverse of the Catholicisation policy came far too late in September, and was rightly seen as an insincere ploy. Had James arrested the peers, such as Danby, whom he thought were plotting against him he might have also disrupted William's plans and averted invasion. Had James accepted Louis's offer of support from the French fleet and requested Louis to threaten Flanders, then William would have been unlikely to invade. All these missed opportunities were the direct result of a failure of intelligence.

Where should the blame lie for a failure so great that it cost the king his crown? James's intelligence staff, which included the intercept section in the Post Office, was much the same as had served his brother so well. It had been re-established at the Restoration and organised into a high state of efficiency by Sir Joseph Williamson who reintroduced the best practices of Cromwell's brilliant intelligence chief, John Thurloe. After Williamson had left, his legacy was continued under Sir Leoline Jenkins who uncovered the Rye House Plot. Middleton was a diligent and reasonably efficient secretary of state who supervised the intelligence department and directed its efforts against the Whig and Republican exiles in the Netherlands. The good state of the intelligence organisation had played some part in the defeat of Monmouth's rebellion, particularly through the arrest of the duke's potential supporters such as Macclesfield. Sadly for James, the intelligence organisation was then to decline when it was most needed.

The power hungry, but lazy, Sunderland then virtually took over the intelligence organisation from Middleton, without having the energy or attention to detail necessary for the task. He had removed the reasonably competent Bevil Skelton from the vital ambassador post in The Hague and replaced him with Alberville who, despite his intelligence background, proved next to useless. Sunderland was an astute politician but refused to accept the information offered by the French on William's preparations for invasion. This is probably because he did not want to cross the king, knowing that James refused to believe his nephew could plot against him. When Alberville belatedly realised that William was about to invade, Sunderland still did not believe him, although it was virtually common knowledge. As late as September, Alberville had rushed to England to convince Sunderland that the invasion was about to be launched but was merely reprimanded for leaving his post. Altogether a long catalogue of fatal errors.

It is true that James refused to accept the intelligence that William was about to invade but Sunderland, his de facto head of intelligence, is culpable of both failing to recognise the intelligence put before him and not attempting to gather additional information on the conspirators until it was completely too late. It is a pity the Sunderland did not take note of the words of Sir Samuel Morland, one of Charles II intelligence experts: 'for want of it [espionage] and intelligence a Prince may lose his crown.'[1]

James may have lost his crown to William and Mary but there was still more for William to do to secure their rule over the three kingdoms. Virtually all Catholics and a significant number of Tories, Anglicans and members of Church of Scotland still regarded James as their rightful king, for all his faults. Such people were given the name 'Jacobites' for their allegiance to James or 'Jacobus' in Latin. It meant that William had become king of a significant number of unwilling and sullen subjects, particularly in predominantly Catholic Ireland and the Highlands of Scotland. William would not have been surprised by this Jacobite objection to his kingship, but regarded it as a minor irritation as long, of course, that their opposition did not extend to active measures to restore

James to the throne. William positively encouraged those who wished to rally around James in France by granting passports to get them out of the way. As a result James soon found St Germain filling up with his supporters. Former royal servants followed him over to regain their jobs, and more importantly, Catholic gentry and peers such as Castlemaine, Powis, Stafford and Melfort arrived at the Chateau. A royal court in exile had begun to form.

William had let James have his carriages and horses sent over to him and even added '45 couple of hounds'.[2] Presumably, this was in the hope that James would settle down to a comfortable retirement and concentrate on his passion for hunting. Churchill and Grafton had been tasked by William with reorganising the English army and purging it of those who remained loyal to James. As a result, many of those officers and soldiers who had lost their jobs decided to regain them by travelling to serve James in France. By February 1689, James had an army of over 3,000 and a well-established court with the courtiers, servants and etiquette befitting his royal rank. He was living in some splendour largely financed by the 50,000 livres (£3,000) monthly pension he received from Louis.[3] The exiled king at first appeared content with his comfortable lifestyle and in no hurry to leave his wife and son to lead a force to regain his inheritance.

James had many of the trappings of monarchy, but William had been proclaimed joint monarch and had the task of governing the three kingdoms. Naturally, William's new regime had swept away the past administration. Sunderland who had already been sacked by James had fled to Rotterdam at the time of the invasion. He made an attempt to regain James's favour, but when that failed he had converted back to Protestantism and swore loyalty to William, in the hope of being able to return to England. James had not told Middleton of his plan to escape but merely left him with a letter to use to rally support for his return. The loyal Middleton had done his best to look after his absent king's interest, but had been simply ignored. James's other secretary of state, Viscount Preston, left for the north in an attempt to raise support for James but was arrested and placed in the Tower. William's new secretaries of state were Daniel Finch, the Earl of Nottingham, who was given the Northern Department and Charles Talbot, the Earl of Shrewsbury, was given the more senior Southern Department, which traditionally also led on intelligence. As it happened, this was keeping the post within the family, as Shrewsbury was Middleton's nephew, but unlike him a strong Whig, who it will be remembered, had been one of the seven peers to invite William over and had then gone to The Hague to join in the invasion.

It had been mainly Whig lords who invited William to invade and so they expected that it would be them who would be rewarded with lucrative positions. William acknowledged their help by appointing some of them such as Shrewsbury to his council but had also chosen Nottingham, a Tory, as his other secretary of state and made the Tory, Danby, Lord President and the 'trimmer' Halifax, Lord Privy Seal. William had no wish to rely on either Whigs or Tories and kept the conduct of much government business in his own hands, in particular foreign affairs. He had limited trust in his English peers of either party and understandably used his longstanding Dutch friends as his principal advisers. The most prominent of these was Willem Bentink, his close friend, trusted diplomat and soldier. William made Bentinck First Lord of the Bedchamber, Groom of the Stole, and Treasurer of the Privy Purse and gave him apartments connecting to his own. Bentinck was later made Earl of Portland, but the title mattered little compared to his unique access to the king.

There was considerable dismay as this turn of events became apparent. For example, when William dined formally he would have his general Schomberg at his right hand and the others sitting with him were all Dutchmen such as Bentinck and Zuylestein. English peers would attend the dinner but would remain standing and only watch the proceedings. Even the king's actual dinner appeared alien because he preferred boiled beef and beer to the roast meats and wine favoured by the English aristocracy. It was at times such as this that many began to fully realise that they had given the throne to a foreigner, albeit with Stuart blood.

England was basically under William's control, but the situation was less clear in Scotland. Most of the Scottish Privy Council had travelled to London to show allegiance to William and when the Presbyterian dominated Scottish Convention of estates had been summoned, it had come out in support of William. Although the majority of Scots were Presbyterian, there were a significant number of Catholics and Episcopalians who remained loyal to James. In fact Edinburgh Castle was being held for King James by its governor, the Catholic Duke of Gordon. There was also a potential threat to William from Graham of Claverhouse, Viscount Dundee, who was a popular general and had been

James's enforcer against the Covenanters. This threat appeared to have passed as Dundee had retired to his estate in Dunhope, and in April the estates formally offered William the throne.

Ireland posed a more immediate problem for William as it was predominantly Catholic, except for Presbyterians in parts of the north. The Lord Deputy was James's appointee, the heavy drinking and duplicit Richard Talbot, Earl of Tyrconnell. As an ambitious Catholic he had put considerable effort into James's Catholicisation policy with the result that most posts in the army, government and corporations had been given to Catholics. William wanted to have his new kingdoms settled as soon as possible so he could get on with his main objective of waging war against Louis. He therefore tried to negotiate with Tyrone, offering Ireland freedom of worship and allowing him to remain as Lord Deputy in return for his loyalty. Tyrone pretended to be considering the offer but sent an embassy to James in St Germain, urging him to lead an army to reclaim Ireland and then advance through Scotland to regain England. At the same time, Louis saw the advantage of using Ireland as a second front against William and offered James his support for an armed landing in Ireland. James had begun to accept that losing his throne was God's punishment for his promiscuous past, and was reasonably content in his comfortable and relaxed existence in St Germain. However, he felt that honour obliged him to go along with Louis and Tyrconnell and lead an expedition to Ireland.

So it was that on 16 February 1689, a rather reluctant James set sail from Brest with a force of 4,500 French and Anglo-Irish soldiers, escorted by fifteen French men-of-war. He was accompanied by his bastard son, the Duke of Berwick, and new secretary of state, John Drummond, Earl of Melfort, who had previously been his secretary of state for Scotland. The expedition was supposed to be secret but security had been poor and William must have heard it was to be launched. Possibly because of continued loyalty to James, Admiral Herbert seems to have taken no action to intercept James's fleet, and he landed safely in Kinsale on 12 March. In doing so James became the first English monarch to visit Ireland since Richard II; not a happy precedence. He was met by Tyrconnell and moved to Dublin where he received an enthusiastic welcome and then summoned parliament and took over the reins of government.

This turn of events was a setback for William who was busy setting up his own government and preparing for his joint coronation with Mary on 11 April. This ceremony did not go without a hitch. William Sancroft, the Archbishop of Canterbury, refused to officiate as he regarded himself bound to his oath of allegiance to James. Fortunately, the redoubtable Henry Compton, Bishop of London, took the ceremony, but over 400 Anglican clergy agreed with Sancroft and refused to take the new oath of allegiance. Included in that number were five of the seven bishops imprisoned by James. Many office holders also felt they could not break their sworn allegiance to James and together with the clergy became known as 'non-jurors', and both groups were removed from their posts. Such people and their families would become natural recruits for the Jacobite cause.

There had been another potential upset to the coronation. Just as Mary was putting on her coronation robes a letter arrive for her from James, saying: 'You being crowned is in your own power, if you do it and I [*sic*] and the prince of wales are living the curses of an angry father will fall upon you, as well as of a god who commands obedience to parents.'[4] Fortunately Mary did not see the letter as it was intercepted by one of her gentlemen and discreetly consigned to the archives undelivered. Although unread, the letter made the breach between father and daughter now irrevocable.

The joint coronation provided the appropriate occasion for William to begin to reward those who had helped him seize the throne. Churchill was made Earl of Marlborough; Gilbert Burnet: Bishop of Salisbury; Danby: a marquis; Devonshire: Lord Steward and later a duke; Henry Sidney: a viscount, and so it went on, with Macclesfield becoming a Privy Councillor, Lord President of the Welsh Marches and given five lord-lieutenantships. William naturally rewarded his principal foreign supporters with Marshal Schomberg becoming a duke and Willem Bentinck being made Earl of Portland. William gave out rewards of patronage as well as titles and did not forget his intelligence agents. William Carstares was made Moderator of the Church of Scotland and later Principal of Edinburgh University. James Stuart was made Lord Advocate, James Johnson was sent as envoy to Berlin and would later become Secretary of State for Scotland, Dr Hutton received medical honours including being made fellow of the Royal College of Physicians, and the inveterate conspirator John Wildman, became Post Master General, where he could supervise the intercept operation for the new regime.

Inevitably some of William's supporters were overlooked, or felt they did not get the recognition they deserved. Some such people were likely to join those opposed to the new king's policies. Unfortunately, Princess Anne became one of these. There had been a genuine joyous reunion between Anne and her sister when Mary came over to England, but it quickly soured thanks to the influence of the ambitious and scheming Sarah Churchill, now Countess of Marlborough. William had given Anne and her husband Prince George large apartments in the Palace of Whitehall, but Sarah persuaded her that she also needed the adjoining apartments to accommodate her servants. As these additional apartments had already been promised to the Lord Chamberlain, William refused and Anne angrily said that if she could not be treated with the respect due to her status she would just remain in her Cockpit apartments. So from the very start of William and Mary's reign, relations between them and Anne had become strained. As Anne was next in line to the throne, it meant that the Cockpit became a potential focus for opposition to the new regime.

At about the same time as the coronation, news arrived in London, that Graham of Claverhouse, Viscount Dundee, had raised James's royal standard in Scotland. Claverhouse drew recruits particularly from the north east, which was largely Episcopalian, and during the next four months increased his force to 3,000 strong. He carried out a series of successful skirmishes against the Williamite government forces, playing for time in the hopes that James would land in Scotland. On 27 July Claverhouse won a major victory against the government troops at the Battle of Killiecrankie, but at great price, as a third of the Jacobite army were killed, including Claverhouse himself. James had sent Colonel Alexander Cannon with 300 Irish to support Claverhouse, and following the latter's death, appointed him as commander in Scotland.

Despite the death of Claverhouse, the victory at Killiecrankie boosted Jacobite morale and meant that Cannon's army increased to 5,000, but they were largely untrained and brought with them the problem of supplying such a large and poorly organised force. Nevertheless, they appeared such a threat that, although the Duke of Gordon had by now surrendered Edinburgh Castle, the Williamite government in the city were considering flight. They ordered the newly raised 1,200-strong Cameronian Regiment to hold Dunkelt at all costs against Cannon's advancing Jacobites, who attacked the town on 21 August. After sixteen hours of fierce fighting in the narrow streets around Dunkelt Cathedral, the Jacobites not only failed to take the town, but suffered such major casualties that they withdrew disheartened. Cannon did not have Claverhouse's charisma or military ability, and within weeks of the battle his dispirited army had melted away. James later sent a new commander over from Ireland to lead some Highland clans who had joined the Jacobite cause, but in spring the next year this 800-strong force was soundly beaten at the Battle of Comdale. This ended any armed Jacobite threat and Scotland came under the firm control of Williamite forces.

There was still the matter of James in Ireland, where virtually the whole country was under Tyrconnell's control, except for Protestant Londonderry. In mid-April James left Tyrconnell in Dublin and led an army to Londonderry to snuff out this last outpost of resistance but had been met by cries from the city walls of 'no surrender'. A rather crestfallen James then returned to Dublin and a three-month siege of the city began, which only ended when William sent three armed merchant ships to break the blockade. William had retained a Protestant foothold in Ireland but clearly needed to take the kingdom from James. He sent Schomberg with a force of 15,000 to carry out this task and they landed in Bangor Bay in August. Schomberg was an experienced general but he was 73 years old and it has to be said, was rather past his best. Nevertheless, Schomberg captured Carrickfergus and then advanced to Dundalk. There he remained and decided to make it his winter quarters, rather than risk battle with Tyrconnell who had the potential to throw a 30,000 strong army against him.

While these events were occurring in his other two kingdoms, William was still trying to stabilise his position in England in preparation for returning to the Continent to take part in war against Louis. James's French-backed expedition to Ireland meant that in April parliament had petitioned William to declare England at war with France. William naturally agreed and dispatched Churchill, now Earl of Marlborough, as commander of an 8,000 strong English expeditionary force army to the Low Countries. Marlborough and his men then came under the command of the Prince of Waldeck, who William had appointed as field marshal of the Dutch army to protect the United Provinces if Louis moved his armies from the Rhine to attack Flanders.

William was not finding it easy to govern England. He had expected that he would receive gratitude as the saviour of Protestantism, but instead seemed to be thwarted at every turn. His ministers divided on party lines to oppose each other. The Whig Shrewsbury felt that the king took the advice of the Tory Nottingham and his friend Halifax, rather than his own, thus straining the relationship between the two secretaries of state. More importantly the Whigs in parliament were blocking his efforts to introduce religious toleration for Catholics and Unitarians and holding up his Act of Indemnity in a bid to purge local councils of Tory rivals. Even more irritating, the Whigs had turned the Declaration of Rights into a bill. William had rather assumed that the Declaration was a general guideline for the prevention of absolute monarchy. Making it an act of parliament would mean that he and his successors would be legally bound to its limitations on royal power.

If the Whigs were proving difficult, so were the Tories. The question arose over what income should be granted to Princess Anne, who was William and Mary's heir presumptive and who in July had had given birth to her own heir, William, Duke of Gloucester. William had offered to pay her £30,000 a year from his own parliamentary grant; urged on by Sarah, now Countess of Marlborough, Anne refused this offer on the grounds that it was insufficient and she did not wish to be beholden to her brother-in-law. The avaricious and scheming Sarah then managed to enlist the support of Tories in parliament and the end result was that parliament agreed to giving Anne a parliamentary grant of £50,000 a year for life. William had increased his offer to £50,000 and was furious that parliament was prepared to give Anne a grant for life while his own grant was subject to an annual vote.

William had never liked Anne and regarded her as an unintelligent, fat, glutton. Mary, who supported her husband in all things, became further estranged from her sister. William was not easy to like. He was aloof, cold and calculating by nature, and this, together with his coughing and wheezing from chronic asthma, did not make him the best of company. He was also an obvious foreigner who never learnt English, and spoke to his subjects in French. Anne began making reference to William's small, hunched physique and abrasive manner by referring to him as 'Mr Caliban'. Another rift had opened up in the Stuart family on top of the major split between James and his daughters.

The rift with Anne would have been an irritation to William, but of little consequence compared with frustrations over delays in achieving his principal objective of countering Louis's military aggression.

The dawn of the new year of 1690 may have occasioned William to reflect on the progress he had made in his great design since he had landed at Torbay over a year previously. There were positives and negatives; the positives had been of his own making and the negatives had been caused by his new English subjects. On the positive side, he had achieved great diplomatic success in forming a Grand Alliance against Louis. By January 1690 England and the United Provinces had been joined by Austria, Spain, Bavaria and Denmark. Good though this was, the Alliance needed his presence and leadership, as there was quarrelling among his Dutch Generals and the lack of a uniting figurehead. On the negative side, parliament had been very slow in voting him money and had obliged him to sign the Bill of Rights, placing limits on his royal powers. Still worse, William could not leave England to join the forces of the Grand Alliance with James still in control of much of Ireland. He was becoming increasingly impatient with Schomberg's lack of progress and the fact that about a third of his force had been lost in the winter as disease swept Dundalk.

William decided to go to Ireland himself, and having received £200,000 funding for the expedition from parliament, dissolved it in February. Shrewsbury had become increasingly exasperated by William running the country singlehandedly, and resigned as secretary of state. This left Danby, now Marquis of Carmarthen, and Nottingham as the main figures in the administration, although neither would have much of a free hand as William continued to keep tight personal control of government, dealing directly with his heads of department without others present. All decisions on both finance and foreign affairs were taken exclusively by the king and so ministers felt they were implementers of the king's decisions rather than decision makers themselves. The question arose of how England should be ruled when William departed for Ireland. A new parliament had opened in March and William obtained its agreement that Mary should be regent in his absence and have a council of nine advisers. By this time William had mustered an army for the Irish expedition comprised of English, German, Dutch, Danish and French Huguenot troops. Having established Mary as regent, he departed for Ireland.

William's fleet of 300 ships carrying his army and its supplies arrived at Carrickfergus on 14 June. As always, when he was with his troops, William became a changed person. Gone was his reserve and asthma and he became an energetic, courageous and inspiring leader. Having linked up with Schomberg's force, he advanced with 36,000 troops toward Dublin reaching the River Boyne on 30 June. Across the Boyne he was faced by James and his Jacobite army of 23,500, composed of some 6,000 well-trained soldiers of French regiments, but mainly consisting of raw Catholic Irish levies with insufficient muskets and powder. The next day the battle began with William sending some regiments to make a diversionary crossing a couple of miles upstream. This resulted in James deploying a large part of his army to meet it, only to find that William's main body crossed the Boyne to attack the depleted principal Jacobite position. There was heavy fighting during which Schomberg was killed but William crossed the river and pushed back the Jacobites to take their position on the high ground of the far bank. Jacobite Irish infantry began to flee and James ordered retreat as he thought his army was about to be surrounded.

William had displayed considerable personal bravery in the fighting and had won the battle in so far as his force had received less casualties and remained in possession of the battlefield. For all that, the engagement was not decisive; about 1,500 Jacobites had been killed compared to 500 Williamites, but the majority of James's force remained intact. For some reason James lost confidence and rode off with his escort to Dublin, in effect deserting his men. At 5 am the next morning, James left Dublin with his escort and rode to Duncannon; the following day he sailed to Kinsale and from there set off by ship to Brest on 4 July, with Melfort and a few others. He was never to return to any of his kingdoms. James's demoralised army retreated to Dublin, only to abandon the city and then march to Limerick under Tyrconnell and the 19-year-old Duke of Berwick. William made an unopposed entry to Dublin on the same day that James had set sail for France.

James had obligingly removed himself from Ireland and once again avoided William the embarrassment of possibly having to take his father-in-law prisoner. With James gone and his army in low morale there was every chance that the war in Ireland might be brought to an end. Unfortunately, William published the Declaration of Finglas offering pardon to the Jacobite rank-and-file soldiers, but excluding the officers and Irish Catholic landed classes. Those excluded realised they had no option but to fight on in the hopes of securing a better peace settlement in the future. And fight on they did; with determination from their main base in Limerick and repulsed a siege by William in August, causing such casualties that William withdrew from the West of Ireland to concentrate on pacifying the south. William was aware that his victory at the Boyne and the flight of James meant that it should just be a matter of time before the Irish Jacobites could be brought to submission. However, he did not have time to spare, so decided to leave the Dutch Baron van Ginkelt to complete the operation while he returned to England to face a new emergency.

Just before William left for Ireland there had been some disturbing intelligence. Mary of Modena had sent letters to supporters in England and knowing of the Post Office intercept system, had them carried by two couriers. The letters were written in invisible ink (probably lemon juice or urine) and hidden inside the courier's buttons in case they were arrested and searched. One of the couriers was William Fuller, a Catholic who had been a page to Lady Melfort and had accompanied her to St Germain. The other was a young Jacobite called Matthew Crone. They had landed at Dungeness and Crone had gone on to London to deliver his letters, but Fuller went to William and Mary's court at Kensington. Unbeknown to Mary of Modena, Fuller had decided to sell his services to the Williamite government. The letters were removed from his buttons and placed against a candle to reveal the secret ink and their subversive wording. Clearly the intended recipients of the letters were Jacobite sympathisers and very likely engaged in treason. It was important to identify similar enemies of the state by finding the addressees for the other courier. The search was on for Crone. He was not difficult to locate because he was found rowdily drinking toasts to King James in a tavern in Gracechurch Street. Crone was taken before Secretary of State Nottingham for examination and denied everything, until Fuller was brought in and he realised he had been betrayed. Crone still refused to talk, but his resolution was shaken as he realised he was to be tried for treason. While Crone was in custody, another Jacobite agent called Tempest was captured on the Dover Road carrying letters to supporters in England. It was at this point that William had left for Ireland, just when there were clear signs of preparations for a Jacobite rising in England.

While William had been in Ireland the threat had become clearer. Crone was sentenced to death for treason, but the day before his execution he asked to see Nottingham and offered to provide information in exchange for his life.[5] Crone was brought before the privy council and told them of an intended Jacobite uprising in London which would capture Queen Mary and proclaim James II king. At the same time, it was planned that a French fleet would sail into the Thames. This came at the time when a French fleet under Admiral Tourville was sighted off the Devon coast and it was believed that French troops were concentrating in the Dunkirk area, possibly in readiness for invasion. Considerable alarm ensued. Crone mentioned various prominent people involved in the plot such as the queen's own uncle, the Earl of Clarendon. Arrests were made and Clarendon and others were placed in the Tower. The roundup of suspects was extensive and included innocents such as Samuel Pepys, who found himself in the Gatehouse Gaol because he was a non-juror who had resigned his position at the Admiralty rather than take an oath of loyalty to William and Mary.[6]

Charles II's widow, Queen Catherine, was a Catholic and had a small court at Somerset House so was thought to be a possible focus for Jacobite plotting. To prevent this possibility, she was bundled off out of the way to Windsor Castle. Military measures were also hurriedly put in hand. Marlborough who had been left in command of the army in England, gathered together 6,000 regular troops and organised the militia for the defence of the realm and Admiral Herbert (recently created Earl of Torrington) was ordered to intercept the French fleet. As word spread about the imminent French/Jacobite threat, it seemed that the Glorious Revolution might be about to be undone. Then came a major blow to the government.

The very day before William's victory at the Boyne, there had been another battle many miles away out at sea off Eastbourne. This was the Battle of Beachy Head where the combined English and Dutch fleet under Torrington had suffered a major defeat by Admiral Tourville. Queen Mary and her council had ordered Torrington to attack the advancing seventy-five-ship French fleet, despite the English/Dutch fleet having only fifty-six ships. The result was disastrous, with six Dutch and one English ship lost. Fortunately Tourville did not successfully pursue Torrington, who managed to bring the remnants of the fleet limping back to the safety of the Thames. The victory gave France the command of the Channel, which meant that they had the potential to mount an invasion of England and even cut William off from crossing the Irish Sea to return to England. The luckless Torrington was blamed, branded a traitor, and sent to the Tower.

On top of this, dispatches were arriving that France had won a major victory against the Grand Alliance at the battle of Fleurus, which had resulted in the French occupation of eastern Flanders. Tourville demonstrated France's new naval power by landing at Brixham with 2,800 men and burning the village of Teignmouth. If he had hoped that he would be welcomed by local Jacobite gentry, he was disappointed. He heard that the county militia were advancing against him, so re-embarked and put back to sea. Tourville's withdrawal, and the glad tidings of William's victory over James at the Boyne gave Mary and the council cause to hope that the immediate emergency had passed, but anxiously awaited what Louis might do next in support of James.

James's defeat at the Boyne and ignominious flight from Ireland does not seem to have much concerned him. His safe return was welcomed with relief by Mary Beartrice and he could resume his opulent life style at St Germain. He was encouraged by the news of the victory at Beachy Head which had given the French command of the Channel and full of ideas for launching a French-backed invasion of the south coast and the marching on London while William and his army were still in Ireland. He was delighted when Louis came to visit him as soon as he had returned to St Germain, but then crestfallen to discover that Louis showed no enthusiasm for the suggested invasion. Louis left and James sent numerous messages to him at Versailles suggesting another meeting but having been repeatedly put off by the response that Louis was slightly unwell, came to realise that Louis was keeping him at arm's length. James began to understand that Louis, his only friend, would support him with money, ships and soldiers, but only if it suited him. The fact was it did not suit him at that time. The Duke de Louvois, his secretary for war, was completely opposed to invading England. Louis himself, was far more interested in his Flanders campaign than helping his cousin who had squandered the troops he had given him for Ireland.

James felt humiliated by Louis's rebuff and realised that there was no option but to put off any invasion of England until Louis became minded to give it his backing. As it was clear that there would be no speedy return to England, James began getting his court at St Germain on a permanent footing. He confirmed appointments with Lord Melfort as his secretary of state and intelligence coordinator, Sir John Neagle responsible for Ireland and Fr Louis Innes responsible for Scotland. James's troops were still fighting on in Ireland but the remnants of his army in Scotland had been destroyed at Cromdale and there was no one in arms for him in England. James's strategy was therefore to try to give what little support he could to Ireland and to send money and agents to England to try to organise an uprising for when a French-backed invasion might become possible,

In September William returned to England, but by then the crisis was over. Apart from the futile gesture of burning Teignmouth, Tourville had kept his fleet in Le Havre and failed to exploit the situation. Louis was furious and Tourville was dismissed, but by then the English fleet had reformed and had risen to ninety vessels cruising the Channel and so brought the brief French command of the sea to an end. Shortly after, William sent Marlborough on an expedition to Ireland to capture the Jacobite towns of Cork and Kinsale. Marlborough achieved this with his customary efficiency, and in doing so took possession of two ports that might have been used by the French to land reinforcements for the Jacobites. With England safe from invasion and the Irish Jacobites cut off from French help, William could at last arrange to join the Grand Alliance in Flanders.

In January 1691 William returned to The Hague after an absence of two years, during which he had become king of England, Scotland and Ireland and created the Grand Alliance against Louis's aggressive expansion. He received an enthusiastic welcome home and having restablished himself in control of the United Provinces, assembled a congress of representatives of the Grand Alliance. He persuaded the congress to oppose Louis with a 220,000 strong army and agreed to provide a 20,000 force as the Dutch/English contribution. This done, in May he took his army with Waldeck as his second in command and Marlborough as one of its generals, to begin operations in Flanders.

With William gone, Mary was again left as regent. She assumed this role with courage and success. Mary was a woman of intelligence, determined to do her best to fulfil the policies of her beloved husband. She was also a person of charm and beauty who courtiers found a welcome change from to her cold and authoritarian spouse. It was really only at the beginning of 1691 that England could return to something approaching normal government. Since William had landed at Torbay there had been the huge upheaval of the Glorious Revolution, uprising in Scotland, James's bid to regain Ireland and the threat of a French invasion.

Government had been a matter to reaction to each crisis and the reins of that government had been held tightly in the hands of William.

The secretaries of state were largely ignored or reduced to merely writing letters announcing the king's decisions. Although William conducted government with great energy, often working late into the night, it was too much for one man. His management style resulted in backlogs in government business and some important matters became neglected. Among these was the effective running of intelligence. Information was reactive. It came in from lords lieutenant, sheriffs and magistrates when uprisings took place and military intelligence on the disposition of Jacobite forces was provided by army scouts, but there was little or no pre-emptive collection of intelligence. One reason why the Battle of Beachy Head was lost was lack of intelligence about the French combining the Brest and Toulon fleets.

The responsibility for intelligence management traditionally rested with the secretary of state for the south, although occasionally it was undertaken by the secretary of state for the north. William had appointed the Earl of Shrewsbury secretary for the south, but this had not been a total success. As we have seen, Shrewsbury was a strong Whig often at loggerheads with the Tories in the Council and frustrated that William gave him little responsibility. He had resigned partially through ill health, and partly because the new parliament of 1690 had a Tory majority. Such was the man and such were the circumstances of his time in office, that he did not get to grips with the effective management of the government intelligence service. He had been replaced in June by Nottingham who was not succeeded as Secretary for the Northern Department until Henry Sidney was given the post in December.

Sidney had been created a viscount for his excellent work in organising leading figures to support William's invasion. In many ways his experience of covert activity would have made him an ideal choice to be given responsibility for intelligence, but that was not to be. Nottingham was nominally responsible for intelligence and had managed the turning of Crone and the arrests that followed. However, after William left for Flanders it was Danby, now Marquis of Carmarthen, the Lord President of the Council who was Queen Mary's principal minister. Both William and Mary trusted Carmarthen more than their Whig ministers and he began to take a more prominent part in intelligence matters; 1691 would see the government intelligence service being better aligned to meet the threats posted to the new dual monarchy and their Glorious Revolution.

Chapter 8

An Invasion Threatens
1691–5

'Much apprehension of a French invasion, and of a universal
rising, our fleet begins to join with the Dutch.'
Diary of John Evelyn, entry for 24 April 1692.

The Glorious Revolution had brought a revolution in intelligence
requirements. In James's reign the threat was from a few diehard
Republicans and Scottish Covenanters, but mainly Whig extremists and
their exiled brethren in the United Provinces. Intelligence was largely
directed against the activities of these dissidents in the United Provinces.
As we have seen, little attempt seems to have been made to monitor the
activities of Whig peers such as Macclesfield in England, or appreciated
that William of Orange was planning an invasion until very late in the day.
When William and Mary became joint monarchs the threat was reversed.
Whigs, Covenanters and Republicans had supported William's invasion
and were therefore loyal to the new regime and the United Provinces had
not only become an ally, its Stadtholder was also king of England.

The threat now came from the former king and those who had until
recently been the monarchy's most loyal subjects. These Jacobites
consisted of Roman Catholics, some Quakers and those Anglicans
who clung to their traditional support of an anointed monarch. The
latter category were usually Tories such as the Earl of Ailesbury, but,
of course, not all Tories were Jacobites. Some, such as Carmarthen,
were fiercely loyal to the crown – as long as it rested on a Protestant
head. The other change was that France, which had been a semi-ally
during James's reign, was now the enemy with which the country was at
war. It was a complex situation but the end result was that for the next
hundred years the threat to England would be posed by the Jacobites and

their French allies. It was the task of those responsible for the country's security to realign intelligence collection to target the two new threats.

One reason government intelligence was slow to redirect itself against the new threats was that whereas the French state and its forces were a clear target, Jacobites were often more difficult to discern. The Whigs found it convenient to unfairly brand their Tory political opponents as Jacobites. Many Tories did retain Jacobite sympathies, but the majority put their Protestantism before support of a papist king. Indeed the Tories were the party that traditionally supported the monarch, whereas it was the Whigs who were normally opposing the monarch and seeking to limit royal power. On top of this, there were those who had changed sides during the Glorious Revolution to support William. Some had done so out of religious conviction, but many had changed sides out of self-interest. How far could they be relied upon if it looked as though James might regain the throne?

Some Jacobites were well known to the government as they were prominent people who had openly supported James during his Irish expedition. When James returned to St Germain he established several of these in a group called the 'Select Number'. The role of this secret group was to look after the exiled king's interests in his former kingdoms and provide him with intelligence. The members were James's former secretaries of state Charles Middleton, Earl of Middleton, and Richard Graham, Viscount Preston. The other members were Thomas Bruce, Earl of Ailesbury; William Herbert, Viscount Montgomery; Sir John Fenwick; Lieutenant Colonel John Parker; Major-General Edward Sackville and Sir Theophilus Oglethorpe.

On the face of it they should have been a strong team. Ailesbury and Montgomery both provided potential Jacobite supporters in Wales. Montgomery was the son of the Marquis of Powis and during James's reign had been a colonel of a regiment and deputy-lieutenant of six Welsh counties. Ailesbury had been a Lord of the Bedchamber to James and Lord Lieutenant of Bedfordshire and Huntingdonshire. Middleton was Scottish and a former secretary of state for Scotland. Fenwick was a Northumberland baronet and soldier who had risen to major-general under James. Oglethorpe came from an old Yorkshire family, MP for Morpeth, and had fought bravely against Monmouth at Sedgemore, he had followed James into exile but was continually returning to England. Parker was a Catholic convert and officer in James's guards who had fought at Sedgemore and the Battle of the Boyne. He had since served in Flanders with the French before returning to England. Major-General Sackville was the Jacobite leadership's chief link with Marlborough. Between them the Select Number offered considerable military experience and had the potential to raise supporters in many parts of England, Scotland and Wales.

Their problem was that the Williamite authorities were only too well aware that they posed a threat to the new regime and so they could seldom meet as they were either wanted for arrest or under surveillance. The main method of contact between them and St Germain was through a Protestant Jacobite called William Berkenhead who had kept his office as surveyor for Dover by falsely swearing allegiance to William. He was able to use his position to facilitate covert communication across the Channel using a remote landing place in Romney Marsh owned by a Jacobite famer called Hunt. Ailesbury had recruited Berkenhead and so established this important means of communication. That was about the only positive action taken by the Select Number at this stage, however, because not only did they find it difficult to meet, but when they did it resulted in arguments. They were split between Compounders, such as Middleton, who wanted to bring Tories back into allegiance to James, and the majority who were Non-Compounders, such as Ailesbury, who were pressing for James to invade with the support of the French army. On top of this, there was considerable personal rivalry and distrust between many of them.

The one leading Jacobite who had been very active ever since James had fled England in December 1688 was Viscount Preston. In March 1689 reports were received that he was in the north of England trying to get support for the restoration of James with some financial help from the French treasury. This led to him being arrested, brought to London and committed to the Tower where he remained without bail until 25 October. He was released in November and soon was back to conspiring for James's return, although this was not known by the authorities. Once Carmarthen had become principal minister he decide to get a grip of intelligence. One of his actions was to put a watch on Preston in September 1690. With surveillance and the recruitment of some informants, Preston's activities soon became apparent. Preston convened secret meetings of Protestant Jacobites at a house in Covent Garden. There they developed a plot to bring about the restoration of James, with the help of a French invasion in 1691, if the exiled king agreed to protect the Church of England and govern according to the law. This proposal was agreed, and it was decided that Preston would travel to St Germain to obtain James's agreement.

On the stroke of New Year 1691, Preston set off down the Thames for France in a fishing smack called *The James and Elizabeth*, hired from a Quaker in Wapping, after promising a large sum of money should they reach France safely. Preston was accompanied by a Major Edmund Elliott and John Ashton, a former servant of Queen Mary of Modena, whose father-in-law's house had been used as the Covent Garden meeting place. What Preston and his accomplices did not know was that the owner of their boat had been so suspicious of the large sum offered for its hire, that he had gone to report it to Carmarthen.[1] It had not come as a surprise to Carmarthen, who had Preston under close surveillance, so he decided the sailing should go ahead to catch them red-handed.

Blissfully unaware of this, Preston and the others were relieved when their ship slipped past the government frigates at Woolwich and Gravesend and celebrated by opening a seasonal hamper of roast beef, mince pies and wine. At that moment they were boarded, arrested and the ship searched. Preston had been delivering correspondence to James from various dignitaries showing their support, and because these were so treasonable they had been tied together and fixed to a lead weight so they could be jettisoned overboard if the ship was searched. The boarding had happened so quickly there was no time for this, and despite Ashton trying to hide the correspondence under his coat, the incriminating documents were seized. Preston tried to bribe the boarding party, but to no avail and the three were taken ashore and transported to the Tower.

Elliot was released, probably as a result of a deal, but Preston and Ashton were condemned to death for high treason and Ashton was hanged on 18 January. Ashton had gone silently to his grave, but Preston was eventually induced to give evidence against his Jacobite accomplices in exchange for his life. Preston implicated many people, the most prominent of which were the Earl of Clarendon; Lord Dartmouth, James's former admiral; Francis Turner, the Bishop of Ely and William Penn, the Quaker leader. Clarendon and Dartmouth were sent to the Tower where the latter died of a stroke, probably induced by the thought of a traitor's death, and Turner went into hiding. Penn was arrested and remained in prison for four months until he managed to prove his innocence; Preston's only grounds for accusing him were based on something he had heard from the untrustworthy source of James's secretary of state, Lord Melfort.

After all information had been extracted from Preston, he was released in June and lived out the remaining five years of the life he had bought at the cost of his honour. Clarendon, being the queen's uncle, was also released and retired to his Cornbury Park estate at Oxfordshire. Although the incriminating documents and Preston's testimonies only resulted in one execution, they had far greater impact. It neutralised a plot to overthrow the government and reminded the country of the very real threat posed by Jacobites, while at the same time identifying to government intelligence most of the active conspirators. These could be either arrested if there was enough evidence, or placed under surveillance. Carmarthen's Whig enemies found it highly irritating that his masterly intelligence operation had reinforced William and Mary's trust in him, and further strengthened his position as their principal minister.

The year 1691 had begun with an intelligence success that had left the English Jacobites in disarray. Whether this would mark the beginning of the end of the Jacobite threat would depend on King Louis. William's return to England was brief, and having established that the immediate threat to the country was over, he returned to the war in Flanders. Mary was back as regent with Carmarthen as her head of administration, but with no influence over finance or foreign policy. William wanted Carmarthen to concentrate on managing a fractious parliament to support the crown's interests. Carmarthen's cold and arrogant manner meant that he was almost universally disliked, but was nevertheless respected for being an astute politician. He might fail to win support through charm, but he was adept at obtaining it through bribery. Apart from dangling lucrative government appointments to gain support, he also offered hard cash. For this, the secret intelligence fund was a handy source of income. It has been calculated that some £160,000 was misappropriated from the fund for one reason or another during William's reign.[2] This does not mean that Carmarthen failed to use the secret intelligence fund for its proper purpose, but rather that he also used his expertise in bribery with the same skill he employed to recruit informants.

The spring of 1691 was quiet; the Jacobites kept a low profile after the arrests following Preston's confessions. There was some Jacobite propaganda being circulated, including verses written by the dying Aphra Behan, but few people were openly toasting King James in

Jacobite drinking dens such as the Boy in Drury Lane, the Half Moon in Cheapside and the Blue Posts in Spring Gardens. The government had decided not to close such establishments as it was more productive to have them infiltrated by informers.[3] Apart from the earlier arrests, the government felt confident enough to only take a few minor restrictions such as banning performances of Shakespeare's *King Lear*. Despite this, Queen Mary and her council knew that it might only be a matter of time before Louis would decide to support James with an invasion and the currently dormant Jacobite supporters would rise up to support it. Intelligence was needed on what James was planning in St Germain and, perhaps more importantly, Louis's plans in Versailles, as well as Jacobite activity in the three kingdoms.

One of the most important means of intelligence gathering was through postal interception. Nearly all mail went through the General Postal Office in Lombard Street. Since Cromwell's time, intelligence staff had been employed there to identify mail that might be subversive by recognising either the seal or handwriting of the sender, or the address of a suspect recipient. The letter was read, checked for any secret ink, decrypted if it was in code, translated if in a foreign language, then transcribed. The letter (envelopes had not yet been invented) was then resealed and allowed to continue its journey to the addressee who would have no indication that its contents had been compromised.

As we have seen, postal intercept could be circumvented by couriers such as Matthew Crone, but as in Crone case, the courier might be identified and arrested. William Berkenhead's network was in place, but it was not easy to find loyal Jacobites to travel between England and France without arousing suspicion that they might be couriers. Jacobites tried different ways of hiding clandestine correspondence, for example Lord Griffin wrote letters to St Germain hidden in the false bottom of a pewter bottle, but searching arrangements were so thorough that they were discovered and he and his wife were arrested. Although there was a continued use of letters being sent by couriers or concealed in innocuous containers, sending letters through the Post Office remained the main form of communication between Jacobites in England and the Court of St Germain.

John Wildman was the man whom William had made responsible for the Post Office. In Cromwell's time the intercept process had been partially automated by one of Thurloe's secretaries, the inventor Samuel

Moreland, who built 'machines of intelligence' to open letters, copy the contents and create any type of seal. These ingenious machines were destroyed in the Great Fire, but Wildman paid Moreland to reinstall them, thus greatly improving the time spent on the intercept process. Despite this contribution, there was a risk in employing Wildman not only to carry out interception, but to ensure the safe transmission of the sensitive correspondence of the king and his ministers. Wildman had spent his life intriguing against authority, whether it had been Charles I, Cromwell, Charles II or James II. He had supported William and been rewarded by him, but could he be relied upon now William represented authority?

Before long rumours arose that Wildman was plotting with disaffected Scottish Presbyterians. Carmarthen decided to investigate Wildman and found that there was some evidence of this but that Wildman had been using his position to discredit the Tory adherents of William by fictitious letters which he pretended had been intercepted. As a Tory, Carmarthen was particularly infuriated by this partisan distortion of intelligence and Wildman was dismissed. The Post Office intercept service henceforth carried out its duties with honest intelligence assessments. The only set back was that Wildman destroyed the 'machines of intelligence' before leaving and as no one knew how they worked they were never replaced.[4]

The other important source of intelligence for Carmarthen and Mary's regency government was from agents and informers. There was always a ready supply of informers not just to government but to local government, lords lieutenant, sheriffs, JPs, mayors, indeed anyone who was likely to part with money for information. Some of this information was of value but much was gossip, invention or motivated by a grudge. Of more value was that of regularly paid agents, who were either on a salary or paid by results. At the bottom end of this market were those employed on static surveillance and reporting at foreign embassies or Jacobite taverns and coffee shops. Further up the ladder were those tasked with the mobile surveillance of targets such as Viscount Preston. At the top of the tree were those who managed to penetrate enemy organisations, whether they were rings of Jacobite conspirators in England, the court of St Germain, or the French government through its embassies, army in the field, or Versailles itself. The court of Versailles was huge and that of St Germain large, so it was not that difficult to find agents who had the suitable background to be able to merge in as courtiers. The difficulty was for the agent to then get access to valuable enemy planning information, either by ingratiating themselves into positions of trust, or more likely bribing others who had such access.

The English agents who had managed to gain entrance to St Germain had not as yet been able to become privy to high level Jacobite planning, but they were able to make useful reports on matters which were common knowledge in the court. One of these developments was that James's court was beginning to split into two factions. As in England, there were 'Compounders' who wanted James to undertake to preserve the Church of England and promise any amnesty to Williamites. This was very much the approach that had been advocated by Preston and his English Protestant Jacobite conspirators. The other faction were 'Non-Compounders', who wanted James to stick to his pro-Catholic policies regardless of the cost. James and Melfort were both firmly of the view that they were prepared to support religious toleration, but the policy of Catholicisation must continue. Under these circumstances, the Compounders had little option but to wait in the hope that James might come to realise that his inflexible position would be a major obstacle to him receiving widespread support if he landed back in England.

The main event the spring of 1691 was Louis's long siege of Mons for which Louvois had made such meticulous preparations that it was almost bound to succeed. James had hoped to burnish his somewhat tarnished military credentials by attending the siege, but being out of favour with Louis, he was not invited. This was all the more galling for James because he had recalled his son Berwick from Ireland, but as soon as the young man returned, he had gone off to Mons as a gentleman volunteer. William was also making for Mons at the head of an allied force of 38,000, but his advance was blocked by a French force of 46,000 under Marshal Luxembourg, protecting Louis's army besieging the city. After devastating bombardment the great fortress surrendered to Louis in April. Louis returned to Versailles triumphant, leaving his generals to continue the war and William to return to The Hague.

Louis's triumph boosted Jacobite morale, but the summer brought a serious setback for James in Ireland. Louis had withdrawn the French contingent from Ireland the previous September, and had no intention of sending reinforcements. However, he did dispatch a good general, the Marquis de St Ruth, to lead the Jacobite force in Ireland now that Berwick had left. In June Baron van Ginkell, William's commander in Ireland, began to besiege the Jacobite stronghold of Athlone. St Ruth was unable to relieve Athlone before it surrendered, and so a frustrated St Ruth decided to win back the initiative by forcing Ginkell to a pitched battle. St Ruth took up a strong position on a ridge near the village of Aughim, between Athlone and Limerick. When Ginkell's force attacked on 12 July the fighting resulted in St Ruth gaining the upper hand, but just as a Jacobite victory was in sight, St Ruth was decapitated by a cannon ball. This demoralised the Jacobite army, their position collapsed and they began to flee, only to be hacked down by Ginkell's cavalry; 6,000 of the 20,000-strong Jacobite army were killed, wounded or taken prisoner, whereas Ginkell lost 600, with 1,000 wounded.

The town of Galway surrendered without a siege to Ginkell, who then set off to besiege the Earl of Tyrconnell, in the final Jacobite stronghold of Limerick. Tyrconnell died of a stroke before the siege began, which only lasted for five days before the town surrendered on 30 October. As the campaigning season was coming to an end, and Ginkell had insufficient men for a successful assault, he had offered generous terms for the surrender. In what would be called the Treaty of Limerick, the Jacobites were promised that toleration for Catholicism and all Catholic landowners who swore allegiance to William and Mary could keep their estates. The Jacobite troops were offered the choice of returning to their homes, joining William's army, or being transported to France to join James's army. A thousand joined the Williamite army, 2,000 returned home and 4,000 decided to be transported from Cork with their weapons, equipment and families to join James.

Jacobite resistance in Ireland was now over. James was despised by most Catholics for deserting them after the battle of the Boyne and his army was gone. Ireland became completely under Williamite control. The parliament was dominated by Protestants who soon disregarded promises of religious toleration, banished Catholic clergy and introduced penalties against Catholics. The Catholic Irish were to become sullenly subservient to Protestantism and the English monarchy. This gloomy quiet remained for about a hundred years until resistance was again relit inspired by the French Revolution.

William had achieved military success in Ireland, but things had not gone so well with his war in Flanders where he was leading a 56,000-strong Grand Alliance force against Marshal Luxembourg's French army. The conflict had consisted of sieges and manoeuvring, with no engagements of consequence and William returning to England every so often to run the country, leaving Waldeck in command. It was in one of his absences in September that Luxembourg received intelligence that William had gone to England and Waldeck was beginning to pull back to winter quarters, which made him decide to attack the Alliance rear guard at Leuze. The smaller Alliance force were defeated and lost about 1,800, dead or wounded, to Luxembourg's loss of 400. It was by no means a strategic victory, but it was a victory nonetheless, and like any French victory, it gave encouragement to English Jacobites.

It was not just Jacobites who noted Louis's continued success and therefore likelihood of backing James's return. There were many Protestant Englishman who had reason to dislike William for his cold manner, Calvinist religion and favouritism to the Dutch at the expense of his English supporters. Some of the more prominent of these had congregated around Princess Anne and her little court in the Cockpit. These included Marlborough, Baron Sidney Godolphin and Admiral Russell, who had replaced Torrington as Lord High Admiral. Russell was a Tory who had become irritated with the Dutch and blamed their navy for not doing more to blockade the French coast. Godolphin was a Tory and William's First Lord of the Treasury, but hated Carmarthen. Marlborough had become disenchanted with William because despite this military success in Ireland, he had only been given subordinate commands, not offered the Garter and passed over when the lucrative post of Master-General of the Ordnance became vacant. To them William's position as king was by no means assured and they decided to hedge their bets by making overtures to James in St Germain. They all had contacts at St Germain, and even Marlborough, who was despised by James for deserting him, could still communicate via his nephew Berwick, or his wife Sarah's sister, Lady Tyrconnell.

William's intelligence organisation made him well aware of the illicit correspondence taking place with St Germain by the Cockpit group and others such as the Earl of Shrewsbury. William regarded this as nothing more than people using it as an insurance policy, and did not think any of them would actively support the return of James and Catholicism. Of greater concern to William, had he been aware of it, was that Princess Anne was in correspondence with her father. The already poor relationship between Anne and her sister and brother-in-law had been steadily deteriorating. Anne resented that her husband Prince George had been given no command when he had accompanied William to

Ireland, and instead of travelling with William in his carriage, was left to ride with the troopers. Prince George had later asked for a post at sea, but William had removed his consent at the last minute and when Anne had requested to move from the Cockpit to the unoccupied Queen's House in Richmond, this had been turned down. Anne's burning anger over genuine grievances had been fanned by Sarah, who took every opportunity to increase the breach between William and Mary and their heir to the throne.

In December 1691, Anne wrote to James begging forgiveness for deserting him in 1688: 'If wishes could recall that which is past, I had long since redeem'd my fault', and promising that she was 'very desirous of some safe opportunity to make you a sincere and humble offer of my duty and submission to you wishes'.[5] This was indeed a change of heart for Anne, and one that could have treasonous consequences.

Meanwhile, Marlborough was continuing to make life difficult for William by pressing parliament to address the Crown against the employment of foreigners, and openly criticising the Dutch officers. By January 1692 William and Mary had had enough of Marlborough and the poisonous effect his wife, Sarah, was having upon Princess Anne. Marlborough was dismissed from all military and civilian offices on a charge of taking bribes. Mary then wrote to Anne instructing her to dismiss Sarah. Anne, refused and flew into a fury. Sarah had long been her closest friend in a relationship so close that some considered it to be lesbian. Mary's response to Anne's defiance was for the Chamberlain to inform Anne that she must vacate her Cockpit apartments. Anne was so incensed that she decided to leave the court and persuaded the Duke of Somerset to let her use his residence at Sion House. She never spoke to her sister again and instead of referring to William as 'Mr Caliban', began calling him the 'Dutch abortion'.[6] Another bitter breach had occurred in the Stuart family.

For James, 1691 had been a difficult year. He had irreparably lost Ireland, had no army in Scotland and his last supporters in the Highland clans had been bribed into taking an oath of allegiance to William. His hope of landing in England with French backing had evaporated. Skelton had arrived at St Germain, and James appointed him envoy to Versailles so he would have a trusted diplomat in place in the unlikely event of Louis being prepared to consider an invasion. However, in January 1691 the situation suddenly brightened. Louvois had died in September and had been replaced as minister by the Marquis de Chamlay, who was not opposed to an invasion of England. French agents, such as the abbé Renaudot in London were sending reports of William's mounting unpopularity arising from the cost of the war and favouritism to the Dutch. In particular, it was known that Princess Anne had fallen out with William and Mary, and a number of powerful Tories had made overtures to James. Most important of all was the change in the French attitude to James. He was no longer seen as a mere drain on the royal purse, but someone who had his own army. Following the Treaty of Limerick the Jacobite Irish Brigade had just arrived in France. These were seasoned troops who would later win renown as 'the Wild Geese'.

With the situation changed, Louis decided to support his cousin in an invasion. James, who had been kept at arm's length, now found himself closeted with Louis at Versailles in long planning meetings. They came to a conclusion that an invasion would receive widespread support. If it received the backing of Princess Anne, then it would likely to be supported by Anglican clergy. Marlborough was popular with the army and could probably bring a large section of it over to James, and Admiral Russell might bring over a good section of the navy. The operation was agreed, and James began concentrating his force of nine regiments of infantry, two regiments of dragoons, twelve regiments of cavalry and two companies of Scots infantry, in Normandy. They were to be joined by an equal number of French troops, making a total of 15,000. The Wild Geese were re-equipped and the infantry issued with scarlet tunics to preserve the fiction that they were the legitimate British Army. They were given intensive training with Berwick, who had returned from Mons, putting the cavalry through its paces.

William was as yet unaware of the planned invasion and had departed for the Continent in March. With William occupied in Flanders, Louis and James's preparations progressed. Admiral Tourville had been reinstated and the plan was for him to combine with the Toulon fleet and attack and defeat the English navy before it had time to unite with the Dutch navy. Tourville was then to provide protection for the troop transports of the invasion force to sail from Normandy to their south coast landing site. In April, James joined Marshal Bellefond, the French commander, in Normandy. Mary's government had received intelligence that there was a build-up of forces in Normandy, but believed that this was with the intention of attacking the Channel Islands. On 5 May,

Admiral Richard Carter captured a French privateer and discovered from one of the prisoners that a joint French/Jacobite force was preparing to embark at La Hougue with the intention of landing in Sussex and marching on London.[7]

Following this information the government took rapid steps to ensure that the Dutch fleet joined Russell's fleet as soon as possible and made preparations for the defence of the kingdom. Several suspect Jacobite sympathisers were arrested, including Marlborough. The militia was mobilised, troops about to be sent to Flanders were kept in England, orders were given for all Catholics to remove themselves at least ten miles from London, and cattle were driven fifteen miles from the coast, so they could not be used to feed invaders. James then dropped a bombshell by announcing that Mary Beatrice was heavily pregnant and sent letters to leaders in England inviting them to travel on safe conduct to St Germain to witness the birth. None took up the invitation, but it made the point that Mary Beatrice was capable of childbearing and by implication, the Prince of Wales was legitimate. With William and Mary childless and Anne with just one sickly son, many Tories might believe the future lay with the stronger royal bloodline of James and his two children. Anne wrote back to her father that she could not travel as she was herself pregnant, but added that should he land in England she 'would fly to his side'.

James made preparations for a Jacobite rising in England to support his invasion. With the help of William Berkenhead's network, Melfort's agents brought signed blank commissions for Jacobite gentry to use to raise regiments. These were given to people such as Viscount Montgomery and distributed to Catholic families in Cumberland, Lancashire and Cheshire. James then issued a proclamation that if he returned as king, he would grant religious toleration and a political amnesty for all except some named traitors. Jacobites had reason to hope that with so many tired of rule by a Dutchman, there was a real chance that James's proclamation and potential proof of his son's legitimacy would result in him receiving a general welcome if he landed in England. With such a potential danger, much would depend on Russell and his navy preventing the crossing.

The unnerving question for the council was whether they could depend on Russell and the navy. Russell was known to have been in contact with St Germain and many naval officers felt a loyalty to their former king who had been so supportive of his navy. In a brilliant stroke,

Mary sent Nottingham down to the fleet with a message saying that she had heard rumours of their disloyalty, but she did not of course believe them, and was certain that they would all do their duty. The inspiring message was read out to all captains and had the desired effect. Russell and all senior officers assemble on his flagship immediately signed a declaration of loyalty to the queen and the Protestant religion.

Tourville left Brest having been given specific orders by Louis to attack the English fleet at all costs. Russell also took to sea and rendezvoused with thirty-six Dutch ships. He captured a Guernsey Privateer who told him that Tourville's fleet of forty-four men-of-war and eleven fireships was sighted off Portland.[8] Russell sent out reconnaissance vessels and they returned with their top gallants hoisted, signalling that they had located Tourville. The two fleets met twenty miles north east of Cape Barfleur on 29 May. The Toulon fleet had been delayed and Tourville had just forty-four fighting ships, whereas Russell's combined English/Dutch fleet had eighty. The French minister of marine had received intelligence that Dutch ships had joined Russell's fleet and on 9 May countermanded Louis's orders to attack, but the new instructions did not arrive in time.

Although outnumbered two to one, Tourville followed Louis's orders and attacked. He had been given intelligence that about fifteen English ships would defect to him when battle was joined, but soon found that was not the case. The battle was inconclusive with considerable damage to both fleets but no ships lost. The next day Tourville disengaged in the fog, Russell later pursued. The French fleet became scattered and three ships were beached at Cherbourg, a few returned to Brest and twelve made for the safety of La Hougue's batteries and the support of the troops awaiting embarkation. Over 3 and 4 June, Russell sent fireships and longboats into the harbour which destroyed all twelve French ships of the line and most of the transports. The threat of invasion was over, and England was to have permanent command of the Channel.

The Battle of La Hougue was the Trafalgar of its day. James's planned invasion had been his best chance of taking back his crown. If Tourville had been joined by the Toulon fleet and managed to defeat Russell before he had linked up with the Dutch fleet, James's 15,000 French/Jacobite force could have landed on the south coast. It is doubtful that they would have received much of a welcome. The majority of the population might have tired of William, but they feared James and Popery more. James's declaration had been clumsily written by Melfort and the aggressive tone and long list of those exempt from pardon suggested retribution was to come. Worst of all, although promising freedom of worship, it did not undertake to support the Church of England. Mary and her council had made considerable propaganda of this and gave James's declaration and the government response very wide distribution in the three kingdoms.

James had hoped that once he landed, Marlborough would bring the army over to him, but Marlborough was in the Tower and despite irritation with the Dutch troops, there were few Jacobites in the army or militia. William had a royal yacht on standby to return him to England if James landed, and we may assume he would have rallied enough military to have opposed James's force of only 15,000. Possibly the most likely outcome would have been a civil war. Louis's ministers had had already considered this and supported the invasion because a civil war would at least keep William away from leading the Grand Alliance against France in Flanders.

The events after the triumph of La Hogue were something of an anti-climax. William had wanted to follow up the victory with an invasion of France but a failed harvest, administrative mismanagement and lack of troop transports led to this being abandoned. William continued with the war in Flanders, but most of his energies were spent on trying to keep the coalition together with the Nordic states threatening to leave and the new Pope wavering. William was a good general, but it was his misfortune to be up against a great general, in the form of the Duc de Luxembourg. The French had captured Namur and in August William was defeated by Luxembourg at the Battle of Steenkerque, south west of Brussel, with the loss of 10,000 killed or wounded. The war with France dragged on with Louis making ground, but not achieving a victory of sufficient magnitude to force the Grand Alliance to accept his terms for peace. In November, William was back home to open parliament and discovered that it was becoming less inclined to continue supporting the ever increasing cost of the war.

When William became king of England he had already exhausted his credit to finance his invasion. In order to build the ships and expand the army for his war with France he needed a colossal £1.2 million. This problem had been overcome by the creation of the Bank of England in 1694 which raised the £1.2 million and took over the management of government debt. By establishing a Central Bank, the English government put its finances on a firm footing, but of course taxation had to be high to cover the interest and the increasing expenditure of the war. High taxation would be a cause of government unpopularity for the next twenty years. The only consolation was that it was equally unpopular in Louis XIV's France.

After the La Hague defeat James at first remained optimistic that the Toulon fleet would arrive to take his troops to England. Not only did this not happen, but Louis sent orders for the invasion army to be broken up and dispersed to his armies in Flanders, Savoy and Catalonia. James was devastated and believed that the failed invasion was a sign of God's displeasure. He returned to St Germain deeply dejected, but just in time for his spirits to be raised by Mary Beatrice giving birth to a baby girl, Louisa Mary. Having been abandoned by the daughters of his first marriage, the arrival of Louisa Mary promised a new start. However, there was no disguising the fact that there was little chance of him regaining his thrones in the foreseeable future. Money was getting short and when about a hundred Scottish Jacobite officers made their way to his court, all he could offer them was to enlist in the French army as privates. It was clear that Louis was not considering another invasion of England. Berwick had gone to join Marshal Luxembourg and led the charge that broke William's line at Steenkerque. Apart from providing troops to support Louis, there was little James could do other than to use agents to maintain contact with Jacobites in England.

The one area James was able to exploit was propaganda against William. William was unpopular for his favouritism to the Dutch, in particular Willem Bentinck, now Earl of Portland. Bentinck was an old and loyal friend of William and was much in his company, but was employed as an important implementer of the king's decisions rather than having any power. William was always his own man and kept the reins of government tightly in his hands. The one person whose advice he sought above all others was that of an English man, the Earl of Sunderland. Amazingly, Sunderland had been allowed to return to court in 1692, and William began to make use of his considerable political experience. But James's propaganda effort against the unpopular Dutch was aided when a perfect target presented itself in the good-looking young Arnold van Keppel. He had entered William's household and had been granted extensive lands by the king in 1692. This provided an opportunity to accuse William of having a homosexual relationship. This slur would be magnified during the rest of William's reign and widely believed, as

Keppel was later promoted to Groom of the Bedchamber, then Master of the Robes, baron, viscount and finally Earl of Albermarle in 1697.

Little had changed at St Germain other than Middleton joined James in 1693 and was appointed as a second secretary of state with responsibility for correspondence with England and Scotland. The hard-line Catholic Melfort remained principal secretary of state and responsible for intelligence, but as Middleton was of the more moderate Compounder Jacobite group, it meant that his conciliatory line could help broaden Jacobite support in England and Scotland. The same year also saw changes in the secretary of state in England, owing to a failure at sea. A combined English/Dutch merchant fleet of 200 ships was attacked by a French fleet in the bay of Lagos on the way to Turkey. Admiral Rooke's escorts could not protect them and about three quarters of the ships captured or lost. It was judged the greatest loss to the city of London since the Great Fire.

Nottingham was blamed because he had fallen out with Admiral Russell, causing him to resign, and then filled the senior naval posts with his Tory cronies such as Rooke. When William returned to England in the autumn he reinstated Russell, dismissed Nottingham and replaced him with the Whig Sir John Trenchard. William knew the Tories normally supported the crown but were against the war, whereas the Whigs often wanted to limit the power of the crown but supported the war. William needed parliament to vote money for the war. He retained the Tory Carmarthen as Lord President, but on the advice of Sunderland appointed Whigs to main positions in his cabinet. These included Charles Montague, Thomas Wharton and the most prominent, Sir John Somers the Lord Keeper. These gentlemen were to be called the 'Whig Junto', and would dominate the government for many years.

Apart from exploiting some slurs on William's character it seemed the Jacobite cause was getting nowhere. William and Mary appeared secure on their joint thrones, but events were about to bring a resurgence in the Jacobite threat.

Chapter 9

A Single Sovereign
1695

'The small pox increased exceedingly, and was very mortal,
The Queen died on the 28th … There never was so universal
a mourning.'

Diary of John Evelyn, entry for 29 December 1695

Louis, like William, was finding it difficult to continue covering the cost of the war. France did not have the advantage of the Bank of England to manage its debts, on top of which the failed harvest of 1693 had caused widespread famine and unrest. Louis decided to prepare for peace, but first wanted to achieve a successful offensive as a prelude to peace negotiations. In July 1693, Luxembourg's masterful manoeuvres resulted in him having superior numbers when he brought William and allies to battle at Landen. William fought very bravely as usual and received bullet holes through his hat, sleeve and sash knot, but Luxembourg won the battle. William organised a disciplined withdrawal, but had lost about 15,000 killed or wounded. Luxemburg's army was weakened, having lost about 10,000, and so prevented him from achieving a decisive follow up. He captured the fortresses of Vauban and Charleroi but William saved Liege. The war dragged on inconclusively with both sides taking up defensive positions.

James was unable to do more to regain his crowns until he received Louis's support for another invasion. Throughout 1694, Louis's armies were achieving no notable success while creating ever greater government debt. Melville had resigned in June 1693 and Middleton became James's single secretary of state and head of intelligence. He was trying to keep Jacobite spirits alive in England and Scotland, but there was little that could be done other than pushing out propaganda against

William, his favouritism to the Dutch and the cost of the war. Even the fact that Mary Beatrice had given birth did not seem to have won any new support. Prominent Jacobites knew that they were likely to be watched by government informers and all talk of plans for uprisings came to an end.

This uneasy equilibrium was shaken by a surprise event in December 1694. Queen Mary died of smallpox. Unconcerned about his own health, William had personally nursed her and was totally heartbroken at her loss. There was general grief at the popular queen's death. She had ruled with distinction as regent for a total of thirty-two months. She could be seen as being rightful queen as the daughter of James II, who was regarded as having vacated the throne. William was now sole monarch, whose claim to the throne was merely that his mother was the daughter of Charles I. Princess Anne, with a far stronger claim, was his heir but hated him and was now reconciled with James. On top of that, William was unpopular for his cold foreign manner, favouritism to the Dutch and the crippling cost of his wars. This all made for a very dangerous situation that was ripe for exploitation by the Jacobites.

There was some celebration among a few Jacobites in Bristol at the news of Mary's death, with toasts to James and singing of 'The king [James] shall enjoy his own again.' Otherwise English Jacobites merely awaited developments. At St Germain, the death of James's daughter was marked by neither rejoicing nor grief. James let it be known that there would be no mourning as she had ceased to be his daughter in 1688. James's lack of paternal feeling did nothing to endear him to either his British subjects or the French court, but then he was turning into an introverted religious obsessive. He was convinced that God was punishing him for the sexual promiscuity of his younger days and spent large portions of his time in religious devotions. He still remained passionate about hunting and had taken to writing his memoirs, but was withdrawing from his public life. Mary of Modena was left to manage the court and Middleton ran the government in exile.

The resignation of Melfort in June 1694 had left the moderate Middleton as sole secretary of state and head of intelligence. Middleton was a Protestant and a Compounder who tried to persuade James to have his son brought up as an Anglican in the hopes that this would allay Protestant fears about James's support for Popery. This was not something to which James could agree having become an ever more devout Catholic. Middleton did, however, persuade James to issue a new declaration to replace the disastrously vengeful proclamation drafted by Melfort in 1692. The declaration drafted by Middleton was much more conciliatory, promising to uphold the Church of England, pardon those who had supported William and undertaking that James would rule under parliament's guidance. James gave his half-hearted assent to the declaration, but it did nothing to revive Jacobite support. The Protestants of James's former kingdoms did not trust him to keep his word and the Catholics felt that he was selling them out to the Anglicans. In short, the Jacobite cause was at a low ebb as 1695 drew to a close.

The sombre news of Mary's death gave rise to a hope that it might provide an opportunity to topple William. Jacobite morale had been suffering, with Louis failing to win victories and in no position to support another invasion of England. Ireland was a lost cause and Scotland was firmly under Williamite control with the Jacobite army destroyed and new government strongholds such as Fort William built to dominate the Highlands. In addition, the potentially rebellious clans had been bought off into swearing allegiance to William after the distribution of £12,000 in bribes. It was in England that Middleton felt that the Jacobite cause might at last prosper, as now Mary was gone, there might be a real chance of encouraging an insurrection against the unpopular William. With Anne known to detest William and at least partially reconciled to her father, her support might be the deciding factor.

Anne's health was poor, she was becoming obese and had been weakened by her numerous pregnancies. It had been generally assumed that although Mary was three years older, her good health would result in her outliving her younger sister. With Mary's death, the situation was transformed. As William was a chronic asthmatic and fifteen years older that Anne, she was very likely to outlive him and become queen. She also had a 5 year old son, Prince William, Duke of Gloucester, to continue the dynasty after her. Unfortunately, relations had further deteriorated since the final breach between Anne and William and Mary over her refusal to dismiss Sarah, Lady Marlborough. William had removed Anne's personal guard and given instructions to civic dignitaries that she was not to be accorded any royal courtesies if she visited their towns. Anne had moved from Ham House to Berkley House and courtiers were instructed not to see her. Despite this, she was still visited by the Tories who had supported her in the past and Berkley House became a focus for opposition to William, much as had been the case when Anne lived in the Cockpit. Sarah was, as ever, by her side as was Marlborough, who had been released from the Tower, but like Godolphin, was still in communication with St Germain.

These communications with St Germain bordered on the treasonous, as was shown when a Jacobite agent, Captain David Lloyd, saw Marlborough when he visited London in March the previous year. It seems that Marlborough was so angry at his treatment by William that he warned Lloyd that the English navy was planning to attack the French naval squadron in Brest. The attack took place in June 1694 and was a complete failure. The French had removed their squadron to the Mediterranean and strengthened the port defences having received prior intelligence of the landing. It seems probable that the intention to attack Brest had become common knowledge and Marlborough did no more than to pass on what was already known. However, Marlborough's conduct would have given James and his ministers grounds for hope that he would support an insurrection to restore James. If Anne would give James her backing, then there was a real chance of success.

Anne had broken off communication with James after his failed invasion, but she had come to believe that James Francis Edward might actually be her brother, and that she had deserted her father unfairly. It was known that she hated Catholicism, but Jacobites might hope that this was counteracted by her hatred of William and she would return to being a dutiful daughter. Unknown to James, Mary's illness and death was to be the cause of an eventual reconciliation between Anne and William. Anne had been moved by her sister's illness and tried to see her before she died saying she would 'run any hazard' for a meeting. William sent a polite message saying that Mary was too ill. A few days after Mary died Anne wrote to William regretting that she had 'fallen into her [Mary's] displeasure.'[1] Anne was having one of her phantom pregnancies at the time and on 13 January was carried to Kensington Palace to pay her respects to the king. William was still in a state of deep despair over Mary's death and received her kindly. He had been advised by the Archbishop of Canterbury to mend the rift between them. Seeing Anne sharing his grief for Mary, made him begin the process of reconciliation. Anne's guards were restored and Mary's jewellery was passed on to her. A little later, Sunderland persuaded William to give Anne St James's Palace as her residence and establish a court as heir to the throne.

Sarah had not wanted Anne to be reconciled with William, but was eventually persuaded by Sunderland that it would be in her best interests. The reconciliation transformed Marlborough's situation. On 25 March he kissed hands with William, thus demonstrating his loyalty and William's preparedness to forgive his past opposition. This did not stop Marlborough and his friend Godolphin continuing to maintain polite contact with St Germain. Despite this, he and the other erstwhile dissidents of the former Berkley House group realised their interests now lay with being true subjects of King William.

It was a disappointment for Middleton to learn that Anne and her followers appeared to have become reconciled to William. Nevertheless there was still the hope that William's unpopularity would be enough to give rise to a Jacobite rebellion. That unpopularity could be increased by effective propaganda. There were a number of good Jacobite propagandists. Included among them was Robert Ferguson, the Radical plotter who had been Monmouth's chaplain then fled to Holland and later provided propaganda supporting William's invasion. Ferguson had felt his loyalty to William had not been rewarded and so transferred his writing skills to the Jacobite cause.

There was another Jacobite pamphleteer who had even greater impact in 1695. This was Charles Leslie, a non-juring Church of Ireland priest, who had moved to London in 1690 and began churning out pro-Jacobite pamphlets. He wrote a pamphlet titled: *Gallienus Redivivus, or Murther will out, &c. Being a true Account of the De Witting of Glencoe, Gaffney.* Despite the unpromising title, the contents were incendiary. It recounted a previously little-known event that had taken place back in 1692 when the Scottish clans had to swear allegiance to William by 1 January but Maclain Macdonald, the chief of the Macdonalds of Glencoe, had been unable to do so until a few days later. Leslie's pamphlet said that government soldiers following William's orders had requested shelter from the Macdonalds and having received their hospitality for two weeks, began killing their hosts in the middle of the night – including thirty-two women and children, after which they burned their village to the ground.

The nation was appalled to hear of the massacre of Glencoe and a parliamentary commission was set up to establish the facts. This eventually revealed that the blame lay with those Scots who wanted teach the unruly, marauding clans a lesson and had covered up the fact that Maclain had sworn allegiance, albeit slightly late. Sir John Dalrymple, the secretary of state for Scotland, had given William a warrant on which was written, 'this set of thieves should be extirpated', which the king had signed – unread. Dalrymple then wrote to Sir Thomas Livingstone, the commander in Scotland, to carry out the order and 'not to trouble the government with any prisoners'. Richard Campbell of Glenlyon was the officer selected for the task. The shooting of some outlaw clansmen would have been soon forgotten had it not been for Campbell's pretence at friendship, acceptance of hospitality, and massacre of women and children.

The commission exonerated William and laid the blame on Dalrymple, who was forced to resign as secretary of state. The king gave no compensation to the Macdonalds, there was no punishment for the perpetrators and Dalrymple remained an important political figure in Scotland. William's involvement with the massacre and his failure to take action against those responsible, was to forever blacken his name and provide valuable material for future Jacobite propaganda.

Apart from exploiting William's unpopularity, the English Jacobites had remained in disarray since the Preston arrests. There nominal coordinators, the Select Number, lacked a single dynamic leader and were beset by personal rivalries. They had not even cooperated with each other at the critical time back in 1692 when there had been a real prospect of James mounting a successful invasion. A quarrel between Sir John Fenwick and Major General Sackville over who was the most senior paralysed preparations for a rising in London. With Preston gone, the two most prominent members were Ailesbury and Middleton who detested each other, not least because Ailesbury was a Non-Compounder and Middleton was a Compounder. Both went to see James in St Germain in 1693. Ailesbury tried to persuade James to lead an invasion force and recommended that he should secretly take a new declaration to the officers of the Fleet to win them over. James disliked both the idea and Ailesbury's rather hectoring manner, and preferred Middleton's smoother and more conciliatory approach. Ailesbury was dismayed to find that it was his rival Middleton who had won the king's ear and so had an audience with Louis XIV. Ailesbury's plan for an invasion was equally rejected by Louis. When James made Middleton his secretary of state, Ailesbury realised that he was beaten and returned crestfallen to England. He resumed his position in the Jacobite leadership but his enthusiasm was greatly depleted.

Another problem was that most leading Jacobites did not attempt to hide their continuing support for James and so had only themselves to blame for becoming prime suspects during periods of increased Jacobite threat. Some even flaunted their opposition to the reign of William and Mary. For example in 1691, after William had failed to prevent the French capture of Mons, Sir John Fenwick had publicly insulted Mary when she was in her coach in Hyde Park. He had approached the coach and made a supercilious bow in which he waved his hat in her face. William was furious when he heard about it and said that if he had not been king, he would have called Fenwick out for a duel.

The behaviour of arrogant, overconfident Jacobites such as Fenwick made it relatively easy for William's intelligence apparatus to counter their amateurish threat. That said, there was room for improvement. The Tory Nottingham had been a diligent and loyal secretary of state but was inclined to turn a blind eye to the activities of his Tory former friends who felt that they could not in conscience swear loyalty to William. Carmarthen was also a Tory, but had few friends and no soft feelings for anyone, so had stepped in to uncover the Preston Plot. Nottingham had been replaced as secretary of state for the south by Sir John Trenchard in November 1693. This was part of William's new policy, recommended by Sunderland, of making the Whigs dominant in the Council, as they were the party most supportive of the war against France.

Trenchard was a man who regarded all Tories as closet Jacobites and took his duties as head of security very seriously. He brought into his employment Aaron Smith and Hugh Speke as his principal instruments to hunt down Jacobites. Speke was Trenchard's brother-in-law and a fanatical radical who was solicitor to the Treasury, but finding himself short of money was more than eager to unmask Jacobites in the hope that he might profit from their confiscated estates. He presided over a mercifully short period in which search warrants were issued often against unspecified persons for suspected crimes. Indiscriminate searches resulted in documents being seized and innocent people cast into prison while the documents were checked for anything incriminating. Fortunately, a discreet payment to Speke could ensure the release of those against whom there was no evidence.

There was money to be made in identifying Jacobites. Word got round the world of informers and before long they were queuing outside the secretary of state's office after easy money. One of the many informants who came forward was an Irishman and former Catholic priest called John Taaffe, who had been chaplain at Standish Hall in Lancashire. Following the Glorious Revolution he had thought it politic to convert to Anglicanism and win credit with the new regime by providing information on places where Jesuit and Benedictine money had been hidden in London. Although by now married, he had continued to pose as a Catholic priest as cover for his work as an informant. Taaffe had fallen in with a Jacobite agent called John Lunt, who had been working to organise the gentry in Cheshire and Lancashire to revolt. Lunt had been arrested, but then released through lack of evidence and later been turned by Taaffe into a government informant. Taaffe presented Trenchard with lists of northern gentry who had either Jacobite commissions in their possession or had caches of weapons. On receiving this, Trenchard sent Aaron Smith, accompanied by Taaffe and some men to Lancashire with search warrants.

News of the intended searches spread before their arrival and some Jacobites fled while others buried or burned incriminating material. Nevertheless, Smith and Taaffe's house searches uncovered sixty cavalry swords, thirty trooper's saddles and some muskets hidden in garrets, up chimneys and behind wainscots. Taaffe also took the opportunity to enrich himself by stealing any communion plate and other valuables which he could get his hands on during the rummaging. The searches were greeted with outrage by many of the northern gentry and the whole matter was taken up by Jacobite propagandists. These pamphlets poured scorn on the allegations and said the searchers had found nothing more incriminating than some hunting saddles and old fowling pieces. This propaganda was believed by many who likened the allegations to those of Titus Oates's lies in the Popish Plot. As a result, most northerners rallied to the defence of their mistreated gentry. Nevertheless, in October, nine of those found in possession of the weapons or other incriminating material were brought for trial before four judges in Manchester.

Taaffe had expected to be richly rewarded by Trenchard for finding this damning evidence against Jacobite gentry. Taaffe was to be disappointed. Trenchard had heard about his thefts during the searches and was so disgusted with the way Taaffe had carried out the operation that he dismissed him without payment. Taaffe was furious and decided to obtain money by a different method. He contacted the families of the accused Jacobites and offered to withdraw his evidence against them in exchange for a substantial bribe. This was eagerly agreed by the families and as a result the trials turned into farce. Firstly Lunt gave evidence, but became so confused that he showed himself to be an unreliable witness. Then Taaffe was called to give evidence and said that the whole matter had been fabricated by him and Lunt. The judges immediately released the accused, resulting in much cheering from the crowds outside, who then proceeded to pelt the prosecution and his witnesses out of Manchester.

Parliament reassembled the next month and Trenchard was attacked for believing the accusations of Taaffe and Lunt. Aaron Smith appeared before the House for investigation and parliament eventually came to the conclusion that some of the northern gentry had indeed been acting treasonously. It came to light that Leiutenant Colonel John Parker had been sent to the north to help the Tory gentry raise mounted regiments in preparation for any uprising. Parker had managed to establish the nucleus of nine cavalry regiments one of which was under his command with half of its the troops in the north and the other half in London. As Parker's preparations were still in the early stages they did not pose an immediate threat, but rather a potential danger for the future. Parliament then began to blame Trenchard for mishandling the whole affair which had resulted in treacherous northern Jacobite gentry evading justice. Parliament imprisoned Taaffe for his duplicity and made so much ridicule of Trenchard for his handling of intelligence that his health began to give way and he later resigned as secretary of state in April 1695. So also ended Hugh Speke's anti-Jacobite witch hunts.

Trenchard was replaced by Charles Talbot, Earl of Shrewsbury, one of the seven who had invited William over for the Glorious Revolution. It will be remembered that Shrewsbury had previously been secretary of state but had resigned in June 1690 through ill health. Shrewsbury resumed responsibility for intelligence, but did not pursue it with the misplaced enthusiasm of Trenchard. He carried out his duties loyally but had no interest in harassing Jacobites for the sake of it, indeed while out of office he had himself been in correspondence with St Germain. Although the Lancashire and Cheshire Jacobite gentry had been shown to pose no immediate threat of uprising, a more serious type of threat was resurfacing towards the end of 1695.

We have seen that Louis was not prepared to support James and invade England unless there was first an uprising. Jacobites in England were not prepared to rise up unless Louis supported an invasion by James. One way out of the impasse was to arrange for William's assassination as a spark to bring about both an uprising and Louis's agreement to an invasion. Assassination had been considered on several previous occasions. For example, in 1692 Louis's war minister, Marquis Barbezieux, engaged a junior French officer called Barthelemy de Grandval to carry out William's assassination at his army headquarters in the Netherlands. Naturally no one used the unseemly word 'assassination'. When Grandval visited James at St Germain prior to his mission, the former king told him he was aware of the 'business' and that if he was successful 'he should never want'.[2] Grandval recruited two accomplices to shoot William: a Catholic former Dutch officer called Leefdael, and a Walloon adventurer called Dumont. They turned out to be poor choices.

Garndval and his accomplices met in Brambant then made their way to William's headquarters. Once they arrived, both Leefdael and Dumont independently decided to betray the plot. Grandval was arrested, confessed all, was sentenced and executed. There were other arrests in England of those suspected of being party to the plot, including Lieutenant Colonel John Parker, who later escaped and then, as we have heard, had gone to the north of England to raise Jacobite cavalry regiments. After Trenchard's disruption of the northern Jacobites, Parker had returned to London to concentrate on building up the London squadrons of his secret cavalry regiment. He was again arrested and put in the Tower while evidence could be found against him, but he was never brought to trial because he escaped again in August 1694 after Sir John Friend, a wealthy Jacobite brewer, had used £300 to bribe some of the yeoman warders.

Williamite propaganda had been able to make good use of Grandval's confession to demonstrate that James and Louis had been implicated in the attempted assassination. As a result, Jacobite plots for William's assassination was put on the back burner – for a time. Lieutenant Colonel John Parker fled back to St Germain after his escape from the Tower, but before leaving appointed his senior captain, Robert Charnock, to command the London squadrons of his regiment. Charnock had an unusual background. He had been a Catholic priest and Vice President of Magdalen College in James's reign, after which he was expelled, left the priesthood, married, and followed James into exile, then became a soldier and served under Parker in the Battle of the Boyne. After Parker had left England in the summer of 1694, most Jacobite officers in London regarded

Fenwick as the overall military leader in Parker's absence. Charnock had no time for Fenwick and against his orders began developing a plan to kidnap William and take him to France.

Charnock's main associates in this conspiracy were two of the other squadron commanders of Parker's nascent cavalry regiment. These were the rather unreliable Catholic pair, Captain George Porter and Cradell 'Scum' Goodman. Porter was a fat debauchee who had got through a fortune of about £15,000 inherited from his maternal grandfather, the Earl of Newport. He was prone to duels and quick-tempered, not helped by the discomfort of his venereal disease. Goodman was an actor and conman who had financially exploited Charles II's old mistress, the Duchess of Cleveland, as her lover, and then had a couple of spells in prison on trumped up charges of highway robbery and attempted murder brought by Cleveland's son, the Duke of Grafton. He appears to have fully merited his nickname 'Scum', but despite his behaviour had been pardoned by James when king and so had become a Jacobite. St Germain were in no haste to authorise this rather ramshackle assassination plan and the opportunity passed when William left the country for Flanders in April 1695.

Middleton's new declaration had failed to rekindle Jacobite support, so his best hope was that William's unpopularity in England would increase to such an extent that Jacobite leaders in Britain would feel that there might be enough support for an uprising. The causes for grievance against William had been mounting up. There were the old ones about the cost of the war, William's favouritism towards the Dutch, and accusations of homosexuality. The Jacobite propagandist, Robert Ferguson, had written a very influential pamphlet, *A Brief Account of the Late Depredations*, which had referred to 'a Dutch King influenced by Dutch Councils'. Added to this was economic disruption due to the lack of coinage and the fact that so many silver coins had been clipped that there was little confidence in its value.

In June some Jacobites were confident enough to conduct a propaganda event by openly celebrating the birthday of James Francis Edward, the Prince of Wales, in the Dog Tavern, Drury Lane. What began as a defiant toasting of the prince's health with drums beating and a few banners, was rapidly turned by Captain George Porter into a drunken riot. This led to the arrest of Porter, along with a number of others including Sir John Fenwick, the Jacobite military commander for

London and the south east. Fenwick was briefly imprisoned, but was released when the court accepted his defence he had been too drunk to stand up, let alone take part in the riot. While Fenwick was briefly in custody, command passed to his deputy Sir George Barclay. Barclay was a Scottish army officer who had been knighted by James in 1688 and joined Claverhouse's uprising in Scotland. He had been promoted to major general for continuing to help lead Jacobite resistance after Killiecrankie, until the army had melted away. Since then he had gone to James at St Germain and then returned to England to support Fenwick in providing military professionalism for any Jacobite rebellion.

The situation regarding William's unpopularity was slightly changed as a result of him capturing the great fortress of Namur in August 1695. He was at last a victor in the long running war and welcomed with bell ringing and cheers when he returned to England in October. The loss of Namur was a wake-up call to Louis that he had reached military stalemate in Flanders. His overstretched and now unsuccessful armies were bringing France to bankruptcy. Louis began considering peace negotiations. He had already put out feelers to William for peace via his Danish allies, but these were rejected as Louis had stated he was not prepared to recognise William as king. Louis then thought that his best way ahead was to place James back on the throne of England and so remove his main enemy, William, and be in a position to negotiate peace terms from a position of strength.

An opportunity presented itself because the French troops in Flanders had gone into winter quarters and so some could be made available for an invasion of England. This was a complete change of policy. James and Louis had flatly turned down Ailesbury's recommendation for an invasion in 1693, and then again as recently as the spring of 1695, when Ailesbury and some of the Select Number sent Robert Charnock over to make a case for an invasion. Now Louis was all for an invasion and James began to muster enthusiasm for an operation that could be his last chance of regaining his thrones.

Louis began planning the deployment of some of his forces from Flanders to the Channel ports as an invasion force to be led by James. As the majority of William's navy were deployed off Cadiz, there was a good chance that a French fleet to could sail to England unopposed. However, Louis believed that such an expedition would only be feasible if William had become sufficiently unpopular, for there to be a widescale rebellion against him. English Jacobites were reporting on William's unpopularity back to St Germain and Louis was receiving similar information at Versailles from Abbé Renaudolt, his intelligence chief. The many grievances against William had remained, despite the recent Namur uplift to his popularity. From the autumn of 1695 Louis began moving troops from Flanders to the Calais area and assembling troopships in the port. He let it be known that the purpose for assembling this overseas expeditionary force was to carry out an attack on the coast of Zeeland.

While making preparations for an invasion, Louis had always made it clear that it would only be launched if there was first an uprising of Jacobites in England. The Duke of Berwick informed James that he had been assured that Jacobite leaders could raise at least 2,000 cavalry in London and the south east, but more recent information from a Jacobite agent called Mr Noseworthy (alias Powell) said the numbers were much smaller and widely scattered. Worse still, any rising was conditional on James landing in England with an invasion force. In the past James had always assured Louis that English Jacobites were ready to rise up for him, so, not wishing to lose face, he decided not to share this intelligence with Louis when they met in early January. The plan was confirmed for James to land near Dover and advance on London, and it was agreed that Berwick should secretly travel to England to liaise with Jacobite leaders on the organisation of the uprising.

The start of 1696, therefore, saw a substantial increase in the Jacobite threat. Intelligence had already been coming in to the government from various sources. Although Carmarthen had been made Duke of Leeds in 1694, his power was on the wane and his many enemies had closed in on him. The Whigs falsely accused him of Jacobism, and in April 1695 he had been impeached for taking bribes. The impeachment was abandoned through lack of evidence when the chief witnesses were mysteriously spirited away to France. Despite this, Carmarthen was unable to bounce back. He continued as Lord President of the Council until dismissed in 1699, but had lost the king's ear and retained little real power. As a result, Leeds was no longer playing an active part in intelligence and the work reverted to the secretaries of state. That is, the Duke of Shrewsbury for the Southern Department and Sir William Trumbull, who had taken over the Northern Department in May 1695.Trumbull was a very experienced, but rather timid, government servant who did not enjoy his new position of responsibility which became more burdensome than normal because of Shrewsbury's poor health. Trumbull found himself taking over Shrewsbury's responsibility for intelligence and so it was he who received the first rumours of a new Jacobite plot.

In August 1695, Trumbull heard information that a serious Jacobite plot was afoot. He tasked agents and informers to find out more but then handed over the investigation to James Vernon. Vernon was the 48-year-old younger son of a Cheshire gentry family, who had built up considerable experience in government service. From 1671–2, he had worked for Sir Joseph Williamson, Charles II's secretary of state and head of intelligence, gathering information in the United Provinces. This was followed by participation in a diplomatic mission to France, then secretary to the Duke of Monmouth until 1678, when he joined the office of the secretaries of state and became editor of the *London Gazette*. From that he became secretary to Shrewsbury when he was southern secretary for the first time (1689–90), and when Shrewsbury resigned he became secretary to Sir John Trenchard and spent time in Flanders reporting troop movements, but became Shrewsbury's secretary again when he resumed power in March 1694. Moreover, this capable government servant had greater influence than this because he was also the secretary to the Lords Justices, which was the body running the country whenever William was abroad. In short, with an ailing Shrewsbury and an over-faced Trumbull, Vernon was the right man to be given the lead role for intelligence.

Vernon found himself in receipt of large quantities of source information about Jacobite plots, but with it came the difficult task of separating hard intelligence from idle rumour and information fabricated by informants to receive payments. The great majority of Catholic or Tory gentry suspected of Jacobite sympathies were by now well known locally, as were the former officers, non-jurors and others of doubtful loyalty to King William who associated with them. It is hard to put a number of such suspects but it was about 5–10 per cent of the population. In fact, only a small percentage of these were actively engaged in subversive Jacobite activities, but all were potential suspects and might be the target of informant's reports.

The other principal source of government information about Jacobites was St Germain. A few Williamite agents, such as John Macky, managed to get themselves accepted in the Jacobite court. Macky had provided the valuable intelligence that the 1692 invasion was planned to land on England's south coast rather than Scotland, as had been believed by the Admiralty. That said, it was difficult to gain access to James's inner councils as his secretaries of state were very security conscious. On the other hand, it was relatively easy to arrive at St Germain with a cover story and gain some access to the court. After all, numerous former soldiers, Catholics and English and Scottish non-jurors had made their way to James's court to express their loyalty, and if possible, seek employment. In fact, virtually all royal positions were already occupied and James was finding it hard enough to continue paying his existing household staff. The expatriates who had flocked there merely hung around hoping that something might turn up, if not in James's court, perhaps the French army. There was no room for them at the St Germain chateau, which was already massively overcrowded, so they had to find lodgings in the nearby town, which almost doubled in size. The French landlords made the most of the situation, charging high rents which led to many of these expatriates getting through what little savings they had brought with them.

Not only had a considerable number of Jacobites moved to the town, but James had also encouraged Catholic religious orders to move there. This was a shrewd move as it meant that many of the priests, monks and nuns who became established there dispensed charity to the needy. James and Mary of Modena also implored all their senior contacts in the Catholic Church to provide any assistance they could to their unfortunate supporters. As a result, some children of their faithful, but impoverished adherents were given places in convents if girls, or education and possible entry to priesthood or a monastery, if boys. Those who failed to obtain employment through the court, army, or religious institutions were likely to be very disappointed with their situation. Added to the general poverty was the instability in the town, where fights and duels were frequent, especially in the winter months when proud but poorly paid Jacobite soldiers returned for winter quartering. It was no surprise that many of these people became bitter that the loyalty they had shown to the exiled king was bringing destitution rather than reward. As a result they were a perfect pool in which Williamite agents could fish to recruit informants. Desperation led many to volunteer their services to provide information for the small financial rewards, and it is fair to say that St Germain was swarming with Williamite agents and informants.[3]

Although a large quantity of useful but relatively low level intelligence was coming from St Germain, as in England, it was not always reliable. For example, there was John Simpson who sold information, but it was to both sides. Then there was William Fuller who had been a page of Lady Powis and later a Jacobite courier taking messages across the Channel. He had been arrested on his tenth trip to England and brought to Secretary Shewsbury for questioning, where he described the various methods of concealing messages (such as inside buttons) and agreed to become an informant in exchange for his release. This worked well to begin with, but greed made him start to fabricate reports in order to boost his covert income.[4] For all that, the large number of low level informants at St Germain meant that the Williamite intelligence received information on at least major activities at James's court. With Louis having decided upon an invasion of England it was difficult to hide the troop movements, logistic and naval preparations that began to take place. As the joint invasion force was to be 16,000 strong, this could hardly be accomplished in secret. From August 1695 onwards, Vernon was receiving reports of the beginnings of a build-up of French and Jacobite forces at Calais and Dunkirk. Information was also coming in about French troop transport vessels being brought to those ports.

What Vernon did not as yet know was that a plot was about to be hatched to assassinate William before the invasion took place. Sir George Barclay travelled to St Germain to encourage James to provide some support for the English uprising, even though he was having serious misgivings about Fenwick's hopes of raising sufficient numbers. Barclay may at this stage have already begun to consider that the assassination of William might provide the necessary catalyst to launch both a rising and an invasion. However that might be, Barclay had several audiences with James and may have intimated the possibility of assassination, but this is not known. All that is certain is that he was given £800 to help finance operations in England, most of which was to be spent on purchasing horses. He was also given a royal warrant authorising English Jacobites, 'to rise in arms, and make war upon the Prince of Orange … and such other acts of hostility against the Prince of Orange … as may conducive to our service, we judging his the properest, justest, and most effectual means of procuring our restoration.' This vague wording might, or might not, be interpreted to include authorising William's assassination.

In January 1696, Barclay returned to England and landed at Romney Marsh near the isolated house of Hunt, the Jacobite farmer and smuggler used by Berkenhead, and then set off in disguise to meet his Jacobite associates in London. Barclay's disguise must have been good as he was tall, slim, with large hooked nose and a crippled right hand which made his distinctive appearance well known to the authorities.[5] Nevertheless, he remained undetected by continually changing his lodgings and only coming out when darkness was falling. A week later Berwick, escorted by Berkenhead, landed at Romney Marsh and he too made his way to London to contact Jacobite leaders. A few days later, twenty Jacobite officers from James's guards at St Germain landed in the same place, with orders to support Barclay in his operation. The most prominent of these were two Catholic officers, Ambrose Rookwood and Major John Bernardi, a Catholic of Genoese decent who had previously been leading some of the Jacobite troops in Scotland. These officers had been told to rendezvous with Barclay in Covent Garden's piazza and were to recognise him by the fact that he would have a white handkerchief hanging out of this pocket.

The Duke of Berwick managed to make contact with Ailsebury, Viscount Montgomery, Fenwick and other Jacobite leaders without coming to the attention of government security. These meetings had been disappointing because Fenwick and others had been adamant that they would indeed raise Jacobite forces, but only if James landed in England at the head of a combined French/Jacobite force. The impasse remained. Barclay, for his part, had got together with Robert Charnock, Captain George Porter and 'Scum' Goodman, who had been planning the earlier assassination attempt. It seems they convinced him that the assassination of William was the best way to initiate a rebellion and uprising. From then on Barclay and the others began planning the assassination, but without informing Fenwick, Barclay's official superior for the uprising, or Ailesbury and Montgomery, members of the Select Number.

Berwick met Barclay in London and become aware of the plot for assassination, or 'kidnapping' as it was described. The plan was to assassinate William, then raise James's standard to formally launch a Jacobite uprising. A beacon would be lit from the cliffs of Dover to notify the French/Jacobite invasion force waiting in Calais and Dunkirk. Berwick may well have thought that the assassination might provide sufficient confusion to result in an uprising and convince Louis to invade. Whatever the case, he returned to France to report back to his father. Berwick caught up with him while James was travelling to Calais in readiness to join the French general Boufflers and the invasion force. The news that English Jacobites would only rise if there was an invasion made James even more despondent, but it seems unlikely that Berwick told him anything about the plot to 'kidnap' William, even though this could be the catalyst for both uprising and invasion. James's chance of success in this major operation to regain his thrones now largely rested on William being assassinated.

Chapter 10

Assassination and Retribution 1696–9

'There was a conspiracy of about thirty knights, gentlemen, captains, many of them Irish and English Papists, and Non Jurors and Jacobites to murder King William.'
Diary of John Evelyn, entry for 26 February 1696

During Berwick's journey to get a ship to France he met Lieutenant Colonel John Parker, who had just returned to England to resume command of his regiment and the London uprising. There had been an unresolved dispute over whether he or Sir George Barclay should be the senior London Jacobite leader. Berwick seems to have persuaded Parker to return with him to France, thus leaving Sir George Barclay with the command. Barclay was making excellent progress in organising the assassination operation. The twenty Jacobite officers who had landed after Barclay had joined him thanks to the handkerchief recognition signal. However, they were surprised and dismayed when told that they were to be assassins rather than to lead armed groups in an uprising, the role for which they had originally volunteered. With some reluctance they agreed to carry out their unsoldierly and dishonourable assignment, but accepted that it was authorised by the wording of the warrant James had given to Barclay. They were first tasked with conducting surveillance of William to identify a suitable location to carry out the attack. It was decided that the best opportunity to assassinate William was when he was returning by coach to Kensington following his weekly Saturday hunting in Richmond Park. William would, of course, have his twenty-five-strong cavalry escort so this presented a significant problem.

Further reconnaissance provided a solution to the difficulty of having to overwhelm so many guards. It was found that when William and his coach crossed the Thames by ferry, his guards remained at the bank side for the ferry to return and transport them over and then catch up with him. The conspirators agreed that William should be attacked when he was separated from his guard soon after making the Thames crossing, as his coach travelled on the muddy lane from Chiswick to Turnham Green. The lane was also suitable because it was so narrow that the royal coach and its six horses would have no room to manoeuvre and attempt escape. Barclay decided that he would need thirty to forty men to accomplish the task and they would be divided into four groups led by Captain Porter, Robert Charnock, Brigadier Rockwood and Barclay himself. Porter and Charnock's groups would take on the guards and Rockwood and Barclay would attack the coach, with Barclay's party responsible for killing everyone in the coach.

This was a good plan but it was then a matter of implementing it and coordinating it with a general Jacobite uprising. The latter was a complicating factor because Fenwick, the uprising leader, had not been given any details of the assassination plot. The more immediate problem was that a large number of people would have to be brought into the joint conspiracies and this meant that there was an increased risk of the plot being reported to the authorities. Charnock asked Porter to organise the assassination operation and Porter instructed his servant, Thomas Keyes, to carry out the recruitment of about twenty volunteers for the attacking force who, with the twenty that had landed with Rookwood, would bring it up to about forty. Keyes had been a trumpeter in the Blues Regiment of guards and persuaded a couple of serving Catholic troopers to join the plot. The majority of the recruits were men such as Major Robert Lowicke who were members of the clandestine London cavalry regiment that Charnock had taken over from Lieutenant Colonel John Parker.

One of these was Sir William Parkyns, whom Parker had made a captain in his regiment. He was a prominent London lawyer who had been privy to Charnock's assassination plot of the previous year. Parkyns was an inveterate Jacobite but had taken the oath of allegiance to William in order to retain his office of clerk of the Court of Chancery. Although he was a captain in the regiment, he was suffering from gout and so was unable to take an active part in the operation. However, he did provide horses, saddles and weapons for forty members of the attacking force. Every effort was made to maintain security and the horses were kept in different stables so as not to arouse suspicion. When all was more or less in place, it was agreed that the assassination should take place on 15 February.

With the well-organised assassination operation about to be launched, William's intelligence organisation needed to hear about it as a matter of the greatest urgency. Although intelligence was the responsibility of the secretaries of state, William tended to treat them as minor functionaries and relied upon the advice of his boyhood friend, the faithful Willem Bentinck, who had been made Earl of Portland. Portland had developed his clandestine skills when organising English Whigs to rise up against James in 1688 and had increased them while gathering military and diplomatic intelligence to support the war in Flanders. As a result he was used to employing agents and informants and, being fiercely loyal to William, took it upon himself to be his unofficial head of internal security. This strange situation was generally known and so it was Portland who received the first intelligence about the impending assassination. On 13 February, Fisher, one of those who had been recruited for the attacking force, decided he wished to be no party to assassination and so requested to see Portland and told him in very general terms that there was a threat to William as he travelled for his Saturday hunting in Richmond. Rather surprisingly, Portland took little notice of this important, though uncorroborated, information, probably because Fisher just appeared another low-grade informer after money.

The next day the real danger of that threat was made manifest. At 9 pm, Captain Thomas Prendergast, a Catholic gentleman from Limerick, asked to be admitted to Lord Portland's lodgings in Whitehall. Prendergast had been a Jacobite cavalry officer in Ireland, then transferred to William's army after the Peace of Limerick and served in Flanders. He left the army and linked up with Captain Porter to make money by conducting highway robbery in Hampshire. In February, Porter had called Prendergast up to London from Hampshire and asked him to take part in the assassination plot and be in the group responsible for killing everyone in the royal coach. Prendergast agreed, but the next day a fit of conscience brought him to Portland's door.

On being admitted, Prendergast told Portland that there was a plot to assassinate William the next day at Turnham Green as he returned from hunting. Prendergast explained to Portland that as a Catholic he supported James, but he regarded it as completely dishonourable to allow an assassination to take place and so he had come to report the plot to the authorities. He went on to say that while he wished to prevent the plot, he was not prepared to divulge information that might incriminate any of the conspirators. Portland could see that Prendergast was a gentleman and appeared a credible source. He immediately rushed to see William and briefed him on what was now corroborated intelligence of the threat to his life. William was incredulous about the threat and was reluctant to let it get in the way of good hunting. It took considerable persuasion on Portland's part to eventually obtain the king's agreement to cancel the next day's outing.

The conspirators were all ready for the operation on 15 February when they heard that William had decided not to hunt that day. It was given out that the cancellation was because of bad weather. They therefore decided to postpone the assassination to the next Saturday, 22 February. As neither Portland nor the secretaries of state knew the identities of the conspirators, it was not possible to take any action against them. Fortunately, on Friday 21 February, a French professional gambler and double agent called De La Rue, provided more details of the plot to Portland. William was informed and became at last convinced that there was indeed a plot on his life. Prendergast was summoned to see William and Portland in the king's closet. William spoke to Prendergast kindly and gave him an assurance that if he provided the names of those conspirators known to him they would come to no harm, but their plot would be foiled. Prendergast agreed to this and gave all the information he knew about the assassins and the preparation for an uprising and invasion.

The next day the main conspirators met at the lodgings Porter shared with Charnock in Norfolk Street off the Strand. Portland had instructed Prendergast to join them as agreed, so that they would not think there was anything amiss. They were just getting ready to launch their operation when their lookout in Kensington came back to report that the king's coach had gone back to the stables and his escorts were returning, shouting that something terrible had been discovered. The conspirators were dismayed, but sufficiently confident that their identities were not known and made no attempt to escape. Charnock encouraged their continued determination to destroy William by squeezing an orange into a glass for them all to take a sip and declaring: 'What cannot be done today can be done tomorrow.'[1] They then began discussing plans to make another attempt on the king's life. Later that day their bravado came to an end when those who remained were arrested, and a general round up of suspects took place. The assassination plot was foiled and with it the intended Jacobite rising and therefore James's invasion. Once news reached France of the arrests, Louis abandoned the invasion and a dejected James was left standing at the Calais quayside. As we shall see, Jacobites in England were to face stern retribution for involvement in something as base as a royal assassination.

Thanks to Prendergast's information, seventeen of the principal conspirators were rapidly arrested including Charnock, Rookwood and Bernardi. However, the leader of the assassination plot, Sir John Barclay, managed to remain in hiding before making his way to Romney Marsh and escape to France. In fact the arrests included Prendergast himself in order to disguise his betrayal. Apart from a general rounding up of suspects, William took action to secure the nation from invasion. The Lord Mayor was told to put the city in readiness for defence, two line regiments were ordered to return from Flanders, lords lieutenant were instructed to put the trained bands and county militia on high alert and the fleet in home waters were ordered to concentrate in the Channel under Admiral Rooke. These were sensible precautions, but there was now no question of Louis authorising the invasion to proceed.

On Monday 24 February, William summoned both houses of parliament and told them of the discovery of the assassination plot, uprising and invasion. Commons and Lords immediately voted an address of thanksgiving for the king's safety. Two bills were then passed, one suspending Habeas Corpus, and the other that parliament should not be dissolved if the king were to be killed, but should continue and be empowered to set the disposal of the crown 'according to the late settlement at the Revolution'. That is, ensuring the crown passed to the Protestant Princess Anne. Other measures were brought in, such as a proclamation that all Catholics should remove themselves at least ten miles from London. In order to flush out those conspirators not already arrested, a £1,000 reward was offered to anyone offering information leading to their discovery and apprehension. To ensure that there was sufficient evidence for convictions, a further £1,000 and a free pardon was offered to anyone involved in the plot who gave themselves up and were prepared to provide information on their fellow conspirators.

There then followed a series of arrests and trials. Having done his duty by discovering the plot, Portland took a back seat and the organisation for locating the conspirators was left with James Vernon. Following a hue and cry, Captain George Porter was captured in Leatherhead on 27 February together with Prendergast and Porter's servant, Thomas Keyes. Prendergast was taken to prison with Porter and Keyes in order to preserve his cover. Almost immediately after capture, Porter saved himself by making a full confession and offering to give evidence against his accomplices. To make his confession particularly valuable, he even falsely implicated James in the plot. Porter's cooperation was a major breakthrough for Vernon and would eventually lead to the conviction of Charnock, King, Friend, Parkyns, Lowicke and Keynes. A little later, a member of the assassination group called George Harris gave himself up for a free pardon and agreement to provide evidence against his former colleagues. Harris's testimonies would lead to the conviction of Bernardi and Rookwood. The policy of offering money and free pardons to those who prepared to betray their comrades had certainly worked.

Searches were made for Sir William Parkyns at his house in Covent Garden and his country seat in Warwickshire. The search party did not find Parkyns, but did discover arms and accoutrements sufficient to equip a troop of cavalry. This find was a reminder that at least some Jacobite gentry had been making preparations for an uprising. Further searches continued for Parkyns, who was eventually arrested in the Temple on 10 March and committed to Newgate Prison. Vernon also supervised the general rounding-up of known Jacobites, whether they were believed to be involved in the plot or not. Some had already been arrested, such as James Graham, the brother of Viscount Preston and King James's former keeper of the Privy Purse. Jacobite leaders such as the Earl of Ailesbury were placed in the Tower, and known agitators such as the pamphleteer Robert Ferguson found themselves in the less salubrious Newgate. The wide-ranging round up of suspects continued for many months in order to apprehend those who had gone into hiding. Some, like Viscount Montgomery, were declared an outlaw but managed to avoid arrest until December, when he gave himself up and was taken to Newgate.

Among those arrested were William Berkenhead who had set up the Jacobite link to St Germain via Romney Marsh. He had also been acting as a French naval spy reporting to the French naval minister Comte de

Pontchartrain. He was imprisoned in Newgate in April, but escaped four months later having invited his keeper to supper and drugged his wine. The enterprising Berkenhead then travelled to Romney Marsh, discovered that Hunt had begun informing on Jacobites, so kidnapped him and made his way to France where James rewarded him by making him Clerk of the Kitchen at St Germain. It is unlikely that the pay for his new post made up for what he had received as surveyor of Dover and the £200 a year he had received as a Jacobite agent, augmented by money given to him as a French agent.

On 4 April parliament drafted an oath of loyalty to William; all those who refused to sign would be liable to the forfeitures and other penalties inflicted on Catholics. This 'Association' as it was called required the signatories to recognise William as their 'lawful and rightful sovereign'. Signing the Association was required of all MPs and office holders both military and civil and all Anglican clergy. This was indeed a test for all those Tories who had been prepared to live under the rule of William, but regarded James as the rightful monarch. As it happened, most Tory office holders had accepted the need to pay lip service to allegiance to William and only about a hundred Anglican clergy resigned.

The majority of Tories who had held moderate Jacobite sympathies were horrified that James had planned to invade the country with French troops, igniting a civil war and that he had stooped so low as to authorise the assassination of his son-in-law. That James quite possibly did not even know of the assassination plot was lost in the general revulsion against it. Local copies of the Association were spontaneously drawn up in the regions and municipalities around the country and thousands of citizens clamoured to sign them. Many of those who signed took to wearing a red ribbon to display their loyalty to William. This was not so much a boost to William as a person, as the grievances against him remained and had been added to by the economic chaos caused by the reissuing of the coinage. What it represented was a disgust in James's action, and recognition of William as the 'lawful and rightful sovereign', irrespective of his perceived faults.

The outpouring of dislike for Jacobites was a considerable assistance to Vernon and his king's messengers in securing the arrests of suspects. The next task of bringing those suspects to trial had begun in March. The first to be tried for high treason on Porter's evidence were Robert Charnock, Sir Edward King, and Porter's own servant Thomas

Keyes. It only took one hour of the court's time to secure their conviction. They were all executed on 18 March, with Charnock showing some style by purchasing a new wig and coat for the big occasion. Next was Sir John Friend who was arraigned at the Old Bailey on 23 March, two days before the Treason Act of the previous year came into effect allowing the accused the assistance of a defence council. Friend, a Protestant, pleaded not guilty and protested that because Porter, who gave evidence against him, was a papist, he should not be believed against his word as a Protestant. This did not move the court and he was convicted after a fifteen-minute hearing and executed at Tyburn along with Sir William Parkins on 3 April. Their quarters (heads, arms and legs) were placed on display at Temple Bar. Parkins's trial had begun two days after Friends and he too had been denied a defence council and had Porter as the principal witness against him. Both men had been visited in prison to try to get them to save their lives by providing information on the other conspirators, but both had refused. Vernon's work of arresting and convicting conspirators continued.

On 21 April, Rookwood was brought before the King's Bench along with Robert Lowick and Charles Cranburn, a Jacobite quartermaster. George Harris joined Porter as prosecution witnesses and Rookwood and Lowick were executed at Tyburn on 29 April. This ended the initial trials. A total of 3,000 Jacobite suspects had been arrested and it had become clear that most had no connection with the plot. Releases of those who had been rounded up began to take place, but this did not include the more prominent Jacobites. The Earl of Ailesbury, who had not been involved in the assassination plot but was the principal Jacobite leader, spent a year in the Tower before being released on bail and allowed to retire to live in Brussels. Nor was release possible for those who were suspected of being conspirators, but there was insufficient evidence to secure a conviction. Fortunately parliament had suspended Habeas Corpus so it was possible to detain these men without trial. Included in this category were Major Robert Cassels, Major John Bernardi, Captain James Counter, James Chambers and Robert Blackbourn. Of these only James Counter was to be released, but that was not until the next reign. The rest remained in prison till the end of their days. Bernardi died in 1736 aged 80 and Blackbourn died in King's Bench Prison in 1748 after more than fifty years detention without trial.

Vernon could congratulate himself that nearly all those who had taken a significant part in the assassination plot had been executed or imprisoned. Despite this, it must have been irritating that he had failed to apprehend two of the most important Jacobites. Sir George Barclay, the leader of the plot, had escaped to France, and Sir John Fenwick, the senior Jacobite military commander, was still at large. Vernon had deployed informants to conduct surveillance on Fenwick's likely haunts and must have been pleased when this led to his capture on 11 July in New Romney as he attempted to escape to France. It must have been even more pleasing when Fenwick was taken to the Tower and began offering to reveal 'vital secrets' to the king in person in exchange for his life. Unfortunately for Vernon, any pleasure he felt soon turned to dismay when Fenwick began to accuse some of the greatest in the land of being Jacobites. These included the Earl of Marlborough, advisor to Princess Anne the heir to the throne; Baron Godolphin, the First Lord of the Treasury; Admiral Russell, the First Lord of the Admiralty; and Vernon's own superior, the Duke of Shrewsbury, the senior secretary of state. As we shall see, Vernon would find himself wrestling with even more complex problem of Fenwick for the next six months.

While James's supporters were being harried by Vernon in England, the former king had been having an almost equally difficult time since the failed assassination in February. He had been in no hurry to return to St Germain and face his courtiers as a failure. He remained with his troops until nearly the last regiment had marched off to Flanders under Louis's orders, in the forlorn hope that France would still mount an invasion. James knew that he was unpopular in England, but discovered that he was also unpopular in France. In March, Parisians had carried out protests against him at the Pont Neuf, demanding that he should not return to St Germain and complaining about the amount of French money that was squandered on supporting him and his court. Perhaps worse still, derogatory pamphlets and songs were circulating about him, poking fun at his failures.

James did return to St Germain in May, and hit back by blaming the failed operation on others: the British Jacobites for not rising; Louis for failing to defeat the Grand Alliance; the weather which had delayed the French naval escort ships for the troop carriers; but most of all God, who had declined to support the operation. He accepted that it was his own past sins that had resulted in God's disfavour and this encouraged him to seek forgiveness by becoming even more devout. It pained him that he was being blamed for authorising the assassination plot and he went to some lengths to let it be known that he had no part in it. Despite launching propaganda to this effect, it did little to change public opinion in his former kingdoms.

One reason why James's propaganda failed was that it was very difficult to get it to England and then distributed. Indeed, the Select Number had dissolved and Jacobite infrastructure, such as it was, had been virtually destroyed by the arrests and convictions. The surviving diehard Jacobites had either fled or were keeping a very low profile to protect their own liberty and family estates. Moderate Tories were most reluctant to take any action that might taint them with having Jacobite sympathies. As a result of this, it was very difficult for James to get any instructions through to remaining English Jacobites and he was becoming starved of any intelligence from them. James authorised Middleton to spend large sums of money trying to persuade Calais merchants to take letters across the Channel. A Mr Nowell was offered 5,000 livres per annum to undertake this task, but the arrangements fell through as there was there was no reliable means of distributing mail on the English side.

Communication became a major issue for James and his remaining British Jacobite sympathisers. There was the option of using the Royal Mail, but the Post Office's General Letter Office in London had a well-established procedure for intercepting and covertly opening all incoming and outgoing mail connected with suspect senders or addressees. Of course, this could be to some extent mitigated by using encryption. However, the government had a well-oiled system for decrypting and if necessary translating, enciphered documents. The leading figure for this was Dr John Wallis, the Salvian Professor of Geometry at Oxford, and often regarded as England's greatest mathematician before Newton. Having shown his ability to decipher a Royalist document in the Civil War, he had been used by parliament, and later by Cromwell, as their encryption expert. Although a Puritan, he had signed a document protesting at the execution of Charles I and this saved him at the Restoration. He had resumed his role under Charles's minister, the Earl of Arlington, and remained in royal pay under James and William, all the time increasing his experience until he had become probably the greatest cryptanalyst of his age.

There was no way in which Jacobite encryption could defeat Wallis. In fact the ciphers used by James, and Jacobites generally, were of a particularly low quality. This may have been a reflection on the powers of concentration of the users. The use of a complex key to either encrypt or decipher a document is a painstaking activity that may not have been entirely suitable for use by hot-headed Jacobite gentry. They used simple codes such as denoting Melfort by '16', Middleton by '10', James by '300', and the queen by '302'. Or codewords such as 'Good Farmer' for James, 'Bold Britain' for the Prince of Wales, and even 'Mr and Mrs Churchill' for Princess Anne and her husband Prince George of Denmark – amusing perhaps, but hardly subtle.[2]

The situation at St Germain looked pretty bad with James becoming a religious recluse and Middleton having very poor communications with what was left of the Jacobite leadership in England. In June something turned up that could change everything. Jan III Sobieski, the king of Poland, died of a heart attack. Sobieski had left no obvious heir and the power in the country rested in the hands of the Francophile Michael Radziejowski, the Cardinal Primate of Poland. Louis wanted to ensure that the next king of the huge country of Poland was an ally and felt that James would be ideal for the role. This scheme was readily accepted by Radziejowski and most of the Polish nobles as they knew James to be both a pious Catholic and a friend of France. The plan had the additional advantage to Louis of getting James off his hands and ending the need to cover his expenses.

In September an envoy from Louis put the proposition to James, thinking that he would jump at the opportunity of regaining his regal status and obtaining the resources of Poland to help him return to his British thrones. James flatly turned down the offer. He felt that claiming a throne that was not his by right was impossible when he was trying to regain a throne that was rightfully his. A personal reason was that he was now 66 years old and did not want to make the effort of trying to gain the throne. Also, even if he succeeded he might not live long enough to establish himself sufficiently to ensure the crown was inherited by James Francis Edward, who was then only 8 years old. Louis was annoyed at James's response and put forward the Prince de Conti as the French candidate, but Conti was slow to move to Poland and the Polish nobles had by then give their backing to August of Saxony as their new king.

William was also thinking about who was to succeed him. After Mary's death a second marriage had been considered and some candidates had been put forward, but he had no intention of marrying again.

The succession lay with Princess Anne, but beyond that it became doubtful. Her only surviving child was the sickly little William Henry, Duke of Gloucester. William liked the boy but was concerned that fits were wracking his weak frame and fluid on the brain was making his skull increasingly disfigured. As William began to fear that the boy would not live long, he came up with a plan to heal the family rift and ensure the Protestant succession. In August, William sent agents to St Germain to spread the word that he might be ready to recognise James Francis Edward as Prince of Wales and adopt him as his son and heir. The less welcome part of the offer was that James should renounce the throne in favour of his son, who would be brought up as a Protestant. This was not very different from the suggestion made to James by Middleton and the rumoured proposal was well received by many courtiers, in particular the Duke of Berwick. Perhaps unsurprisingly, it was scornfully rejected by James and Mary of Modena. There was no question of James renouncing his right to the throne, handing over his son to his greatest enemy and allowing William Henry to be brought up as a heretic and therefore condemning his soul to damnation.

A more devious politician such as his grandfather, Henry IV of France, would have grasped at this opportunity to exchange his religion for the crown. James might have hoped that his son would have privately remained a Catholic while outwardly subscribing to the rites of the Anglican Church. He might even have hoped that the arrangement would effect a reconciliation with his daughter Anne, and that he could end his remaining days as a respected but retired monarch. However, James was too devout and too honourable to accept the conditions, and in rejecting them destroyed the best chance of his heirs succeeding to his thrones.

While James had been considering the two offers, the Duke of Shrewsbury and James Vernon were grappling with Sir John Fenwick's allegations of treason in high places. The allegations had not been made public, but the substance of them had leaked out. The big problem was that it was basically true that Shrewsbury, Marlborough, Godolphin and Russell had remained in communication with St Germain, while pretending loyalty to William. As far as William was concerned this was not news and he was well aware that these men were just keeping their options open. Shrewsbury was so ashamed that William had heard about his disloyalty that he stayed away from court and offered his resignation as secretary of state. William, for his part, valued the services of all those accused by Fenwick; he pretended he did not believe the allegations and refused to accept Shrewsbury's resignation. Shrewsbury was still reluctant to return to court and so it continued to fall on James Vernon to sort out the mess.

The whole matter dragged on with Fenwick continuing to make offers of information in exchange for a pardon, including having a personal interview with William. This all led to nothing as Fenwick provided no revelations other than the general allegations against Shrewsbury, Marlborough and the other prominent Whigs. One reason for this is that Fenwick had played no part in the assassination plot so had little information to provide on the matter. Irrespective of this, it was important for the government to get him out of the way by bringing him to trial for high treason, unfortunately that also presented the difficulty of his allegations coming out in open court.

The matter was further complicated because Fenwick had friends and family connections among the aristocracy and there were some who were prepared to offer him assistance. The most obvious of these was the Earl of Ailesbury who, like him, had not been involved in the assassination plot but was also held in the Tower. Fenwick's greatest asset was his own wife, Lady Mary. She was an active Jacobite and had led a weavers' strike as a demonstration of opposition to William. Lady Fenwick began obtaining financial support from Ailesbury and others to prevent a prosecution taking place. In order to obtain a conviction for High Treason it was necessary to produce two witnesses. Lady Fenwick decided her best approach was to suborn the witnesses.

The obvious witness for the government to use against Fenwick was Captain George Porter. As Fenwick was innocent of the assassination plot, Porter had no evidence against him but this was of little matter as Porter was more than happy to invent evidence for his government paymasters. There still remained the matter of getting a second witness. Porter came up with the idea of using Scum Goodman, who was awaiting trial in the Gatehouse Prison. It was put to Goodman that he would receive a free pardon if he concocted evidence against Fenwick. Goodman grabbed hold of this lifeline and was released in October pending the trial. All was looking good for a swift conviction, but Vernon had not taken account of the determination of Lady Fenwick. She arranged for trusted Jacobites to track down Goodman. This was not difficult as he was frequenting his old drinking haunts, the 'Fleece' in Covent Garden and the 'Dog' in Drury Lane. Goodman was offered £500 if he went to live permanently in France. This was too good an offer for Goodman to decline and a few days later arrangements were made for him to slip off to France never to return.

Lady Fenwick had disposed of one prosecution witness, but there remained the principal witness, Porter. It would probably be only a matter of time before the government dredged up a second 'witness' who was willing to provide purged evidence. Porter needed to be removed and Lady Fenwick employed the services of an Irish barber called Clancey to contact Porter and put a similar proposition to him. When Clancey met Porter he said that he was authorised to offer 300 guineas down and a further 300 when he landed in France, together with an annuity of £1,000 a year. Porter agreed, but on mulling the offer over decided that financially, he was likely to do just as well working for the government without the risk and inconvenience of moving to France. Porter therefore informed Vernon of the offer and on the day appointed for his departure to France, he met Clancey at a tavern in Covent Garden. Government officers had been put in place and arrested Clancey, who ended up being sentenced to the pillory. Lady's Fenwick's plan was foiled.

Vernon was still left with the problem of only having one witness for the prosecution. This is when the Whig dominated House of Commons stepped in to protect their own. On 6 November they passed a motion declaring Fenwick's allegations 'false and scandalous', and then proceeded to pass a bill of attainder against Fenwick. Attainder meant that Fenwick would be pronounced guilty of High Treason by parliament without the need for a trial. This was a neat way out of an embarrassing situation. Leading Whigs had come to the same conclusion as Marlborough's brother, George Churchill, that 'dead men tell no tales'. The bill of attainder was passed by the House of Lords on 23 December and then given royal assent by the king. Consideration was given to the fact that Fenwick was a baronet with family connections to the aristocracy, so he was granted the privilege of being beheaded. This took place on 28 January of the New Year, 1697.

Fenwick's estate was confiscated and given to his wife Mary's nephew, the Earl of Carlisle. Everything down to Fenwick's own horse 'White Sorrel' was disposed of, but fortunately Mary received an annuity from her nephew. The procedure for attainder had proved most useful, but had attracted some criticism as not being entirely in the best spirit of

English justice. Certainly Jacobites regarded it as obnoxious and came to regard Fenwick as one of their martyrs. In fact, as time passed it was generally felt that the use of attainders was oppressive and Fenwick became the last person to be executed by this means.

If Fenwick is included, a total of ten Jacobite activists had been executed. On the other hand, two people connected with the plot ended up doing rather well. Captain George Porter was well rewarded for turning king's evidence. He was granted a pardon, his debts of £1,700 were paid off and he was given an annuity of £260 a year, together with a £70-a-year free rent on a house near Whitehall.[3] The government were making a statement that those who were prepared to betray conspirators would be well rewarded. More deserving favours were given to Thomas Prendergast. He was made a baronet, received a £3,000 cash grant together with the confiscated Gort estate in County Galway worth £500 a year. He later increased his fortune by marrying the sister of the Earl of Cadogen, became an MP and eventually rose to the rank of brigadier, but died leading his regiment at the Battle of Malplaquet in 1709.

Fenwick might have provided St Germain with a martyr who could be used for propaganda purposes, but that was about the only positive thing that had happened for Jacobites since the discovery of the assassination plot. Lieutenant Colonel John Parker had gone secretly to London with the Duke of Berwick in October to try to rekindle Jacobite resistance. This had not been a great success. Berwick had gone to visit his mother, by then wife of Colonel Charles Godfrey, who, like Arabella Churchill, had been James II's mistress. As Arabella was the sister of Marlborough she had no wish to implicate her brother with Jacobite plotting, particularly when he was already embarrassed by Sir John Fenwick's allegations. Arabella therefore informed the authorities of Parker being in England, but he evaded capture and scurried back to France with Berwick, having achieved nothing.

Jacobite morale in England was at a low ebb, but James was being confronted with a greater worry. Louis's whole intention of invading England, ousting William and restoring James to the throne had been to conduct peace negotiations from a position of strength. Peace remained Louis's urgent objective. French forces were spread out, fighting in Flanders, Spain, Italy and Rhineland; the cost was bringing the country to the verge of bankruptcy. The countries of Louis's opponents in the Grand Alliance were also financially exhausted. In the case of England,

Charles Montague had mitigated this by revolutionising public finances by the concept of national debt and exchequer bills, facilitated by the creation of the Bank of England in 1694. After a great deal of difficulty, the problem of clipped and counterfeit coinage had been overcome by all coins being called in and newly minted ones reissued. By the autumn of 1696 England had been put on a sound financial footing, but that did not alter the fact that the country was nearly bankrupt and William was being blamed for high taxation and the chaos caused by the reissue of the coinage. In short, Louis wanted peace and so did William and the other leaders of the Grand Alliance. The difficulty was that there were so many issues to resolve to bring this joint aspiration to fulfilment.

Louis's next step in his peace initiative was to chip away at the Grand Alliance, inducing individual members to make peace. This he succeeded to do with Savoy in August. This was a clear sign to James that Louis was in earnest about peace-making. If James's only ally made peace with England and the Grand Alliance, then there would be little or no chance of him, or his successors, regaining the throne. The situation became very dangerous. In October Louis obtained a long-standing truce in Italy and not long after, negotiations began with members of the Grand Alliance. It took until April 1697 before these were formalised and plenipotentiaries assembled for peace talks at a chateau in Ryswick near The Hague. These negotiations would go on for nearly a year while fighting continued in a rather desultory fashion with neither side gaining advantage after William managed to block an attempt by Louis to capture Brussels and both armies entrenched themselves.

There were several reasons why it was not easy to conclude a peace. One was the sticking point that William, the leader of the Grand Alliance, wanted to be recognised as rightful king of England. A more important reason was the health of King Carlos II of Spain. Carlos was the tragic end product of Hapsburg inbreeding. Described as 'short, lame, epileptic, senile and completely bald before 35, always on the verge of death, but repeatedly baffling Christendom by continuing to live.'[4] Spain was in serious decline but still nominally head of vast empire including the Philippines, large swathes of North and South America, parts of the West Indies, and in Europe: the Spanish Netherlands, Naples, Sicily and Milan. It mattered who ruled Spain and as Carlos was childless and without surviving brothers and sisters, who should succeed him was an issue of some importance. At the beginning of 1697 it looked as though

Carlos was at last about to die and so the question of succession needed resolution.

As it was possible for the crown of Spain to be inherited by a woman or the descendant of a woman, this meant it could pass to the descendants of either of Carlos's deceased sisters. These were Maria Theresa, who had married Louis XIV, and Margaret Theresa, who had married the Emperor Leopold. The situation was complicated by the fact that as part of the treaties for both marriages, Louis and Leopold had renounced claims to the Spanish throne. Neither Louis nor Leopold were concerned about legal niceties and each intended that their own heirs should succeed to the Spanish crown. Louis was impatient to make peace with the Grand Alliance so that it would break up and its members would not be in a good position to obstruct a future attempt to secure the Spanish Empire for his heir. Leopold was equally determined to continue the war and with it the cohesion of the Grand Alliance so that it was ready to support the claim he would be making for the throne of Spain.

The question of the succession to the Spanish throne was to dominate European politics for the next seventeen years and have a major bearing on the Jacobite threat.

Chapter 11

The Death of Princes
1699–1702

'The Death of King James …put an end to that unhappy
Prince's troubles, after a short and unprosperous reign,
indiscreetly attempting to bring in Popery, and make
himself absolute, in imitation of the French, hurried by the
impatience of Jesuits, which this nation would not endure.'
Diary of John Evelyn, entry for 22 September 1701

With the vital negotiations between Louis and the Grand Alliance under
way, James naturally wanted to be part of them in order to influence
the result to his advantage. Louis, on the other hand, had no wish to
muddy the waters by having his own objectives compromised by James.
Louis made it plain to James that he did not want him to send any
representative to Ryswick. James accepted this with bad grace, and then
began dispatching letters and emissaries to the Catholic leaders of the
Grand Alliance, including Emperor Leopold of Austria. This annoyed
both Leopold and Louis. The Emperor was naturally sorry that a fellow
Catholic monarch had lost his crown, but had little sympathy as he
felt that he had brought it on himself. Louis was merely annoyed that
James was trying to go over his head. The result of all this was that these
important negotiations rumbled on month after month with James being
no more than a very distant spectator.

The situation was now getting very dangerous for James. Louis's
eyes were on the prize of securing the Spanish crown for his family,
and so he was prepared to offer almost anything to end the war. He
made overtures to William that he would relinquish all conquests made
during the war, restore Lorraine to its duke, Luxemburg to Spain, and
Strasburg to Austria, return the principality of Orange to William and

acknowledge him as king of England. These were unimaginably good terms for England, but were not acceptable to Emperor Leopold who wanted to continue the war. To make matters worse, the formal meetings at Ryswick were getting nowhere because of arguments over procedures.

William decided to proceed separately with negotiations and empowered Portland to deal direct with the French general Boufflers at a location outside Brussels almost within sight of their opposing armies. The two generals got down to business and after some reference back to their respective sovereigns, an agreement was reached. This was that Louis would no longer provide any support for James in his claim to the English throne, and James and his court should move out of French jurisdiction to the Papal city of Avignon. In return, Louis had requested William grant an amnesty for all Jacobites and allow Mary of Modena her jointure of £50,000 a year to cover James and her living expenses in exile. William refused the first but agreed the second, and it was further agreed that the move of James and the jointure should not be mentioned in the official treaty.

There was some dismay among the plenipotentiaries at Ryswick when they heard of this agreement, but they all came round to it, except for the Emperor. It was decided that the Emperor should have until 10 September to add his signature. Leopold found that he could not persuade his allies to continue the war and, with considerable misgiving, signed the treaty. When William returned to London in early December he was welcomed by cheering crowds, with bells ringing, bonfires lighted, cannon fired and £10,000 worth of fireworks, together with civic ceremonies that lasted for several days, including a public service of thanksgiving at the newly built St Paul's Cathedral.

While much alcohol was being consumed drinking the king's health in England, there could not be a greater contrast with James's court at St Germain. A feeling of the deepest gloom, coupled with anger that they had been completely let down by their French allies. True to form, James turned to God and extreme penitence. Morale at St Germain was not enhanced by the atmosphere of uncompromising Catholicism. Louis had always been a devout Catholic but became more extreme through the influence of his morganatic wife, Madame de Maintenant. Having introduced the persecution of Huguenots, he decided he could no longer allow the Protestant British courtiers at St Germain to practise their religion. James was tolerant to Protestant worship but had no option but to comply with the wishes of his host. As a result, non-Catholics at James's court began to leave. Even Protestants as loyal to James as Sir Theopilus Oglethorpe, who had been one of the Select Number, decided to take the oath of loyalty to William and returned to England in late 1696.

The most prominent Protestant was Middleton, James's Secretary of State. He did remain at St Germain, but ceased to openly practice his religion in order to retain his post. James's compliance with Louis's direction to eject Protestants was a blow to his Protestant Jacobite followers in his former kingdoms. It demonstrated that James might talk about supporting religious toleration and protecting the Anglican Church, but could not be trusted to keep his word. The Jacobite Compounders were thus dealt a serious blow to their cause and many an Anglican Tory squire ceased to toast 'the king over the water'.

1698 began particularly badly for James when he received the news that Whitehall Palace had burned down on 4 January, destroying his former seat of government with its sumptuous historic rooms and the priceless art collection. Jacobites created the rumour that it had been started on purpose by a Dutch laundress. In fact, it was started accidentally by an English laundress who was drying clothes too near a charcoal brazier. For James it meant that even if he or his son miraculously returned to the throne, much of their heritage had gone up in smoke. William, on the other hand, was not too concerned; Whitehall's location next to the river severely aggravated his asthma and he had already moved his residence to Kensington.

In St Germain, Middleton was trying his best to keep the Jacobite cause alive, but morale was low. James's best general, his son Berwick, was spending most of his time at Versailles, therefore depriving St Germain of his spirit, energy and confidence. In England, Sir William Trumbull resigned as secretary of state for the north in December 1694 and William replaced him with James Vernon. As Vernon had already been directing the intelligence service this made little change. With English Jacobites in such disarray, there was little seditious activity to monitor. That said, agents, informants and the Post Office intercept service needed to be managed effectively in case a few desperate Jacobites attempted another assassination of the king. The main intelligence requirement was focused not on internal security, but on the intentions of Louis XIV. Intelligence gathering on France and southern Europe was the province of the Secretary of State for the south, the Duke of Shrewsbury. Ill health continued to dog Shrewsbury and he appears not to have put much effort into monitoring events at Versailles.

The treaty of Ryswick had brought the war to an end, but there was still the matter of the Spanish succession. Carlos II clung on to life, but as soon as his impending death occurred, King Louis and Emperor Leopold could be expected to make their claims to his throne and war would resume. Parliament had been effusive in its praise for William in bringing the war to an end with such a favourable peace. Unfortunately, a recent election had brought a Tory majority to the House of Commons and with it, the demand for a peace dividend. Following a series of bad harvests there was no appetite for continued high taxes. With the threat from France apparently removed, it seemed logical to save money by greatly reducing the size of the army. Parliament had a long tradition of mistrusting a standing army and so were content to leave the defence of the kingdom to the navy and the militia. While considering cuts to the army the demand arose to remove all foreigners serving in it, including William's Dutch Guard. The proposed cuts were enormous. Parliament wanted to reduce the army from 90,000 to 7,000, with a further 12,000 to garrison Ireland. On top of this William would be required to send his loyal Dutch Guard back to Holland. William was so angry about the proposed cuts that he even considered abandoning England and returning to Holland. However, he eventually bowed to the inevitable and gave his reluctant consent.

The peace dividend brought the welcome reduction of the Land Tax from 4*s* in the pound to 3*s*. For William it came at the price of losing much of the army he had put such effort into creating, when another war with France seemed to be approaching. The blow of army disbandment occurred when William was already depressed. He was missing Mary, drinking too heavily and getting irritated with his great friend and confidante, Portland. William was spending more and more time in the company of the young, good-looking Arnold van Keppel, whom he had made Earl of Albermarle and a major general. The devout, serious, middle-aged Portland had no time for the young, frivolous Keppel, who was continually getting himself into scandalous scrapes with his many mistresses. William was wearied by the animosity between the two rivals for his friendship, especially as his health had deteriorated. On top of his asthma, he had gout in the knee, swollen legs and was suffering dizzy spells. To have his two closest companions at each other's throats was really too much.

With the war over, and William recognised as king, it was necessary to appoint an ambassador to France. It could no longer be a middle-ranking person such as Bevil Skelton. William had been the leader of the Grand Alliance that had just concluded a very favourable treaty with France. England had to be represented by someone of stature at the court of Versailles and William chose Portland for the role. Not only was he completely loyal and reliable, but it was Portland who had negotiated the treaty and was aware of the secret clause about the removal of James to Avignon. The other advantage for William of sending Portland to Versailles was that it would put a distance between him and Keppel and so provide a welcome break from their acrimonious rivalry.

Portland left for France with eighty servants and ninety carriages and saddle horses, appropriate to being the close companion of the king of England. He took up residence of some magnificence in the Hotel d'Auvergre in Paris and soon visited Versailles, where Louis received him with courtesy and was impressed by his impeccable manners. This was a good start, but it was galling for Portland to see Berwick and Sir George Barclay accepted in Louis's court despite their involvement in the plot to assassinate William. It was also annoying to find that James was taking every opportunity to visit Versailles or go hunting with members of the French royal family and was always treated as an honoured guest. The link between Louis and James remained close and therefore something that needed careful observation. Portland was very experienced in espionage and soon established an effective network of agents and informants.

The man Portland relied upon to run his covert operations was his able secretary, the poet, Matthew Prior. Prior had spent the previous seven years as secretary at The Hague embassy, largely monitoring the situation during the war with France and keeping an eye on William's Grand Alliance allies. This experienced intelligencer's new role was first and foremost to establish whether Louis was making plans to take the Spanish throne when King Carlos relocated to his mausoleum. It was also necessary to see what diplomatic action was taking place with other nations to seek French alliances in the event of another war. Last, but not least, it was important to keep an eye on James and the court of St Germain to ensure no Jacobite plots were being hatched. One thing it did not take long for Prior and Portland to establish was that there was absolutely no sign of any preparations for the move to Avignon. It became clear that Louis did not intend to fulfil that part of the treaty. How much could he be trusted to honour other parts, in particular continued recognition of William as king?

About the only positive aspect of James's circumstances since Ryswick was that he was not being turfed out of St Germain and sent on his way to Avignon. The end of the war had made travel easier between France and England, so Jacobites could make the journey on the Calais packet boat rather than using a smuggler to land them on an isolated beach. It meant that a number of English gentry had been able to travel in the other direction to visit St Germain, either out of loyalty to their former king or, more likely, mere curiosity. Many of those who visited were charmed by the gracious reception they received from Mary of Modena and some were even able to kiss hands with James when he was not busy with his devotions. Such visitors returned to England, if not Jacobites then at least with increased respect towards the exiled king.

Parliament swiftly put such visits to an end by passing an act forbidding any contact, verbal, written or in person, with members of the former royal family. Anyone who did so after a certain date would not be permitted to reside in England without special licence. Those congenial trips across to France came to an end, but desire to travel in the opposite direction picked up. Many of those who had based themselves around St Germain realised that there was little immediate future for the Jacobite cause. Some began returning to England, but this proved difficult when parliament denied residence in England to anyone who had borne arms for James. Chief among these was James's army, which had to be disbanded. This was composed largely of the 'Wild Geese' Irish Brigade. Louis had been prepared to absorb 6,000 of these excellent troops into the French army, but the rest became unemployed. These men had little option but to find employment in the armies of other Catholic nations such as Spain or the Empire; failing that, they took to highway robbery or tried to make their way back to Ireland as best they could.

A gloom hung over St Germain and with Jacobite morale low it presented a good opportunity for Portland's agents to recruit informers. There were already many Williamite informers in St Germain, but by mid-1698 the place was crawling with them. This was a good position for English intelligence to be in, but sadly there was little worthwhile intelligence produced because Middleton had enough on his hands keeping the impecunious court functioning, without considering any new plots against William. Portland's main efforts at this time was less on intelligence-gathering than on trying to persuade Louis to not only rid his court of Berwick and other Jacobites, but to fulfil the agreement of sending James to Avignon. However, there came a related, but more pressing, matter for Portland to discuss with Louis and his ministers.

With William and Louis well aware that the eventual death of Carlos II would result in war, they took measures to find a diplomatic settlement. William was particularly keen for Portland to broker an agreement now that his army had been decimated, while Louis had kept his huge army intact. Portland became deeply engaged in secret diplomatic activity between France, England and the United Provinces. He returned to England in the summer, having completed the groundwork for an understanding with Louis. Fortunately, Matthew Prior remained at the embassy, continuing his intelligence work for Portland's replacement as ambassador, the Earl of Jersey. Portland had then travelled to Holland with William to complete the negotiations which culminated in the Treaty of The Hague in October 1698. This treaty nominated Emperor Leopold's grandson, the 6-year-old Joseph Ferdinand of Bavaria, as heir to the Spanish empire, including the Spanish Netherlands. The Emperor's younger son, Archduke Charles, would take over the Duchy of Milan. Louis would receive Naples and Sicily. This agreement had one serious drawback. It had been signed only by Louis for France, and William as king of England, Scotland and Ireland and as Stadtholder of the United Provinces. Neither Spain nor the Emperor had been consulted.

The Spanish court had two rival factions, one favouring France and the other the Empire. When news of the secret treaty leaked back to Spain, both factions were furious to hear of the proposed break up of their empire. However, the faction of Carlos II's German wife, Maria Anna, was dominant and she bullied Carlos into publishing a will making Joseph Ferdinand of Bavaria heir to an undivided empire, and herself queen regent during his minority. This did not go down well with the Francophile faction of the Spanish court, but was naturally welcomed by Emperor Leopold. As if this had not complicated matters enough, Joseph Ferdinand died of smallpox in February 1699.

Louis and William then came up with a second partition treaty which was signed just by them in London in November. This allowed

France to have Naples, Sicily and Milan, but made Archduke Charles heir to the Spanish throne and its overseas territories. The Spanish were equally annoyed by this latest carve up of their empire. By then, bread riots and Carlos II's dislike of his queen had brought a change to the balance of power in the Spanish court. With the help of French money, the Francophile group under the Bishop of Toledo became dominant and Carlos was persuaded to amend his will making Louis XIV's younger grandson, Philip Duke of Anjou, heir to an undivided Spanish empire. Charles at last died on 1 November 1700, just a month after this new will. A few days later, Louis proclaimed Philip of Anjou king of Spain. The Treaty of London was forgotten, as the prospect of uniting France and the Spanish empire under a Bourbon dynasty was too much for Louis to resist.

While William had been engaging in what had become fruitless efforts to avoid war, changes had been occurring in his government. Sunderland had continued as an advisor to William as Lord Chamberlain, but had retired through ill health in December 1697. Shrewsbury became Lord Chamberlain in December 1698 and was replaced by James Vernon as secretary for the southern department. Vernon was moved to the northern department in May the next year and then back to the southern department in June 1700. Portland had been unable to stand William's favouritism of Keppel and had broken with William, resigned all offices and gone into retirement. In doing so the king lost a very close friend and the services of his informal but effective head of internal security. It was fortunate that William had an experienced intelligencer like Vernon at the heart of his government over this period. That said, William, as always, kept all decision making to himself and treated Vernon more like a clerk than his secretary. In any case, despite Vernon's efforts, there was little of intelligence interests during this period. France and England were at peace and Louis and William had been trying to cooperate over the Spanish succession.

As far as James was concerned, Louis was allowing him to remain at St Germain and had arranged for him to have some financial handouts, such as 500 pistols to ease the plight of unemployed Irish soldiers to which his brother, the Duke of Orleans, had added a further 200. James had been inspired by the severe Benedictine monastery of la Trappe where the monks carried out extreme penitence and longed for death so they could be united with God. James spent more and more time in his chapel as a suffering penitent. Louis and other highly devout members of his court regarded James's religious devotion with awe and respect. For most of James's own courtiers his behaviour was less than inspiring. However, there were two causes for hope. James might have become an ailing 67-year-old religious obsessive, but his son, James Francis Edward, was developing into a promising Prince of Wales. James Francis Edward was 12 years old in 1700 and was a good looking, lively boy who had become a brave and accomplished horseman. Jacobites could see that the future of their cause rested with him and that future looked all the brighter when comparing him with Princes Anne's ailing son the Duke of Gloucester.

The other cause for encouragement was the situation in Scotland where William had become particularly unpopular. The reason for this was that in 1695 the Scottish parliament had established a company to trade with Africa, the Americas and the Indies, and this had been granted a charter by William. The creation of the company had come at a period in Scottish history called the 'Seven ill years', in which there was an economic slump and severe crop failures. The new company offered a beacon of hope in a particularly dark period. This hope led to an investment frenzy in the company with great lords mortgaging their estates and ordinary citizens committing all their savings. Eventually, the company decided to put its whole effort into establishing a colony at Darien in the Panama isthmus of Central America. There was every hope of finding gold and its position meant that it could create a highly prosperous carrying trade, linking the Atlantic with the Pacific as an overland Panama Canal. In July 1699, four company ships left Leith with 1,200 colonists on board and later landed in Darien and set up a fort. When news of their landing reached Scotland there was general rejoicing with bells ringing, bonfires lighted and stories circulated of the colony finding gold and prospering even beyond the high hopes of its investors.

The problem with this venture was that Darien was a Spanish possession and William was in the midst of negotiating with Louis about the Spanish succession. Spain was angry to hear of the settlement, as was Louis, who was eyeing up the Spanish Empire. In the United Provinces, the Dutch East India Company were also up in arms about a rival. In May 1699 William issued a proclamation denying the colony and banning the governors of all English colonies in the West Indies from giving any assistance to Darien. Louis sent similar orders to French colonies and Spain prepared to send a force to remove the Scots. This was the last straw for the colony which was already failing through disease, lack of supplies and the discovery that the land route between the two oceans was almost impassable because of mountains and forest. They decided to abandon the colony but this was not realised in Scotland, and in August 1699, four ships carrying 1,300 eager colonists set sail for Darien. When they arrived they found the colony deserted and the huts burned. A little later they were forced to surrender to a Spanish landing force.

A few starving survivors eventually reached Jamaica and New York, and word of the disaster was sent to Scotland. The news was a devastating blow to the 1,400 hopeful investors. Among the investors were about thirty-five peers, including the Dukes of Hamilton and Queensbury who invested £3,000 each, then there were ordinary citizens and city corporations, such as Edinburgh, Glasgow and Perth, which together invested £8,000.[1] The full impact of the loss stretched far beyond the 1,400 individual shareholders. The first reaction to the news was astonishment and disbelief, which turned to desperation and was then replaced by anger. This anger was directed against the foreigner William, who was unfairly blamed for bringing about the colony's failure at the behest of the Dutch East India Company. The anger increased when the Scottish Lords begged William to call the Scots parliament, but when he did so he let it sit for only one week; he was more interested in returning to Holland.

Ireland was firmly under the garrison of 12,000 English troops, and James had lost considerable support in England following the assassination plot. The anti-Williamite fury over the Darien colony meant that Scotland became the best hope for an eventual Jacobite uprising. James saw this and considered exploiting the situation by getting Spain to support a force of Jacobites landing in the colony and then to recognise him as king. Nothing came of this rather wild scheme, but in a more practical initiative, James recalled Melville to write to his Jacobite contacts in Scotland to rekindle their enthusiasm for the cause. James also appreciated that for an uprising in Scotland to succeed, he needed to encourage as much as possible of the army in Scotland to follow him. He had special uniform buttons made which could be opened with a screw to reveal a tiny scroll bearing the initials of the rallying call: 'God bless King James and prosper his interests.' These apparently innocuous buttons were smuggled into Scotland and secretly distributed to trusted Jacobites in the army who would encourage others to use them as a replacement for one of their regimental buttons. It is not known whether or not the buttons were distributed, nor whether if they were, they had any effect. What is clear is that the long term, outcome of the failure of the Darien scheme turned Scotland into the best hope for the Jacobite movement.

Jacobite morale was further raised in July 1700 when Anne's only son William, Duke of Gloucester, died of scarlet fever. He was only 11 and she and her husband were stricken with grief as was William, who was in Holland at the time. Anne was already in a bad way, she had severe gout and had to be carried or pushed in a wheelchair, which was becoming increasingly difficult because her sedentary life and ravenous appetite had made her obese. With tears running down her spotty, red, double-chinned face, and foot tied in a poultice, she made a sad spectacle. She had given birth to a stillborn son six months earlier, but after at least seventeen pregnancies, aged 45 and in poor health, she was most unlikely to produce a living heir. This meant that she was the only remaining successor to the throne under the 1689 Bill of Rights. Suddenly the whole Protestant succession came into question and it appeared that James Francis Edward might become heir on the death of Anne.

James seized on this opportunity. He put St Germain into mourning for the Duke of Gloucester, who was after all his grandson, and did all he could to remind potential followers in England that James Francis Edward was the rightful heir. He ordered 7,000 medals to be struck bearing his son's head, which were smuggled to England for distribution to Jacobites and potential sympathisers.[2] The prospect of James Francis Edward becoming heir led some ambitious English aristocrats to come to France to pay their duty to James, who was staying with Louis at Fontainebleau. Matthew Prior's informants soon heard of this, and so the new ambassador to Paris, the Earl of Manchester, made a very public visit to Fontainebleau. The aristocrats then beat a hasty retreat back to England in the hopes that Manchester had not seen them and reported their disloyalty to King William. A different type of visitor to James was James Graham, brother of Viscount Preston, and one of the remaining Jacobite leaders in England. He had an audience with James and made a plea for James to allow his son to be brought up as a Protestant so that he might be recognised as heir to the throne. Needless to say James refused, and this opportunity was lost.

William was swift to remove any doubt about a Protestant succession. King James I's daughter Elizabeth had married the Elector Palatine and had thirteen children, the best known of which was Charles I's nephew and cavalry leader Prince Rupert. By 1701 all thirteen were either dead or converted to Catholicism except for the twelfth, Sophia, who was married to the Elector of Hanover. The 74-year-old Sophia was William's choice for the succession and she had travelled to see him on hearing of Gloucester's death; they agreed that she should be pronounced heir if Anne died without children. This was fine, but it also needed to be agreed by parliament, which was distracted by vicious in-fighting between Whigs and Tories. This included unsuccessful attempts to impeach leading Whigs who had been the king's closest advisers, such as Portland, Burnet and Somers. After several months of parliamentary chaos, the Act of Settlement was eventually passed the next year declaring Sophia and her Protestant heirs the successor to Anne. Scotland, still burning with anger against William, insisted that it would choose its own monarch if Anne died childless.

During this turbulent parliamentary session there was confusion over how to react to Spain and France proclaiming Philip of Anjou king of Spain. William greatly distrusted Louis but did not want war and hoped for a peaceful outcome, so did the Tories and the States General of the Dutch Republic. However, by February 1701 it became clear that Louis was seeking allies to strengthen his position. The Elector of Bavaria had already sided with Louis, this was followed by Swabia and then Milan and Mantua not only recognising Philip as king of Spain, but accepting the stationing of French troops. This was too much for Emperor Leopold who gathered forces to protect his possessions in Italy. At much the same time, the States General realised the Dutch Republic was under threat when French troops took over the garrison of the frontier forts in the Spanish Netherlands in contravention of the Treaty of Ryswick.

The English merchants feared that Louis's takeover of the frontier forts meant that France could control the Scheldt and be able use Antwerp and Ostend to blockade British trade. In the space of a couple of months Louis's actions changed the approach of Europe's rulers from seeking peaceful solutions, to preparation for war. The Whigs and Tories in parliament for once united and voted that William should assemble a 10,000-strong force in the Netherlands, and while still attempting an accommodation with Louis, seek allies among the former Grand Alliance. In July, William left for the United Provinces and sent Marlborough as a commander of the assembling British force and Ambassador Extraordinary to The Hague. William had begun to rehabilitate Marlborough soon after his reconciliation with Anne following Mary's death. The king was well aware of Marlborough's former connections with St Germain but felt that Marlborough's spirit of self-interest would ensure his loyalty. William had made Marlborough governor of the ill-fated Duke of Gloucester and restored him to the Privy Council, but placing him back in command of troops showed that he was at last trusted.

William was delighted to escape England and its fractious parliament. Although his spirits had been lifted by returning home to Holland, the States General were dismayed to see how much he had changed since he last addressed them. He had become a slow walking, hunched and haggard figure. For all that, he threw himself into preparations for war and concluded a pact between England, the United Provinces and Austria, recreating the Grand Alliance. William was not the only member of his family whose heath was failing. In March 1701 James had suffered a stroke while saying mass in his chapel at St Germain. A few weeks later he became partially paralysed down his right side, but recovered enough to travel to Bourbon to take the waters. Louis had paid the expenses for the visit and instructed all the mayors on the route to Bourbon to accord James the honours due to a king. On returning to St Germain in September James collapsed again, took to his bed for what was to be a long drawn-out period of dying.

Louis showed true compassion and kindness for his cousin. Louis liked James, for all his failings, and had deep respect for his religious zeal. He made three visits to James's bedside. On the second visit, Mary of Modena had begged Louis to acknowledge James Francis Edward as king of England, Scotland and Ireland when James died. Louis considered this and on the next visit entered James's bedchamber and made a speech to the dying James and the assembled courtiers which ended: 'I will take your family into my protection and will treat your son in the same manner I have treated you and acknowledge him as he will be then King of England.'[3] At this, the assembled company gave a spontaneous shout of 'God save the King!'

Three days later, on 16 September, James died of a brain haemorrhage. He was 67. To some, his death brought an end to an arbitrary, papist ruler who was rightly removed from the throne. To others, it was the sad demise of a brave soldier and devout Catholic monarch who believed in religious toleration, but was usurped through the treachery of his family and Whig aristocracy, then rose above this tragedy with a dignity and saint-like piety. He may have been a mixture of both.

Certainly Louis held the latter view and proved to be a man of his word. Immediately after James's death he had James Francis Edward proclaimed as James III of England and Ireland and James VIII of Scotland. As James Francis Edward was only 13 years old, his mother, Queen Mary of Modena, was declared regent, but the government in exile continued to be run by Middleton. Louis immediately began to treat James Francis Edward with all the courtesy due to a king when he visited Versailles. The young man was soon recognised by Spain, the Papal States and Modena as the *de jure* sovereign of England, Scotland and Ireland. Suddenly the Jacobite position was transformed. James had become an elderly religious extremist, presiding over a gloomy debt-ridden court with all hope of regaining his throne utterly extinguished. Suddenly a young and promising Prince of Wales was recognised as king by the rulers of two of the greatest powers in Europe who were in a position to support his claim with money and military manpower.

Jacobites could rejoice that Louis had kept his word to their dying king. In contrast, the English were cursing the same Louis who had broken his word given in the Peace of Ryswick. When William returned to England from Holland on 4 November he was welcomed back with bonfires and cheers by a country up in arms about Louis's duplicity. William decided to dissolve parliament in the hope that a new Commons would be Whig dominated and provide the financial resources to combat Louis. When he opened the new parliament on 31 December he found that it had returned a roughly equal number of Whigs and Tories. Both parties were furious with Louis and immediately sent expressions of loyalty to William. The Commons voted to impeach James Francis Edward and this was wholeheartedly supported by the Lords, who wanted to go a stage further and also impeach Queen Mary of Modena for becoming the Jacobite regent. Mary's impeachment was defeated in the Commons, but parliament was united in voting the huge sum of £650,000 in preparation for war with France to be raised from a loan at 6 per cent interest and tax on land, and income tax of 4*s* in the pound.

Another matter was concerning parliament: that the Scottish parliament was in a near state of rebellion. The failure of the Darien

Colony had ruined the mercantile classes, disaffected the aristocracy and the £400,000 loss threatened to bankrupt the country. It had coincided with the appallingly cold weather of the 'Little Ice Age'. This had caused harvest failures in 1695, 1696 and 1698–9, in which about 200,000 people abandoned their homes in a forlorn search of work or charity, and 5 to 10 per cent of the population of the country died of starvation.[4] It was thought that a way of pacifying the Scots was to dissolve the Scottish parliament and for England to accept some of the financial burden by uniting the two countries. This received general approval and the House of Commons began drafting a bill.

William's grandfather, James I of England and VI of Scotland, had united the crowns and hoped to unite the governments of both nations, but this had been opposed by parliament. When William came to the throne, he too wanted to establish a single parliament for Great Britain, but that had got nowhere and been lost to more urgent business. He was, therefore, delighted to find that parliament was enthusiastic about the union. In fact, he undertook to address the Lords himself to support the bill. Unfortunately, William was unable to attend owing to a riding accident.

William had been suffering for some time from headaches and shivering fits, but had continued his routine of Saturday hunting. On 20 February 1702, he broke his collarbone after being thrown from his horse when it stumbled as he rode near Richmond Park. He was taken to Hampton Court where the bone was set, but then insisted on returning to Kensington Palace. William's collarbone became displaced during the bumpy coach journey and needed to be reset on arrival. By 4 March he was well enough to take a walk in the Kensington Palace Gallery, but then became so weak that he was unable to write. In order for him to give assent to the bills passed by parliament a special stamp of his signature was made and this was placed on the Bill of attainder against James Francis Edward, thus legally declaring him a traitor and removing all his property and titles. It was now clear that he was dying and he met death with his normal courage and composure.

In fact, as deaths go, it was a good one. Albermarle rushed back from The Hague and brought with him the welcome news that all was proceeding well in forming the combined English/Dutch army. On 8 March William sent for his estranged close friend, Portland. When Portland arrived William was too weak to speak, but took his hand and held it to his heart. William died at 8 am in his fifty-second year, reunited with his oldest friend and with his young friend, Albermarle, at hand. He breathed his last, secure in the knowledge that his lifetime struggle for Protestantism against the ambitions of Louis would continue. After his death the surgeons established that the actual cause of death had been adhesion of the lung cause by his fall, followed by pneumonia. They also discovered a black ribbon round his neck in which was stitched a gold ring and a lock of his wife Mary's hair. The cold, aloof William was sentimental enough not to have forgotten the love of his life.

There was no sentimentality shown by the pushing and shoving courtiers who crowded the ante-rooms awaiting news of William's death. The moment death was pronounced there was then an unseemly rush to St James's to be among the first to congratulate Anne on acceding to the throne. The actual transmission of monarchy went very smoothly. The Privy Council took the oath of allegiance and Anne confirmed that all office holders should remain in their appointments until further notice. Of course it was well known that Anne was strongly influenced by Lady Sarah Marlborough and a staunch supporter of the Tories, so changes were expected. This was manifest when Anne went in state to the House of Lords on 11 March with her husband Prince George at her side, Sarah immediately behind, and Marlborough carrying the Sword of State. Soon after, Marlborough was elevated to an earl, made Captain General of the Army, Master General of Ordnance and a Knight of the Garter. The longsuffering Prince George, who had never been granted any office under William, was at last given his reward. He became Admiral of the Fleet. The fact that he was unacquainted with matters maritime was not considered an impediment to the appointment.

The fat, red-faced Anne did not look very majestic when she addressed her first parliament, but that was no matter. She was indeed a fat, red-faced monarch, but she was a Protestant monarch and what was more, she was an English Protestant monarch. Lords and Commons were more concerned about what their new English Protestant monarch said than with her appearance. Anne spoke extremely well. Her uncle Charles II had insisted that she was given elocution lessons as a young woman and these came into their own. She eloquently attacked the grasping ambition of King Louis and his support of the Jacobite Popish pretender prince. She also declared her commitment to the Anglican Church, and in a snide reference to William, emphasised that she was English and would always put her country first. The speech went down very well, she received the resounding backing of a loyal parliament.

Next there was the matter of Anne selecting her new government. She appointed the Tory Baron Godolphin as her principal minister and First Lord of the Treasury. This had been on the recommendation of Marlborough who had long been a close friend of Godolphin and knew him to have been a particularly effective Treasurer under William. As Captain General of an army about to go to war, Marlborough wanted a friend and ally running the government and making sure there was funding for the campaign. In May, Vernon was dismissed and Sir Charles Hedges was made secretary of state for the north and the Earl of Nottingham returned as secretary for the south. Nottingham was an old hand at being a secretary, having served in the northern department from 1689 to 1690 and then in the southern department from 1690 to 1693. He was, therefore, in a good position to resume his duties as government lead for intelligence.

It might seem that because Anne's accession took place without protest and received the strong support of parliament, there was little threat to monarch or country. On 4 March, however, England, the Empire, and the United Provinces declared war against France, Spain and their allies, who recognised the Pretender as King James III and VIII. Should Louis get the upper hand in the forthcoming war, then he might provide James Francis Edward with a force strong enough to enable him take the throne. Ireland was firmly under Protestant rule, Jacobites in England were in disarray, but the Scottish problem had not gone away. A Scotland suffering severe economic hardship and blaming its woes on the English government was an obvious breeding ground for Jacobite sympathies. Nottingham would have plenty to occupy his intelligencers in combating the combined French/Jacobite threat.

Chapter 12

The Spanish Succession
1702–14

'As I know my own heart to be entirely English, I can sincerely assure you that there is not anything that you can expect or desire of me which I shall not be ready to do for the happiness and prosperity of England, and you will always find me a strict religious observer of my word.'

Extract from Queen Anne's speech to parliament 11 March 1702

William's death had brought Jacobite rejoicing. They thought it an amusing irony that the horse William was riding when he fell was White Sorrell, the horse confiscated from Sir John Fenwick, who had received almost martyr status since his execution. Great mirth was caused by the story that Sorrell had thrown William after stumbling over a mole hill. For many years Jacobites would raise a toast to 'the little gentleman in black velvet'. With William gone there was now a hope that it would be easier for Louis to launch an invasion of England on behalf to their newly recognised King James III and VIII. Queen Anne might even nominate him as her heir. It had been noted that following William's death, Anne had worn black mourning but made it plain that it was not for William, but for the loss of her own father. These were exciting times when anything might be possible.

Mary Beatrice was regent for James Francis Edward's minority, but had never particularly liked Middleton, the secretary of state. It had been one of James's dying wishes that Middleton converted to Catholicism, and he did so in a bid to win Mary's favour. Mary, who had become almost as religiously obsessive as her husband, decided that James merited sainthood. Indeed, there were many who had been moved by

James's deep devotion and considered him a suitable candidate. James's body parts were distributed as holy relics to various religious locations. His heart went to the Convent of La Chaillot, the entrails were divided between the church of St Germain and the English College at St Omer. The body was taken in state at night to the Church of the English Benedictines in Paris, with hundreds lining the route and dropping to their knees as the cortege passed.

It was only ten days after James's death before the first miracle was reported. This was when the Bishop of Autun was cured of an eye infection while saying a mass for the repose of the dead king's soul. Soon eighteen other people claimed they were healed of various ailments having either visited one of James's shrines, or prayed for his intercession. These were swiftly recorded to make a case for canonisation, but Vatican bureaucracy and a new papal policy of severely limiting canonisation meant it never happened. Despite this, the miracles continued and for nearly twenty years, many devout Catholics made pilgrimages to his shrines and sought his intercession for their healing. The piety of James's later life and general recognition of his saintly qualities, may have been an inspiration to Jacobite Catholics. This was not the case for Jacobite Protestants who had no time for saints, relics and miraculous healings. With the Court at St Germain revelling in such Popish practices and Middleton's conversion to Catholicism, it showed that there was little chance of 'King James III' (who in time became known as 'the Old Pretender') being acceptable to English Anglicans.

Back in England, Anne's succession went smoothly and her coronation took place on 23 April. Parliament voted money for the war against France, and Marlborough left to lead the armies of the Grand Alliance. The War of the Spanish Succession that was to dominate the reign had begun. Marlborough began the great period of his career in which his charm, diplomacy and outstanding military ability was used to bring the disparate and quarrelsome states of the alliance into to a coherent force to challenge the great armies of Louis. By the end of the year his efforts brought the first of many allied successes, with the capture of Leige and a dukedom as his reward.

Anne's reign appeared to have got off to a promising start and even the discontented Scots seemed to have accepted her as their queen without demonstrations of any outward resistance. Under the surface, however, sedition was brewing among some of the powerful nobility. John

Hamilton, Lord Belhaven, had been one of those who invited William to govern Scotland and had become a member of the Scottish Privy Council. He had also been a director of the disastrous Darien Scheme, lost his £1,000 investment and blamed England for the failure. He travelled to St Germain to make the offer of helping to raise rebellion in Scotland for James Francis Edward, if the young prince would agree to convert to Protestantism. This plan would have appealed to Middleton, but a conversion was completely rejected by Mary of Modena, the regent. So that was the end of that, and also of Middleton's hopes of securing James Francis Edward's return to the throne by consent of his subjects rather than French might.

Mary Beatrice had never much cared for Middleton, even after his recent conversion to Catholicism. She favoured James Drummond, Duke of Perth, the elder brother of the Earl of Melfort, who was pressing for a French invasion. James Drummond, when Earl of Perth, had been James II's Chancellor of Scotland who had been caught while trying to escape to France then imprisoned as a Jacobite suspect. He was released in 1693 on condition of banishment, after which he had made his way to St Germain. There he rapidly rose to become Guardian to James Francis Edward, then a duke, and finally chamberlain and principal adviser to Mary Beatrice. It became the policy of St Germain to try to engineer an uprising in Scotland supported by a French invasion. Soon a plan for such a scheme was to be put to the exiled court by a new arrival from Scotland.

In December 1703, Queen Anne informed parliament that intelligence had revealed a Jacobite conspiracy, but she could say no more at that stage. The House of Lords decided to investigate it themselves and began to discover the murky dealings of Simon Fraser, 11th Lord Lovat. There is insufficient space to give justice to the extent of Lovat's perfidy. Suffice to say that he would stop at nothing to inherit through his father the title and lands of his uncle, the 9th Lord Lovat, chief of Clan Fraser. The 9th Lord's heir was his daughter Amelia, so when the lord died, Fraser tried to marry her, but she fled under the protection of her mother's family, the Atholl Murrays. The Atholl Murrays chose a husband for her, but Fraser had him captured and threatened with death if he did not break off the engagement (a gallows was built outside the man's cell). Having failed to marry Amelia, Fraser forcibly married her mother, his aunt, the dowager Lady Lovat instead. He ordered bagpipes played throughout the ceremony and subsequent rape to drown her screaming.[1]

In fact, this did not help his inheritance prospects, as Lady Lovat was the daughter of the powerful Marquis of Atholl, and he, and his son, John Murray, Lord Tullibardine, threw their weight behind Amelia's claim to the Lovat estate. Fraser became an implacable enemy of the Atholls and illegally took the title of 'Lord Lovat' when his father died. There was little chance of Fraser confirming his right to the Lovat estate through the law, as this would be opposed by Tullibardine, whose father had died and whom Queen Anne had appointed Keeper of the Privy Seal and made Duke of Atholl. Fraser had some 3,000 followers from his clan and used them to attack the Atholls in every way he could, including ambushing a force of 600 Atholl men and government soldiers near Inverness and forcing them to surrender.

Although Fraser had been pronounced a rebel, he obtained the support of the Earl of Argyll, chief of Clan Campbell, who disliked the Atholls and interceded with William III to obtain him a pardon. The pardon granted him his Lovat title, but the Duke of Atholl controlled the judiciary and not only refused to give him the Lovat estate, but had him proclaimed an outlaw for not coming to trial on a charge of rape. On the advice of Argyll, Fraser decided to go to France to seek support from St Germain. In order to display his Jacobite credentials he converted to Catholicism and soon wormed his way into the confidence of Drummond and Mary Beatrice. Fraser was not without charm; even his reluctant wife eventually came to quite like him – until he married two more times without troubling to divorce her that is. He used all his guile and charm to present Mary with a plan for a Scottish uprising.

Fraser claimed that he could raise 12,000 Highlanders in rebellion against Queen Anne if the French could land 5,000 soldiers at Dundee and a further 500 at Fort William, who would link up with the Highlanders, take Edinburgh, and then march south to London. This seemed very promising and the plan was put to King Louis, who agreed to it in principle. However, Middleton had doubts about the level of support which could be raised in the Highlands and it was decided that Fraser should return to Scotland accompanied by Captain John Murray to confirm just how many Scottish Jacobites would commit to an uprising. The two set off with Murray visiting Lowland Jacobite peers, and Lovat the Jacobite peers in the Highlands. Both carried with them unaddressed letters from Mary Beatrice to Jacobite leaders asking for their support. Neither Fraser nor Murray found there was much appetite for rebellion and Fraser then went to James Douglas, Marquis of Queensbury, the secretary of state for Scotland, knowing him to hate his rival the Duke of Atholl. Fraser accused Atholl of being a Jacobite conspirator and as proof, he showed one of the letters from Mary of Modena in which Fraser had added Atholl's initials as the addressee. Queensbury believed the story and instructed Fraser to return to St Germain to gather more evidence against Atholl and gave him a passport with a false name to facilitate the journey.

Fraser returned to France delighted to have improved his chances of claiming Lovat lands, having virtually convinced the secretary of state that his great enemy the Duke of Athol was a Jacobite conspirator. On arriving at St Germain he falsely reported that there was strong support for a Jacobite rising in the Highlands and that the French invasion should go ahead. At this point his scheme rapidly unravelled. Robert Ferguson, the inveterate schemer who had changed from a Radical to a Jacobite, got wind of Fraser's conspiracy and informed the Duke of Atholl, who then informed the queen, with the result that Queensbury was obliged to resign as secretary of state. News of Fraser's treachery soon reached France and Louis ordered him to be sent to the Bastille; he remained there and other French prisons until 1715. The investigation by the House of Lords discovered that Fraser's Jacobite plot had been little more than the result of a clan feud over the Lovat estate. Nevertheless, although this 'plot' turned out to be a non-event, it did demonstrate Louis's preparedness to deploy an invasion force to Scotland if he thought the Scots themselves would rise up in rebellion.

As we have seen the Scots were not yet ready to rebel, but their grievances against the English government remained and it only needed an additional cause for complaint to increase the likelihood of an uprising. On the other hand, England remained free from any potential Jacobite threat. This did not mean that harmony reigned. The Whigs and Tories continued to struggle for power, and the Lords and Commons were clashing with each other. The Marlboroughs were completely in the ascendant with the queen. This caused them to be attacked by the envious, including members of his own Tory party, and resulted in the Duke of Marlborough changing his allegiance to the Whigs. Apart from the jockeying for power at court and within the government, the period was dominated by the war of the Spanish Succession. Archduke Charles of Austria had proclaimed himself king of Spain with the support of the

Grand Alliance and had landed in Portugal in the hopes of marching on Spain to overthrow Louis XIV's grandson who had become Philip V of Spain. In the summer of 1704 the Franco Bavarian army threatened to take Vienna, but was defeated by Marlborough at the Battle of Blenheim, resulting in Bavaria making peace with the Grand Alliance. There was no major change in the military situation during the next year, but in 1706 Marlborough's forces defeated the French at the Battle of Ramillies and took possession of the Spanish Netherlands for Archduke Charles.

The peers of Scotland remained restless and had been incensed that the English parliament had voted for the Hanovarian succession in the Act of Settlement without any consultation with Scotland. The Scottish response to this came in 1703 when Lord Belhaven persuaded the Scottish parliament to pass the Act of Security, in which the estates of Scotland would choose their own sovereign on the death of Queen Anne, making it unlikely that they would select a Hanoverian. The Act was denied royal assent by the Lord High Commissioner, the Marquis of Queensbury. This infuriated the Scottish parliament who refused to pay taxes or provide troops for the war unless it was passed. The Act, therefore, was given royal assent, but the English government then responded by passing the Alien Act in early 1705. The Act stated that unless the Scottish parliament either repealed the Act of Settlement, or accepted union with England by December 1705, all Scots in England would be regarded as aliens (by this time many Scots peers had estates in England) and tax would be imposed on all exports to England. This was so great a threat that the Scots gave way and agreed to begin negotiations for uniting the two kingdoms, which led to the repeal of the Alien Act.

The English government was determined to do everything to bring about a united kingdom and so guarantee the Hanoverian succession. The Scottish commissioners were appointed by the queen to ensure they supported the succession and the considerable sum of £20,000, and offers of positions were used to bribe members of the Scottish parliament into agreeing a union. The largest overall bribe was the offer to pay £232,884 5s 0d[2] compensation with 5 per cent interest to shareholders in the Darien scheme, which included virtually all the ruling families. Some peers, such as the Dukes of Hamilton, Atholl, and Lords Annandale and Belhaven, were prepared to accept a federation with England, but completely opposed a union. They were backed by hundreds of citizens who came out on the streets in their support, but to little effect. Their calls for members of parliament to display patriotism could not compete with the allure of English gold, and the Act of Union was eventually passed in March 1707. Scotland and England became one country called the 'United Kingdom', with a single parliament at which the Scots would send representatives to both houses.

Queen Anne had been a strong supporter of the Union, but that view was not shared by most English Tories. In Scotland there was considerable anger about their loss of nationhood and the disgraceful way in which the English government had brought it about. Melfort exploited the anti-English sentiment by writing to the Duke of Hamilton saying that 'King James III' would cancel the Act of Union if he regained the Scottish throne. This became generally known and the many who objected to the Act of Union were drawn to a Jacobite restoration as the best means of reclaiming independent nationhood.

While the protracted negotiations for the Act of Union had been taking place, there had been changes in the English government. In May 1704, Robert Harley replaced Sir Charles Hedges as secretary for the north and Hedges was moved to the southern department. Queen Anne favoured the Tories and was pleased to have both her secretaries from that party. Someone who was not happy with this was Sarah, Duchess of Marlborough, who was a staunch Whig, and was highly irritated that the queen had made the appointment against her advice. Sarah was the queen's closest confidante, but Anne was beginning to find that her friend was becoming imperious and bullying in her manner towards her. For all that, Sarah's influence remained strong and she had Hedges replaced as secretary for the south by her son–in–law, the Whig Charles Spencer, 3rd Earl of Sunderland. Anne detested the arrogant Sunderland and blamed Sarah for forcing him upon her. Godolphin, like the Duke of Marlborough, had become a Whig to retain support for the war and with their influence, and that of Sarah, Anne reluctantly appointed senior Whigs to her government, including making Baron Somers Lord President; the Earl of Wharton, Lord Lieutenant of Ireland; and the Earl of Orford, First Lord of the Admiralty. Sarah, Duchess of Marlborough, remained triumphant, but she had not noticed that her demure cousin Abigail Hill, a mere bedchamber woman, was well on her way to supplanting her in the queen's affections.

With such anti-English feeling in Scotland, Melfort decided to send an agent over to meet sympathetic Scottish lords. He chose Colonel

Nathaniel Hook, a highly experienced agent. Hook had been an agent for Monmouth in London during his rebellion, then fought under Viscount Dundee in 1689 and had subsequently served as a Jacobite agent in Ireland, Flanders and Scotland. Hook travelled to Scotland in 1707, and having met various dissident lords, returned to France to report to Louis's minister, Michel Chamillard. Like many agents he was prone to exaggeration and said that the Earl of Errol, and many Scottish peers, would rise to support 'James III' if he landed with French support. Louis was convinced and agreed to provide troops and ships for an expedition which would divert English troops away from Marlborough's forces in the war. In March 1708, thirty French vessels carrying 6,000 troops set off from Dunkirk bound for Scotland. The supreme commander was Admiral Comte Claude de Forbin, who had been reprimanded for telling Louis plainly that he did not think the expedition had any hope of success. In the event it was went worse than Forbin imagined.

The Pretender, now an enthusiastic 19-year-old who was to join the expedition, caught measles and the sailing had to be delayed until his recovery. As a result, there was time for English and Dutch agents in Dunkirk to report back intelligence on the invasion preparations. The British government was able to put in place defensive preparations, the most important of which was ordering Admiral Bing to blockade Dunkirk to prevent the French from sailing. This manoeuvre failed because gales blew the English fleet off station and the French invasion force took to sea with James Francis Edward on board. Forbin's ships reached the proposed landing site near the Firth of Forth, but Bing's ships caught up with them and took *The Salisbury* (formerly an English ship captured by the French) capturing five companies of French troops. With the English fleet now upon him and bad weather preventing a landing, Forbin decided to abort the invasion and sailed his ships around the north of Scotland, passed Ireland and back to Dunkirk. A very disappointed and seasick James Francis Edward returned to France, no closer to regaining his crown.

A month before the planned invasion, Charles Fleming had been sent to Scotland to coordinate the rebellion with leading Jacobites. The plan was to proclaim James III king and raise forces as soon as the French fleet was seen, then seize money from Edinburgh Castle to finance the rebellion. In the event none of this happened. Apart from a few lairds in Stirlingshire rising, no Jacobites stirred. This was perhaps as well because the commander-in-chief of Scotland, the Earl of Leven, had few troops and little ammunition. Had the French landed their 5,000 soldiers with James Francis Edward, then many Jacobites would have probably rallied to his standard and might have taken Edinburgh, but that was not to be. Instead there was government retribution. Although there had been little or no uprising, Leven arrested twenty-one Scottish nobles including the Duke of Hamilton and had them taken to London. Habeas Corpus was suspended but most were eventually released, although Lord Belhaven was to die in prison a few months later.

In England the threat of invasion had caused alarm and led to Catholics being ordered to remove themselves ten miles from London, resulting in ten battalions being transferred from Ostend to England. It soon became clear that the French fleet was retreating back to France and the ten battalions were able to return to Ostend and make a useful contribution to Marlborough's victory at Oudenande. All was to become quiet at St Germain. The Duke of Berwick was off fighting for Charles V in Spain and the Pretender decided that rather than hang around his court he would burnish his royal credentials by gaining military experience in the French army. With the two brothers absent on military duties, Jacobite scheming was on hold.

London life soon returned to normal with Sarah Marlborough and the Godolphin/Marlborough Whig Junta in the ascendant and supporting the continuation of the war. Earlier in the year the Whigs had managed to remove their Tory rival Harley from government. The opportunity arose when treasonous correspondence was intercepted in Holland between one of Harley's clerks, William Gregg, and Louis's secretary for war, Michel Chamillard. Gregg was employed on intelligence and one of his tasks was to read correspondence sent to France by French prisoners held in England. This included letters from Marshal Tallard, who had been captured at Blenheim and regularly wrote to Chamillard. Gregg decided to write to Chamillard to offer his services as an agent and, to show his potential value, attached a draft letter from the queen to the Emperor. He placed his letter and the queen's draft inside one of Tallard's letters to Chamillard. Gregg was arrested, examined, tried, convicted and later hanged. During his examination Gregg had described the laxity in Harley's office, 'that all papers of state lay so carelessly about the office, that everyone belonging to it, even door-keepers, might read them all.'[3] Although criticising his employer's careless security, Gregg refused to implicate Harley with the correspondence to France. But mud sticks.

Mud also stuck to Harley when, at much the same time, it was found that two of his informants, Valiere and Bara, who he employed as cross-Channel couriers, were in fact French double agents. They were arrested and it was discovered that they had been passing important information on British naval convoys to the French. The Whigs used this to imply that Harley might have condoned their action and that his loyalty was suspect. Marlborough and Godolphin informed the queen that they would resign if she kept Harley on as secretary of state. Other ministers also refused to serve with Harley and so the queen was reluctantly obliged to dismiss him. With Harley also went his friend, another Tory, Henry St John, the secretary for war. They were replaced by Whigs: Harley by Henry Boyle and St John by Robert Walpole.

The Whig ascendency, and with it parliamentary support for the war, was not to last. The queen wanted peace and disliked the party politics of the Whigs. She was also finding Sarah increasingly difficult and was developing a close relationship with Abigail Hill. Abigail married Samuel Masham, a gentleman of the bedchamber to Prince George, and Anne was present at the ceremony. Sarah only heard of her cousin's wedding after it had taken place and was furious that it had been kept from her. Anne had to put up with Sarah constantly attacking her rival Abigail and the more strident Sarah became, the more the queen appreciated Abigail's quiet and kind manner. In October 1708 Anne's beloved husband Prince George died. She was devastated. In the past the queen would have looked to Sarah for sympathy and support, but relations between them had soured. To Sarah's dismay, Anne turned for consolation to the attentive and considerate Abigail, now Mrs Masham. Sarah found herself more and more excluded by the queen. This would have been no more than the sad cooling of a close friendship had it not been for its political dimension.

Abigail was a Tory and Anne had always preferred the Tories to the Whigs, who had been rather forced upon her by Sarah because of their support for the war. Abigail was also a cousin of Robert Harley who was liked by Anne, despite having been forced to dismiss him. With Abigail's assistance, Harley became a frequent unofficial advisor to the queen, visiting her by the back stairs. Harley and his Tory party were pressing for peace, which is exactly what Anne felt the country needed, but which Godolphin, Marlborough and the Whigs would not countenance as they wanted to achieve a complete victory. The war was going badly for

Louis and the cost was driving France towards bankruptcy. He therefore put out feelers for peace, but the terms offered by the Grand Alliance were little more than a humiliating surrender. The war dragged on, to the consternation of Anne and the Tories. In 1709 Marlborough won the bloody Battle of Malplaquet, but at the cost of 20,000 allied dead. James Francis Edward fought in the battle and charged with Maison du Roi against the English redcoats. He displayed the bravery expected of a king, but it was at the expense of fighting against his own countrymen. Jacobites could not help feeling that this act made him appear more like a foreign prince rather than the true claimant to the British thrones.

The queen was dismayed by the level of casualties from the war (the carnage at Malplaquet was not to be exceeded until Borodino) and wanted peace, but hostilities continued into the next year, with Marlborough making slow progress against the French frontier forts in preparation for a breakthrough to Paris. However, Malplaquet was to be his last great victory as he was losing his power base at home. His wife Sarah's overbearing manner had not only lost the queen's confidence, but their deep friendship had turned to hatred and on 6 April 1710, they had a blazing row which irreconcilably terminated their relationship. Sarah was later dismissed from all appointments, removed from her St James's apartments and banned from court. Abigail had replaced her as Anne's favourite and she and Harley were the powers behind the throne. In June, Sunderland was turned out of office and replaced by the Tory William Legge, Earl of Dartmouth, and in August, Marlborough's friend and ally, Godolphin was dismissed as Lord Treasurer and replaced by Harley, who became Anne's principal minister. The next month Henry St John replaced Boyle as secretary for the north. The election of 1710/11 returned a large Tory majority to the Commons clamouring for peace, nevertheless the war still went on, supported by a small majority in the Lords. Harley ran a very successful pamphlet propaganda campaign to discredit Marlborough using the two great writers Jonathan Swift and Daniel Defoe. The result was that Marlborough was accused of embezzlement and on 30 December 1711 he was dismissed as commander-in-chief and from all other offices. The next day Harley persuaded the queen to create twelve new Tory peers (of which Abigail's husband was one) to give the Lords a majority in voting for peace negotiations with France.

The Tories were triumphant and able to press ahead with peace. Marlborough's replacement as commander-in-chief was the Tory Duke of Ormond, who was given instructions to avoid battles and not to take part in sieges. On top of this, 12,000 British soldiers were withdrawn from the Continent. Marlborough's work began to be undone during the protracted peace negotiations. In July 1712, Marshal Villars's French army defeated the Austrian/Dutch force at the Battle of Denain, after which the allies lost as much as they had gained in the previous three years. Louis having strengthened his negotiating position, the principal peace agreement between Britain and France was eventually signed in Utrecht in April 1713. Great Britain acknowledged Louis's grandson as King Charles V of Spain, but was given possession of Newfoundland, Nova Scotia, Gibraltar and Menorca and access to the valuable Asiento (slave trade between Africa and South America). These were sound gains, but Whigs felt that despite Marlborough having won the war, the Tories had lost the peace. Although the Tory party had got its way, cracks were appearing in its façade and had only just managed to hold together until the signing of the Treaty of Utrecht. The queen had made Harley Earl of Oxford, and St John, Viscount Bolingbroke. With Oxford becoming lazy and drinking heavily, St John had begun manoeuvring for the Tory leadership. In fact, the absurd situation arose in which, unknown to Oxford, St John was carrying out separate peace negotiations with France. Indeed he had actually informed the French that the Duke of Ormond had been ordered not to engage in any battles which had led to the French victory at Denain.

There had been little Jacobite threat since the abortive French landing in Scotland of 1708 and the arrests of suspects that followed. The Pretender was away fighting in the French army in a war that had encountered crippling costs with nothing to show for it. During the long drawn out peace negotiations Louis had no appetite for making another attempt at invading Scotland on James Francis Edward's behalf as it would have prejudiced his hopes of a peace settlement. This lack of Jacobite activity meant that the intelligence department and the secretaries of state had little to concern them regarding that threat. Intelligence gathering was instead focused on the war. Marlborough had built up a highly effective intelligence organisation and spent very large sums of money paying agents to provide him with information about both French military intentions and capabilities, and the state of support he could expect to receive for the other nations of the Grand Alliance. Fortunately Matthew Prior had remained in Paris either as an advisor to the Ambassador, or for a time Ambassador himself, but always developing his intelligence network to provide secretaries of state with good information on Louis and the court of Versailles.

Of the many agents and informants at this time, one in particular stands out. This was Antoine de Guiscard, the younger brother of the Count de Guiscard. He had entered the priesthood but left when it was recognised that his extreme debauchery made him unsuitable for that calling, so he made a career change to become an officer in the French army serving at the royal court. He was expelled from the court for some crime (quite what we do not know) and was so annoyed about this treatment that he offered his services to any states which were enemies of France. He found intelligence employment with the Duke of Savoy, then in 1706, he arrived in England and, using the title 'Marquis', was taken on as an agent by Harley. Over a period of time he came up with various schemes to invade Normandy but produced little intelligence of value, and Harley reduced his agent's pay from £500 to £400 a year. Irritated by this, Guiscard decided to offer his services to the French government and used a Paris banker called Moreau as a go-between. Fortunately, the post office intelligence system intercepted his correspondence and he was arrested. Guiscard demanded that, as an aristocrat, he should appear before the Privy Council and this was agreed. On arriving at the Council he took revenge on Harley by stabbing him with his penknife. Harley was injured but his life was saved by the thickness of his brocade waistcoat and the intervention of Ormond and other council members, who stabbed Guiscard in several places with their swords. Guiscard remained alive and was taken to Newgate, where he died a week later of his wounds.

The Guiscard incident provides a cameo of the way intelligence was handled at this time. Guiscard was typical of the type of adventurer who became involved in high level espionage. Motivated by self-interest they were not to be trusted and had a habit of improving their finances by becoming double agents. Nevertheless, the offer of service by a well-connected French aristocrat was not to be spurned and a senior government minister such as Harvey was prepared to pay him substantial sums from the secret intelligence fund. Like the majority of agents and informants the intelligence provided was mediocre, or simply invented, and the really sound intelligence was that provided by the intercept service that revealed Guiscard's treachery. Finally, although it would have been reasonable for Guiscard to be questioned by the Privy Council, it was highly unprofessional not to have searched him beforehand, or to have failed to interrogate him in the Fleet after he had been wounded. The whole Guiscard incident indicates Harley's rather careless manner regarding intelligence management, which had already been shown by the lack of security in his office. Harley, great schemer as he was, had become lazy and was losing the backing of his fellow Tories. His wound from Guiscard was not serious, but he made the most of it by taking to his bed and receiving considerable public sympathy. As a result, his Tory antagonists had to defer attempts to supplant him.

Anne's Tory ministry were good at conspiring against each other and the Whigs, but not so effective in covert intelligence gathering. This was less of a concern after 1713 as need for intelligence on the Jacobite threat had receded. With Marlborough gone and the War of the Spanish Succession over, it seemed the need for intelligence on France was much reduced. This was particularly so because one of the provisions of the Treaty of Utrecht was that Louis should not only acknowledge Anne as queen, but banish the Pretender from the great palace of St Germain and send him out of France to live at Bar–le-Duc as a guest of the Duke of Lorraine. It would seem that with French support removed, and James Francis Edward pushed off to far away Lorraine, the Jacobite cause was just about finished.

With the war ended, another important issue was to dominate public life for the next two years. Anne's health was failing and thoughts turned to the succession. Legally the Acts of Succession and Union named the Dowager Electress Sophia as Anne's heir, and her son George next in line after her. That should have been the end of the matter except that Anne had come to believe that James Francis Edward very probably was her younger brother and so would be her rightful heir if it wasn't for his Catholicism. In addition, she did not like her Hanoverian cousins and in 1711 had opened secret communications with the Pretender about nominating him as her heir, if he converted to Protestantism. In May, James Francis Edward wrote a long letter to her saying that he could not renounce his faith but would grant liberty of conscience to Anglicans and Nonconformists. This was completely unacceptable to the staunchly Anglican queen, and as far as she was concerned, that ended the matter.

This did not end the matter within the Tory Party, which was devotedly Anglican but becoming split by the rivalry between Oxford and

Bolingbroke. Oxford would have supported the Pretender's succession in the unlikely event that he had been prepared to convert to Anglicanism, but Bolingbroke supported the Pretender's succession if he remained Catholic and made some accommodation for the Anglican Church. There were about eighty Tory MPs who supported Bolingbroke in preferring a Jacobite succession. They were outnumbered by Hanoverian Tories, but still represented a substantial group.[4] As time went on Anne tired of Oxford and turned more to Bolingbroke for advice. One reason for this was that Bolingbroke won Abigail over to his side and began a close partnership which included sharing the £30,000 Bolingbroke had made by selling Asiento licences. In August, Bolingbroke strengthened his position by moving from secretary of state for the north to replace Dartmouth as secretary of state for the south. As such, he became senior secretary of state and also head of intelligence. His position as secretary for the north went to another Tory with Jacobite sympathies, Sir William Bromley.

The year 1714 began with the queen in bad health, but she was well enough to open parliament on 16 February. The Whig leaders such as Nottingham, Devonshire and Somers began pressing Anne to strengthen the Protestant succession by inviting George, the Elector of Hanover, over to England and allowing him to attend the House of Lords as 'Duke of Cambridge', the English title that had been bestowed upon him. It was felt that the Elector should be in the country when the queen died, otherwise there was a chance that the Pretender might land in England before George had made the journey from Germany. The queen was extremely angry about this recommendation and had no wish to have the son of her successor waiting around for her to die. As it happened, the Dowager Electress Sophia died on 8 June and her son George, now heir presumptive to the British throne, had to remain in Hanover for the period of mourning. However, as it had become public knowledge that the queen had refused to agree a visit for George, it was taken by many to suggest she favoured the Pretender as her successor. It is likely that both Bolingbroke and Abigail hoped that this was the case, as they were doing what they could to discreetly encourage the queen to name her brother as her heir. The two of them had been doing their best to undermine Oxford and in truth this was not difficult; Anne had come to dislike him, regarding him as lazy, discourteous to her and difficult to understand, especially when he was inebriated. On 27 July, Bolingbroke achieved his goal when the queen dismissed Oxford and made him her principal minister.

Bolingbroke formed a ministry of Tories with Jacobite sympathies. The Duke of Ormond became commander-in-chief and Lord Warden of the Cinque Ports (useful for a Jacobite invasion); the Duke of Buckingham, Lord President and Lord Dartmouth, Lord Privy Seal. The Earl of Mar was made secretary for Scotland; the Duke of Shrewsbury, Lord Lieutenant of Ireland and the Treasury was put in commission to avoid any possible rival taking over the powerful post. It was an extraordinary situation; Bolingbroke, principal minister and head of intelligence, was in league with the Jacobites to engineer the crown passing to the Pretender. The Whig magnates were aware of Bolingbroke's Jacobite scheming and were doing all they could to bring about an orderly Hanoverian succession. There were a few Whigs who wanted to keep their options open. True to form, Marlborough was communicating with both the Pretender and the Elector of Hanover. The Pretender decided to test his fidelity by asking for a loan of £100,000 – he did not receive a reply. Marlborough decided to throw in his lot with the Elector and sent him £20,000 as a token of his loyalty.

Whig magnates rallied and the Dukes of Somerset and Argyll turned up uninvited to the Privy Council. They said that with the queen about to die, it was a national crisis and therefore essential to fill the important post of Treasurer. The person they proposed was the Duke of Shrewsbury, a Tory but a known champion of the Protestant succession, and this recommendation was made to the queen. Anne was lying in her bed having suffered a stroke and was unable to speak, but nodded her consent. She gave the duke the white staff of office with a courtier guiding her hand.

This was a major setback for Bolingbroke. The strongly Protestant Shrewsbury was not only Lord Lieutenant of Ireland, but also Lord Treasurer and so trumped Bolingbroke as senior member of the Cabinet just when Bolingbroke was still trying to muster sufficient pro-Jacobite supporters. While Anne was in a long drawn out process of dying in her Kensington Palace bedchamber, Bolingbroke was further along the corridor in Abigail's apartments desperately scheming with Robinson, Bishop of London and other Jacobites. The Whigs were equally active; for example, James Stanhope who had been a principal Allied general in Spain during the war, but then turned Whig politician, was planning military support for the Hanoverian succession. He began making preparations to seize the Tower and round up known Jacobites. Bolingbroke became genuinely concerned about the queen's deteriorating health as he needed more time to get his plans in place and hoped that Anne might be induced into writing something bequeathing her kingdoms to her brother the Pretender. However, there was to be no time for at 7 am on 1 August, Anne died. She was just 49 years old.

Oxford, Tory though he was, decided to get revenge on Bolingbroke and immediately called all Whig peers in London to attend the Privy Council to ensure the Protestant succession. Bolingbroke discovered that his Jacobite supporters in the Privy Council were outnumbered and his hopes for the Pretender were in ruins. As was required by the Act of Succession, a Regency Council was immediately formed, nominated by George. It was headed by Shrewsbury and consisted mainly of Whigs who acted decisively to ensure the Protestant succession. Four regiments were dispatched to London for the maintenance of order, and the fleet was ordered to sea. A message was sent to the Elector requesting him to go to Holland from where he would be escorted by the navy to his new kingdoms.

Marlborough landed at Dover on the same day as the queen's death and was warmly welcomed by the crowds. His presence provided reassurance that the army would support the Elector, who was proclaimed as 'King George I' without any disorder in England, Ireland and even Scotland. The situation remained so stable that the Elector gave himself ample time to settle his affairs in Hanover and it was not until seven weeks after Anne's death that he arrived at Greenwich. He was not accompanied by a queen, because he had divorced his wife Sophia Dorothia for having an affair with a Polish colonel. Sophia Dorothia was imprisoned for life and the colonel was never seen or heard of again. The new king of England could be expected to be ruthless with those who opposed him.

The Pretender's hopes of gaining the crown were in tatters and the Treaty of Utrecht had made Louis promise to remove his vital French support. The question was, would Louis keep his word. Most people could probably guess the answer to that question.

Chapter 13

The Fifteen and After
1715–89

'A great and joyful shout went up, proceeding in waves up
St James's Street,through the Mall and along the Strand …
and faraway the batteries of the Tower told the City and the
river that George was king.'

H.M.C. Portland Vol. 5 p.482

The Protestant succession went without the slightest hitch. It has to be
said that other than being a Protestant and great grandson of King James
I & VI, there was little about George I that might win the affection of
his new subjects. He was a brave and experienced soldier, but being
rather shy, compensated for this by a gruff manner. Relations were
not enhanced by the fact that he spoke no English, had arrived with a
group of German mistresses and hangers-on, and was deeply distrustful
of the British nobility. He was particularly distrustful of Tories, whom
he regarded as closet Jacobites and responsible for making the Treaty
of Utrecht without reference to Hanover or the other members of the
alliance. Unsurprisingly, the new king appointed a cabinet composed
almost entirely of Whigs.

Charles Townsend became secretary of state for the north and
principal minister, James Stanhope was made secretary for the south
and responsible for intelligence. Marlborough replaced Ormond as
commander-in-chief. There was a similar turnover in Scotland. The
Earl of Mar was replaced by the Duke of Montrose as secretary of state
for Scotland, and the Duke of Argyll was made commander-in-chief of
Scotland. King George's coronation was held on 31 October and was
even attended by Oxford and Bolingbroke. The coronation itself went
without incident, but there were riots in about twenty towns including

Bedford, Birmingham, Chippenham, Norwich and Reading.[1] These were not so much pro-Jacobite demonstrations, but rather an attempted Tory show of strength and were caused by Tory Anglican priests inciting their congregations to attack Nonconformist meeting houses. The riots were soon put down and the three kingdoms appeared to have accepted the Hanoverian succession.

Queen Mary Beatrice had been allowed to remain at St Germain, but her son the Pretender was based in Lorraine with the opportunity of succeeding Anne now gone. His French backing had been removed and Louis had even instructed the Duke of Berwick, as a marshal of France, not to take any action to support his half-brother. Louis wanted to be seen to adhere to the Treaty of Utrecht, but at the same time put pressure on England by providing some aid to James Francis Edward. He got round this by asking his grandson, now Philip V of Spain, to do so for him by providing 10,000 crowns to finance an invasion force using ships purchased from the French Channel ports.

Meanwhile, the new Whig administration was taking no chances with national security. Although rioting had ended, a few months later the Riot Act was passed making it a felony for a group of more than twelve not to disperse within an hour of being ordered to do so by a magistrate. The election of March 1715 resulted in a crushing defeat for the Tories, making it possible for the Whigs to reap vengeance. They began to charge leading Tories with treason. As a result, an anxious Bolingbroke fled to France and became secretary of state to the Pretender. He was followed the next month by Ormond, who had tried unsuccessfully to organise a rebellion in the West Country. The flight of Bolingbroke and Ormond provided excellent ammunition for Whig propaganda to brand leading Tories as Jacobites. Oxford was impeached for his hand in the Treaty of Utrecht and sent to the Tower. And so it went on, with a purge of Tory office holders such as JPs and deputy lieutenants.

The removal of Tories from official positions was a sound policy for the Jacobite-fearing Whigs, but sometimes had unintended consequences. John Erskine, Earl of Mar, was an ambitious man who was very conscious of his status in Scotland. He was therefore furious, not only that he been dismissed as Scottish secretary, but that King George had been discourteous enough to have turned his back on him. On 2 August Mar decided to take his revenge by returning to Scotland to start a rebellion without even consulting the exiled Jacobite court. On 6 September 1715, he raised a standard of King James III at Braemar among his Highland clan members. In doing so he sent out a proclamation promising to repeal the unpopular Act of Union. Such was the anti-English feeling that before long he gathered support in the Grampian Highlands and in the Lowlands north of the River Tay, and his force had risen to 5,000.

Another unintended consequence of the Whigs over-eagerness to neutralise Jacobite sympathisers occurred in parliament. In September, Stanhope obtained the agreement of the House of Commons to the arrest of six MPs suspected of being Jacobites. Thomas Forster was one of these and fled north to join his relation the Earl of Derwentwater in Cumberland. Derwentwater was a Catholic and had heard that he was liable for arrest, so he too fled in disguise to Northumberland. Forster joined Derwentwater and persuaded him to initiate an uprising for the Pretender. This they did on 9 October at Derwentwater's estate in Northumberland, where they raised a small group of friends and servants. They were then rather unsure what to do next so made for the Scottish borders and eventually linked with some Mar-supporting Lowland rebels under William Gordon, Viscount Kenmure.

At much the same time, the Spanish sponsored invasion fleet had been assembling at St Malo. Fortunately for the British government, this Jacobite expedition had been known about since it began in early July. King George had appointed John Dalrympole, 2nd Earl of Stair, as Ambassador to Paris in January to replace Matthew Prior who had been the long standing acting ambassador. The king knew he could trust Stair as a successful lieutenant general who had fought alongside him in the Grand Alliance. The Tory-dominated Commons had set up a secret committee to investigate treason and corruption related to the agreeing of the Treaty of Utrecht. As Prior had been deeply involved in the negotiations he was recalled, questioned, and unjustly imprisoned for a year. This was poor thanks to a dedicated public servant and highly effective intelligencer. As it happened, Stair was to make an even greater success as Ambassador. He was able to effectively take over Prior's agents and informants and add a special dimension of his own. Secretary Stanhope had ordered him to create good relations with the Duke of Orleans, who was likely to become regent on Louis's death. This he did with great effect, to the extent that eventually he received intelligence of Jacobite activities from Orleans's French intelligence assets as well as his own sources. In short, Stanhope was receiving accurate and timely information on the Jacobite expedition.

Stanhope had served with distinction in Spain and Portugal during the War of the Spanish Succession and having received intelligence of the Jacobite invasion, took firm control of a military response. The militia were called out and regular troops deployed to all important towns. Catholics suspected of disloyalty had their arms and horses confiscated, non-jurors were arrested, as were suspect Jacobite leaders such as Lord Lansdown and Sir William Wyndham. Habeas Corpus was suspended to ensure suspects could be detained as long as necessary and so English Jacobite sympathisers found themselves leaderless. The fleet was ordered to blockade St Malo to prevent Spanish ships departing. At the end of October the Duke of Ormond took one of the Spanish ships with the intention of landing in Devon and initiating a western uprising. He managed to avoid the blockade but was intercepted by the King's Customs of the Devon coast and returned to France. At the Pretender's insistence he made another attempt but was beaten back by a storm. Jacobite hopes had to rest on the success of Mar in Scotland and any support that might be received in the north of England.

Mar had gathered a force of about 3,300 rather rag-tag followers and decided to march south. The little army gathered recruits on its journey south, which eventually numbered about 10,000. The Duke of Argyll received intelligence of Mar's movements and deployed his 1,500 trained troops and a further 1,500 volunteers to block his advance at Sheriffmuir, near Dunblane. An indecisive battle took place on 13 November after which Mar claimed victory and withdrew to Perth having failed to dislodge Argyll's troops who were behind a turf wall. At almost the same time, Thomas Foster and the united northern England and Jacobite Lowland force numbering 1,400 foot and 600 horse had advanced as far as Preston. They had gained a few recruits while passing through the northern counties, but these were almost all Catholics – which had not sent a positive message to Tory Anglicans. Townsend had been closely following their advance and coordinated the two government forces under generals Carpenter from the north and Wills from the south, to converge on the Jacobites at Preston. Neither Thomas Foster nor the Earl of Derwentwater had any previous military experience and were horrified by the casualties caused when the government troops attacked the town. Fearing encirclement, they panicked and decided to surrender, much to the anger of the Scots troops. About 1,500 Jacobites were taken prisoner and the rest escaped.

Soon after these setbacks the Pretender travelled to Dunkirk and sailed with a single ship to land at Peterhead in Scotland on 27 December. He had arrived with Melfort and a few followers but no troops. The Pretender was met by Mar and, on 6 January 1716, made a triumphant entry to Dundee, then moved to Scone with the intention of being crowned. However, things did not turn out well. The coronation never took place; Argyll had been reinforced by 6,000 Dutch troops and within a month had occupied Dundee. The Pretender fell ill with a fever, not helped by icy Scottish winter or the realisation that he was receiving only half-hearted support in Scotland and virtually none in England. With government troops approaching, James Francis Edward decided that his cause was hopeless and on a night in February took a small ship from Montrose and sailed back to France, accompanied by Melfort and Drummond. He had abandoned his supporters, leaving them to fend for themselves just as his father had done after the Battle of the Boyne.

The Pretender landed in France to discover that he was not wanted. Louis XIV had died on 1 September the previous year, having predeceased two generations of his heirs who had died of smallpox or measles. While Louis was on his deathbed, his heir and great grandson, the future Louis XV, was brought to him. The king's advice to the 5-year-old boy was not to take part in wars as he had done. Together, the king and his great-grandson were to rule France for 132 years, but being so young, Louis XV would have to wait till his maturity (thirteenth birthday) before holding power. In the meantime, France would be ruled by Louis XIV's nephew, the Duke of Orleans, as regent. Orleans was wary of Spanish expansion in Italy and so wanted England as an ally, encouraged by the détente being fostered by Stanhope and Stair. Orleans's pro-British alignment may have also been helped by the fact that George I was his first cousin, as Orleans's mother was the elder sister of George's mother the Electress Sophia. Orleans was therefore more closely related to George than to his Bourbon cousin, Philip V of Spain. Be that as it may, the next year France concluded the Triple Alliance with Great Britain and the United Provinces against Spain.

Under these changed circumstances James Francis Edward's presence in France was an embarrassment and there was no question of him receiving any French support in the future. As if this was not bad enough, the Duke of Lorraine made it clear that he was not welcome in his territories. The Pretender had to find a residence further away from England in various Papal territories such as Avignon. An additional blow came in 1718 with the death of his mother, Mary of Modena, from cancer. She had been living in a nunnery near Paris. Her religious devotion had been much respected by the French court, indeed many thought she should be a candidate for sainthood. Her death meant the end of any influence that she and her few courtiers might have had at Versailles. It also meant the end of St Germain as a Jacobite base. Fortunately the Pope provided the Pretender with the Palazzo del Re as a permanent home in Rome and sufficient funds to run a small court. This at least gave James Francis Edward a firm base, but it was a long way from England and extremely difficult to carry out any timely communications between there and any Jacobite supporters remaining in Britain. Also, by living in Rome the Pretender appeared to most Englishmen as little more than a minor foreign papist princeling.

In Britain retribution fell on the rebels, but in a much milder form than had been the case after the Monmouth rebellion. The Pretender's army in Scotland had been disbanded after he left for France and the men melted away back to their homes. Only about 700 rebels were brought to trial and they were sentenced to be indentured servants in West Indian plantations. Of the seven peers who surrendered at Preston, only Kenmure and Derwentwater were executed, and there were less than a couple of dozen executions in Lancashire. In total, fifty rebel estates were seized.[2] Many rebels escaped confinement, including Forster in Newgate Prison. He invited Mr Pitt, the prison governor, to dinner then got him drunk and took his keys. He managed to lock up some of the prison staff and make his escape and eventually reached the safely of Paris. The next year there was an act of indemnity to pardon those who had rebelled in Scotland but there were some exceptions, such as the whole of Clan Gregor.

By modern standards the government action against the rebels might seem harsh, but was not thought so at the time. When Forster's surrendered force was marched from Preston to London they were greeted by, 'The mob who insulted them terribly carrying a warming pan before them, and saying a thousand barbarous things.'[3] Apart from some Catholics and High Tory Jacobites the great majority of the population in England wanted peace and stability and had no sympathy for rebel papist. The Tory Party was discredited by the association of some of its leaders with Jacobites and was not to obtain a majority in the House of Commons for a half century. Anti-English feeling would continue to smoulder in Scotland and give rise to Jacobite sympathies, but in England the Hanoverian succession was firmly in place. In the words of Lord Townsend: 'The discontented people are rather cold to the present government, than disposed to venture anything against it.'[4]

The 1715 rebellion had been a botched affair from beginning to end. It was badly coordinated, and badly led by nobles with little or no military experience. Furthermore, it received only half-hearted support in Lowland Scotland and very little in England. With the perspective of time it may be seen that the Hanovarian government was strong enough to withstand any threats from the time of George I's coronation. The death of Louis XIV and the treaty with France brought an end to any realistic chance of a Jacobite monarchy. Of course, this was not apparent at the time as people would be concerned about the Jacobite threat for many years to come and Hanoverian governments would ensure that extensive intelligence resources were deployed against it.

For James Francis Edward, the loss of his French patron was a severe blow, but he lived in hopes of finding the backing of another great power. Spain provided that new patron as King Philip V wanted to regain the Spanish territories lost by the treaty of Utrecht. He captured Sardinia in 1717 and the next year invaded Sicily resulting in France, Great Britain, Austria and the Dutch Republic declaring war on Spain. As Spain was at war with Great Britain, King Philip decided to support the Pretender in an invasion. Spain provided twenty-nine ships and 7,000 men from Cadiz to pick up Ormond and the Pretender at Corunna then make a major landing in the West of England and a smaller landing in Scotland. The British government received timely intelligence of this plan from the sources of the Earl of Stair and Orlean's French agents. Even without the intelligence this small invasion force was doomed to failure because it would have received little Jacobite support in England. As it was, the Spanish fleet was largely destroyed by a storm by the time it reached Corunna in March 1719 and the Pretender and Ormond never embarked. Two Spanish frigates and 300 marines did manage to make a landing on the Isle of Lewis and gather some highland supporters, but were intercepted by government forces at Glen Shiel and after heavy mortar bombardment fled or surrendered.

So ended any hope of a Jacobite invasion of Britain. Another expedition was planned for 1722 but never got off the ground because the Duke of Orleans heard about it and alerted the British government, who rapidly rounded up all Jacobites who might have supported an uprising. The Jacobite cause became so forlorn that the Pretender started having bouts of depression and began to be deserted by some of his principal followers. For example in 1723, Bolingbroke obtained the help of the King George's mistress, the Duchess of Kendal, to receive a royal pardon and returned to England. Although Orleans died in 1723, the British French alliance of 1717 was to last for twenty-five years and effectively removed any prospect of French support for the Pretender during that time. The situation changed when Louis XV reluctantly became embroiled in the War of the Austrian Succession, in which King George II of Britain, as Elector of Hanover, was in the opposing alliance. In 1743 France decided on diversionary action to take Britain out of the war by carrying out an invasion of England led by the Pretender's son, Charles Edward Stuart – 'Bonnie Prince Charlie', the 'Young Pretender'. A fleet of transports and 12,000 troops was assembled at Dunkirk early the next year, but there was a great storm the night before the Young Pretender was about to board which completely destroyed the fleet. Louis cancelled the invasion, but after appeals from Charles Edward agreed to provide two vessels and 100 volunteers from the French Irish Brigade to make a landing in Scotland.

British intelligence had been fully aware of both the intended major invasion and the small two ship Scottish expedition which set sail for the Western Isles with the Young Pretender in July. The two ships were intercepted by HMS *Lion* and after a four-hour battle returned damaged to their French port, but did manage to land the Young Pretender and a handful of followers in Scotland. Prince Charles raised his standard at Glenfinnan and was acclaimed by about 700 Highland supporters. The 25-year-old 'Bonnie' prince was not only tall and good looking, but had a charm and charisma which enabled him to pick up recruits as he marched to Edinburgh and then enter the city unopposed. A government force of 3,000 poorly trained troops advanced on Edinburgh but was surprised and scattered in a daring attack by Prince Charles at Prestonpans. After this there were no other government troops left in Scotland. Knowing that most of the government army was deployed on the Continent, Prince Charles decided to march into England with the intention of taking London.

A total Jacobite force of 8,000 advanced into England as far as Derby, but finding he had received very few English recruits and knowing that government forces were advancing against him, decided to retreat to Scotland. The Duke of Cumberland, the commander of British troops in Flanders, had been recalled together with 12,000 men. He marched 8,000 men to attack the Jacobite force and eventually caught up with the Pretender at Inverness in April 1746. The prince made a long night march in an unsuccessful attempt to surprise Cumberland's troops and his exhausted and depleted army of about 5,000 arrived on Culloden Moor. Cumberland had received intelligence of the surprise attack and was ready to pour cannon fire on the Jacobites. Within an hour of the start of the battle the Jacobites were routed and fleeing for their lives. The Young Pretender told his supporters to fend for themselves and fled to the Highlands, eventually getting a ship back to France. His hopes of winning the throne for his father in tatters and leaving his followers to feel the full force of bloody retribution by 'Butcher' Cumberland.

On his return to France Prince Charles was well received in Paris, but two years later was expelled from French territory by the Treaty of Aix-la-Chapelle which brought an end to the war between France and Britain. The Young Pretender then spent several years wandering about Europe trying to find a backer. In 1750 he visited London in disguise and secretly met about fifty leading Jacobites, but this did not go well. Even after he took Anglican Communion to show he could be a Protestant king, the leaders still advised him that there was no hope of a Jacobite uprising. A couple of weeks after his arrival in England he returned crestfallen to the Continent and the Catholic faith. Prince Charles's life went into a downhill spiral. The charming, dashing young man was replaced by an embittered failure who blamed those closest to him for his predicament, with the result that he became estranged from his father and fell out with those who might help him. In 1754 the Seven Years War began between Britain and France, and in 1759 Louis XV's Foreign Minister, the Duc de Choiseul, considered mounting an invasion of England using Prince Charles as the nominal leader. However, when Choiseul met the drunken and argumentative Young Pretender he was so unimpressed he abandoned the idea. A little later British naval victories resulted in so much damage to the French fleet that an invasion was impossible.

Prince Charles continued his restless peripatetic life with a variety of mistresses and a few illegitimate children, but returned to Rome when his long time invalid father died in 1766. Although Charles was now nominally king in exile, a major blow came when the Pope refused to recognise him as the legitimate claimant to the British throne. In 1772 the 52-year-old Charles finally married, to the 22-year-old Louisa, daughter of the Prince of Salm-Kyrbury, but this did not result in him settling down to a more stable existence. They had no children and Louisa left him when she could no longer put up with his drunken physical abuse.[5] Charles's final years were ones of painful dropsy and alcohol-induced illness, deserted by virtually all his British exiles. He died in 1788 – a hundred years after his grandfather James II had lost his crown. Charles had no legitimate children so the last of the Jacobite Stuarts was his brother, Henry Benedict Clement, but as he had entered the Catholic priesthood he was ineligible to claim the throne. Henry had become Cardinal Bishop of Frascati near Rome, but lost his lands and descended into poverty as a result of the French Revolution; his fortunes revived in 1803, however, and he became Dean of the College of Cardinals, but died four years later. At the end there was a minor form of reconciliation between the Hanovarian and Jacobite sides of the Stuart family. When George III heard of Cardinal Henry's poverty he arranged for him to receive an annuity of £3,000 a year. In 1819 a fine marble monument carved by Canova was erected in St Peter's Basilica to commemorate the Old and Young Pretenders and Cardinal Henry. One of the subscribers to the monument was King George IV.

The thirty-year period from 1685 to 1715 saw major events that have defined the Great Britain that exits today. The country's religion, parliamentary democracy, financial system and the very name United Kingdom all stem from this short span of thirty years. The Glorious Revolution not only ensured that England and Scotland remained Protestant in religion, but also in a culture very different from the Catholic Baroque that influenced art, music, theatre, sculpture, gardens and architecture. The Glorious Revolution also resulted in the Bill of Rights, the cornerstone of parliamentary democracy and the un-coded British constitution. The accession of William III meant war with France, resulting in a major increase in the army and navy, leading to great victories such as Blenheim and imperial expansion with the acquisition of Gibraltar and substantial additional territory in Canada. By the end of the war, Britain's command of the sea made it the primary European commercial power. The war also resulted in considerable expense, but that led to the formation of the Bank of England which became the model for the central bank of other countries. Commercial success brought with it the rise of a merchant urban middle class, which in time would grow in wealth and influence to rival the landed gentry who had traditionally dominated the government of the country. William's victory in Ireland resulted in Protestant political domination, which caused Catholic resentment. This resentment eventually led to partition, the creation of Eire and a Protestant Northern Ireland where 'King Billy' is still celebrated. The death of William raised the fear that Scotland might choose a Jacobite as its monarch to succeed Anne. The English government's pressure on Scotland to accept the Act of Union created the United Kingdom of Great Britain and a bitterness against the English government which exists to this day.

These are some of the major changes that arose from the events that occurred in this thirty-year period. There are many reasons why these important events took place, including the strongly held beliefs in Catholicism and Protestantism which challenged loyalties and were to divide a royal family and a nation; the personalities of James II and William of Orange; the fact that neither William and Mary, nor Anne, had any children to succeed them, and the power of France to first provide vital support for the Jacobites and subsequently withdraw it. However, there was a usually neglected factor which played a significant part in shaping events – intelligence.

Intelligence had given warning of Monmouth's ill-starred rebellion, intelligence and clandestine operations were used by William of Orange to ensure that he would receive support if he landed in England, and a failure of intelligence by James and his government meant that William's invasion was not recognised until it was too late. Once William was in power, it was naval intelligence that meant the English fleet could unite with the Dutch fleet to destroy the French invasion force of 1692. It was intelligence that foiled the 1696 plot to assassinate William. Thereafter, it was intelligence that provided timely information on future Jacobite plots and the Post Office intercept service, which made it very difficult for Jacobites to communicate with each other and organise resistance. In short the effective use of combat intelligence, surveillance, espionage and intercept played a significant part in shaping the history of those exceptional times.

Appendix 1

ROYAL STUART FAMILY TREE

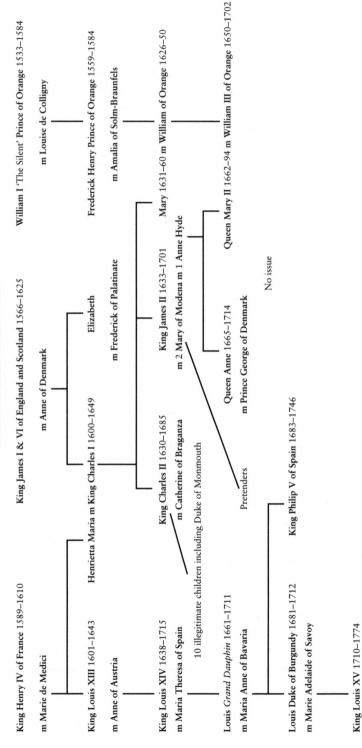

King James I & VI of England and Scotland 1566–1625

m Anne of Denmark

William I 'The Silent' Prince of Orange 1533–1584

m Louise de Colligny

Frederick Henry Prince of Orange 1559–1584

m Amalia of Solm-Braunfels

Mary 1631–60 m William of Orange 1626–50

Queen Mary II 1662–94 m William III of Orange 1650–1702

Elizabeth

m Frederick of Palatinate

Henrietta Maria m King Charles I 1600–1649

King Charles II 1630–1685

m Catherine of Braganza

10 illegitimate children including Duke of Monmouth

King James II 1633–1701

m 2 Mary of Modena m 1 Anne Hyde

Queen Anne 1665–1714

m Prince George of Denmark

No issue

Pretenders

King Henry IV of France 1589–1610

m Marie de Medici

King Louis XIII 1601–1643

m Anne of Austria

King Louis XIV 1638–1715

m Maria Theresa of Spain

Louis *Grand Dauphin* 1661–1711

m Marie Anne of Bavaria

King Philip V of Spain 1683–1746

Louis Duke of Burgundy 1681–1712

m Marie Adelaide of Savoy

King Louis XV 1710–1774

Appendix 2

HANOVERIAN AND JACOBITE STUART FAMILY TREE

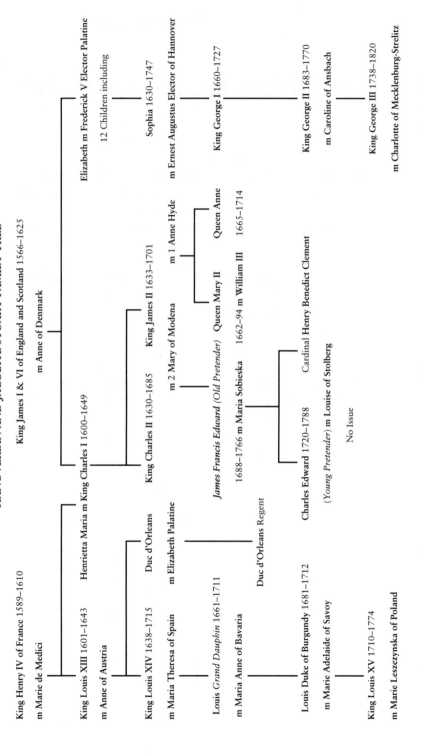

Appendix 3

English Secretaries of State 1685–1715

Year	Reign	Southern Department	Northern Department
1685	James II	Earl of Sunderland	Earl of Middleton
1686	James II	Earl of Sunderland	Earl of Middleton
1687	James II	Earl of Sunderland	Earl of Middleton
1688	James II	Sunderland/ Earl of Middleton	Viscount Preston
1689	William III & Mary II	Earl of Shrewsbury	Earl of Nottingham
1690	William III & Mary II	Earl of Nottingham	Viscount Sydney
1691	William III & Mary II	Earl of Nottingham	Viscount Sydney
1692	William III & Mary II	Earl of Nottingham	Viscount Sydney
1693	William III & Mary II	Nottingham/ Sir John Trenchard	Sir John Trenchard
1694	William III & Mary II	Sir John Trenchard	Duke of Shrewsbury
1695	William III & Mary II	Earl of Shrewbury	Sir William Trumbull
1696	William III & Mary II	Earl of Shrewbury	Sir William Trumbull
1697	William III & MaryII	Earl of Shrewbury	James Vernon
1698	William III & Mary II	James Vernon	James Vernon[1]
1699	William III	Vernon/ Earl of Jersey	James Vernon
1700	William III	James Vernon	Sir Charles Hedges
1701	William III	James Vernon	Sir Charles Hedges
1702	William III / Anne	Earl of Manchester/ Nottingham	Vernon/Hedges
1703	Anne	Earl of Nottingham	Sir Charles Hedges
1704	Anne	Sir Charles Hedges	Robert Harley[2]
1705	Anne	Sir Charles Hedges	Robert Harley
1706	Anne	Sir Charles Hedges	Robert Harley
1707	Anne	Earl of Sunderland	Robert Harley
1708	Anne	Earl of Sunderland	Henry Boyle
1709	Anne	Earl of Sunderland	Henry Boyle
1710	Anne	Earl of Dartmouth	Viscount Bolingbroke
1711	Anne	Earl of Dartmouth	Viscount Bolingbroke
1712	Anne	Earl of Dartmouth	Viscount Bolingbroke

1713	Anne	Viscount Bolingbroke	Sir William Bromley
1714	Anne/ George I	Viscount Bolingbroke/ Stanhope	Bromley/Townsend
1715	George I	James Stanhope	Viscount Townsend

Notes

1. James Vernon was sole Secreteary of State from December 1698 to May 1699
2. Robert Harley became Earl of Oxford in May 1711
3. As well as the Secretaries of State the following often took a lead in government intelligence:
   a. Hans William Bentinck, Earl of Portland – for William of Orange 1686–1689 and for the William III, pariticuarly in 1696
   b. Thomas Osborne, Earl of Danby, Marquis of Carmarthen, Duke of Leeds when Lord President from 1689–95
   c. Robert Harley, Earl of Oxford 1706–13

Bibliography and Sources

Aubrey, Philip, *The Defeat of James Stuart's Armada 1692* (Leicester University Press, 1979)

Ashley, Maurice, *John Wildman, Plotter and Postmaster* (London: Jonathan Cape, 1947)

Baxter, Stephen B. *William III,* (London: Longmans, 1966)

Baynes, John, *The Jacobite Risings of 1715,* (London: Cassell and Company Ltd, 1970)

Burnet, Gilbert, *A History of His Own Time,* (London: British Library reprint Samuel Bagster, 1815)

Calendar of State Papers Domestic (London: Longmans, 1860)

Callow, John, *King in Exile* (Stroud: Sutton Publishing Ltd, 2004)

Carswell, John, *The Descent on England* (London: the Cresset Press, 1963)

Cowper, Lady Sarah, *Diary* (Herford Country Record Office, 1700)

Devine, T.M. *The Scottish Nation 1700-2006* (London: Allen Lane Penguin Press,1990)

Dictionary of National Biography (Oxford Dictionary of National Biography (Oxford University Press, 2004)

Doebner, Dr, (Ed.) *Memoirs of Mary, Queen of England* (Leipzig: 1886)

Durant, Will, *Age of Louis XIV* (London: Story of Civilization TBS Publishing London 1963)

Earle, Peter, *Monmouth's Rebels, The Road to Sedgemore 1685* (London: Weildenfeld and Nicholson, 1977)

Evelyn, John Diary, Guy de la Bèdoyère (Ed.) (Woodbridge: Boydell Press, 1995)

Fraser, Antonia, *The House of Hannover* (London: Cassell & Co, 2000)

Hilton Jones, George, *Convergent Forces immediate causes of 1688 in England* (Iowa State University Press, 1990)

Hatton, Ragnibald, *George I Elector and King* (London: Thames and Hudson, 1978)

Hoppit, Julian, *A Land of Liberty? England 1689–1727* (Oxford University Press, 2000)

Holmes, Richard, *Marlborough, England's Fragile Genius* (London: Harper Press, 2008)

Hussy, John, *Marlborough, John Churchill, Duke of Marlborough, Hero of Blenheim* (London: Weidenfeld & Nicholson, 2004)

Hutton, Raginhild, *George I Elector and King,* (London: Thames and Hudson, 1978)

James II, *Life of James the Second, King of England etc, Collected Memoirs writ of his own hand,* (Royal Archives, Winsor Castle)

Keary, Anna, *The Last Royal rebel – The Life and Death of James Duke of Monmouth* (London: Bloomsbury, 2016)

Kenyon, John, *The Popish Plot* (London: William Heinemann Ltd, 1972)

Kenyon, John, *Robert Spencer Earl of Sutherland 1641–1702* (London: Longmans, Green and Co, 1958)

Lenman Bruce, *The Jacobite Risings in Britain, 1689–1746* (London: Eyre Methiren Ltd, 1980)

Van der Kiste, John, *William and Mary* (Stroud: Sutton Publishing, 2003) Cambridge University Press, 1994)

Macaulay, Thomas Babington, (Ed.) Charles Firth, *Macaulay's History of England* (London: Macmillan and Co, 1919)

Marshall, Alan, *Intelligence and Espionage in the Reign of Charles II, 1660–1685* (Cambridge University Press, 2002)

Mitford, Nancy, *The Sun King* (London; Hamish Hamilton, 1966)

Miller, John, *James II* (London: Yale University Press, 2000)

Miller, John, *James II a Study in Kingship* (Hove: Wayland Publications, 1978)

Monod, Paul, *Jacobitism and the English People* 1688–1788 (Cambridge University Press, 1989)

Pepys, Samuel, *The Diary of Samuel Pepys,* Eds Robert Latham and Willaim Matthews (London: Bell and Sons, 1976)

Portland, Duke of, *H.M.C Portland* (London, H.M. Stationary Office, 1891)

Rouse, A.L. *The Early Churchills* (London: Penguin Books, 1969)

Schwoerer Louis, G. (Ed.) *The Revolution 1688–1689 Changing Perspectives* (Cambridge University Press, 1992)

Somerville, Dorothy, H. *King of Hearts, Charles Talbot Duke of Shrewsbury* (London: George Allen & Unwin Ltd, 1962)

Szechi, Daniel, *The Jacobites Britain and Europe 1685–1788,* (Manchester University Press, 1994)

Tomalin, Claire, *Samuel Pepys, The Unequalled Self* (London: Viking Penguin Group, 2002)

Traill, H.D. *William III* (London: Macmillan and Co, 1897)

Turner, D.C. *James II* (London:, Eyre & Spottiswoode, 1950)

Valance, Edward, *The Glorious Revolution, 1688 – Britain's Fight for Liberty* (London: Little, Brown, 2006)

Whitehead, Julian, *Cavalier and Roundhead Spies, Intelligence in the Civil War and Commonwealth* (Barnsley: Pen & Sword, 2009)

Wormald, J. *Scotland; A History* (Oxford University Press, 2005)

Notes

Abbreviations

CSPD – Calendar of State Papers Domestic
DNB – Dictionary of National Biography

1. A New King – 1685

1. Antonia Fraser, Charles II (London: Weidenfeld and Nicholson, 1979), p. 446.
2. Ibid., p. 452.
3. John Miller, James II (London: Yale University Press, 2000), p. 120.
4. John Miller, James II a Study in Kingship (Hove: Waylan Publications, 1978), p. 122.

2. Conspiracy in the Netherlands – 1685

1. Anna Keary, *The Last Royal Rebel – The Life and Death of James Duke of Monmouth* (London: Bloomsbury, 2016), p. 35.
2. John Van der Kiste, *William and Mary* (London: Sutton Publishing, 2003), p. 74.
3. Anna Keary, *The Last Royal Rebel – The Life and Death of James Duke of Monmouth* (London: Bloomsbury, 2016), p. 327.
4. Ibid., p. 331.
5. Ibid., p. 331.
6. Peter Earle, *Monmouth's Rebels, the Road to Sedgemore 1685* (London: Weildenfeld and Nicholson, 1977), p. 74.
7. Ibid., p. 53.

3. King Monmouth – 1685

1. Alan Marshall, *Intelligence and Espionage in the Reign of Charles II, 1660–1685* (Cambridge University Press 2002), p. 275.
2. Peter *Earle, Monmouth's Rebels, the Road to Sedgemoor, 1685* (London: Weidenfeld and Nicholson, 1977), p. 54.
3. Ibid., p. 55.
4. Ibid., p. 57.
5. Richard Holmes, *Marlborough, England's Fragile Genius* (London: Harper Press, 2008), p. 111.
6. CSPD, dated 20 June 1685.
7. Peter Earle, Monmouth's Rebels, the Road to Sedgemoor 1685 (London: Weidenfeld and Nicholson, 1977), p. 238.
8. Ibid, p. 164
9. CSPD, dated 1 July 1685.
10. John Kenyon, *The Popish Plot*, (London: William Heinemann Ltd, 1972), p. 19.

4. Dissident Survivors – 1685-6

1. Melinda Zook, DNB Vol 27 p.778.
2. Richard Greaves, DNB Vol 23 p. 834.
3. Peter Earle, *Monmouth's Rebels, the Road to Sedgemoor 1685* (London: Weidenfeld and Nicholson, 1977), p. 148.

5. Sleepwalking over the Edge – 1687

1. Alan Marshall, *Intelligence and Espionage in the Reign of Charles II, 1660–1685* (Cambridge University Press, 2002), p. 277.
2. Edward Valance, *The Glorious Revolution, 1688 – Britain's Fight for Liberty* (LondonLittle, Brown London 2006), p.136.
3. A.L. Rouse, *The Early Churchills* (Penguin Books London1969), p. 204.
4. John Carswell, *The Descent on England* (Cresset Press London1963), p. 123.
5. Edward Valance, *The Glorious Revolution, 1688 – Britain's Fight for Liberty* (London: Little, Brown, 2006), p.99.

6. Ibid., p.100.
7. A.L. Rouse, *The Early Churchills* (London, Penguin Books, 1969), p.207.

6. A Protestant Wind – 1688–9

1. D.C. Turner (London: Eyre & Spottiswoode, 1950), p. 412.
2. John Kenyon, *The Popish Plot*, (London: William Heinemann Ltd, 1972), p. 91.
3. Edward Valance, *The Glorious Revolution, 1688 – Britain's Fight for Liberty* (London: Little, Brown, 2006), p.110.
4. John Van der Kiste, *William and Mary* (Stroud: Sutton Publishing, 2003), p. 101.
5. CSPD, James II June 1687 – February 1689, p. 360.
6. A. L. Rouse, *The Early Churchills*, (Harmondsworth: Penguin Books Ltd, 1969), p. 208.

7. A Precarious Dual Monarchy – 1689–90

1. Alan Marshal, *Intelligence and Espionage in the Reign of Charles II, 1660-1685* (Cambridge University Press 2002), p. 301.
2. John Callow, *King in Exile, James II: Warrior, King & Saint*, (Stroud: Sutton Publishing, 2004), p. 55.
3. Ibid., p. 61.
4. Ibid., p.16.
5. T.B. Macaulay, Ed Charles Firth, *Macaulay's History of England*, (London: Macmillan and Co, 1919), Vol IV, p. 1890.
6. Pepys was later released on bail and then charges of being a Jacobite were dropped in October but he remained under surveillance. Claire Tomalin, *Samuel Pepys, The Unequalled Self*, (London: Viking, Penguin Books, 2002), p. 356.

8. An Invasion Threatens – 1691–5

1. John Callow, Richard Graham Viscount Preston, DNB, Vol 23, p. 227.
2. Stephen Baxter, *William III* (London: Longmans, 1966), p. 278.

3. John Callow, *King in Exile, James II: Warrior, King & Saint*, (Sutton Publishing Stroud 2004), p. 162.
4. Maurice Ashley, *John Wildman, Plotter and Postmaster*, (London: Jonathan Cape London 1947), p. 288.
5. Life of James the Second, King of England etc, Collected Memoirs writ of his own hand, (Royal Archives, Winsor Castle) RA/M-4, Vol. II, p. 474.
6. A.L. Rouse, *The Early Churchills*, (London: Penguin Books, 1969), p. 232.
7. Philip Aubrey, *The Defeat of James Stuart's Armada 1692*, (Leicester University Press, 1979), p. 80–81.
8. Ibid., p.89

9. A Single Sovereign – 1695

1. Richard Holmes, *Marlborough, England's Fragile Genius*, (London: Harper Press, 2008), p. 186.
2. H.D. Traill, *William The Third*, (London: Macmillan and Co, 1897), p. 108.
3. John Callow, King in Exile (Stroud: Sutton Publishing Ltd, 2004), p. 227.
4. Idem., p. 227.
5. Paul Hopkins, DNB, Vol 3, p. 766.

10. Assassination and Retribution – 1696–9

1. Macaulay, Thomas Babington, Ed Charles Firth, *Macaulay's History of England*, (London: Macmillan and Co, 1919), Vol V, p.2601.
2. John Callow, *King in Exile* (Stroud: Sutton Publishing Ltd, 2004), p. 228.
3. Paul Hopkins, DNB, *Captain George Porter*, Vol 44, p. 953.
4. Will Durant, *Age of Louis XIV* (London: Story of Civilization TBS Publishing London 1963), p. 164.

11. The Death of Princes

1. Macaulay, Vol VI, P. 2916.
2. John Callow, *King in Exile* (Stroud: Sutton Publishing Ltd, 2004), p. 227.

3. Nancy Mitford, *The Sun King* (London: Hamish Hamilton Ltd, 1966), p. 208.

4. Julian Hoppit, *A Land of Liberty, England 1689-1727* (Oxford: Clarendon Press, 2000), p. 250.

12. The Spanish Succession – 1702–14

1. Edward M. Furgol, DNB Vol 20 *Simon Frazer, 11th Lord Lovat*, p. 863.

2. Bruce Lenman, *The Jacobite Risings in Britain, 1689–1746* 9 (London: Eyre Methiren Ltd, 1980), p. 86.

3. Bishop Burnet, *History of His Own Time,* Vol. 2, (British Library reprint Samuel Bagster, London 1815), p. 210.

4. Julian Hoppit, *A Land of Liberty / England 1689-1727* (Oxford University Press 2000), p. 308.

13. The Fifteen and After – 1715–89

1. Paul Monod, *Jacobitism and the English People* 1688–1788, (Cambridge University press 1989) p. 181.

2. Bruce Lenman, *The Jacobite Risings in Britain, 1689–1746* 9 (London: Eyre Methiren Ltd, 1980), p. 161–2.

3. Sarah Cowper, *Diary,* (Herford Country Record Office, 1700), p. 62.

4. Julian Hoppit, *A Land of Liberty? England 1689–1727* (Oxford University Press 2000), p. 394.

5. Murray G.H. P. Pittock, *Charles Edward Stuart,* DNB Vol 11, p.153.

Index

Index